Value Creation and Sport Management

T0300484

The sports business has become one of the fastest growing industries in recent years. Sports organizations now have the potential to generate massive amounts of revenue through a variety of different channels, including broadcasting rights, advertising and branding. However, the rise of sports-related business has so far received relatively little attention from management scholars and social scientists. This book argues that we can no longer afford to ignore this important economic and social phenomenon. It presents a new conceptual framework based on the concept of value creation to show how we can understand and explain the success and failure of sports organizations. Key concepts are illustrated with case studies of sporting organizations, including Real Madrid, FC Barcelona and the America's Cup. Written by a team of authors from one of the leading business schools in the world, it provides a unique set of theoretical and practical insights for researchers and sports organization managers.

SANDALIO GÓMEZ is Professor and Chairman of the Center for Sport Business Management (CSBM) at IESE Business School, Madrid.

KIMIO KASE is Professor at IESE Business School, Madrid.

IGNACIO URRUTIA is Dean of Antonio de Nebrija University, Madrid.

Value Creation and Sport Management

SANDALIO GÓMEZ
IESE Business School, Madrid

KIMIO KASE
IESE Business School, Madrid

IGNACIO URRUTIA
IESE Business School, Madrid

CAMBRIDGE
UNIVERSITY PRESS

CAMBRIDGE UNIVERSITY PRESS
Cambridge, New York, Melbourne, Madrid, Cape Town,
Singapore, São Paulo, Delhi, Mexico City

Cambridge University Press
The Edinburgh Building, Cambridge CB2 8RU, UK

Published in the United States of America by Cambridge University Press, New York

www.cambridge.org
Information on this title: www.cambridge.org/9781107406179

First published 2010
First paperback edition 2012

A catalogue record for this publication is available from the British Library

Library of Congress Cataloguing in Publication Data
Gómez López-Egea, Sandalio.
Value creation and sport management / Sandalio Gómez, Kimio Kase,
Ignacio Urrutia.
    p.   cm.
Includes bibliographical references and index.
ISBN 978-0-521-19923-0
1. Professional sports–Management.   2. Professional sports–Economic aspects.
3. Sports administration.   I. Kase, Kimio, 1949–   II. Urrutia, Ignacio.   III. Title.
GV713.G59 2010
796.06′9–dc22
2010016803

ISBN 978-0-521-19923-0 Hardback
ISBN 978-1-107-40617-9 Paperback

To my granddaughter Esperanza who has given to all of our family a new reason and a new hope to live – SG

To Mercedes and Uncle Kiyoshi and Aunt Toshie; and in tender memory of Gabriel – KK

To Patricia and my sons and daughters – Ignacio, Patricia, Jorge, Juan, Borja, Elisa and Rodrigo – and my father Juan, and in loving memory of my mother Elisa – IU

Contents

Figures

Tables

Contributing authors

Tanguy Jacopin, PhD   Researcher at IESE Business School, Madrid and Managing Director, Global Born Ltd

Carlos Martí, PhD   Research Associate, Centre for Sport Business Management (CSBM), IESE Business School, Madrid, and Director, Unidad MBA and Executive MBA, Barna Business School, Santo Domingo

Magdalena Opazo   Research Assistant, Centre for Sport Business Management (CSBM), IESE Business School, Madrid

Enrique Tellechea   Director, Marca y Publicidad, Banco Popular, Madrid

Foreword

I have lived my life combining my passions for Inspirational Leadership, Peak Performance, Brand Building, Sustainability and Sport. As the Worldwide CEO of Ideas Company Saatchi and Saatchi, I touch many great organizations and work closely with Procter and Gamble, Toyota, Sony Ericsson, Novartis, General Mills, Visa, JC Penney, Guinness and Lexus. Many of these successful (and great) companies have strong commercial partnerships in the world of sport. As Chairman of USA Rugby I'm involved in leading the charge to inspire Americans to fall in love with the great game of rugby and to bring the United States into the world rugby arena. As CEO in Residence at the Judge Business School of Cambridge University, I'm involved with helping Cambridge MBAs define what it takes to fully realize their potential as tomorrow's leaders. And above all, I'm dedicated to the idea that the role of business is to make the world a better place for everyone.

To do this, all businessmen and students of business have to provide inspirational leadership in four areas: economic sustainability, environmental sustainability, social sustainability and cultural sustainability. I am firmly of the view that sport is the number one medium and vehicle for achievement globally and locally in all these four areas.

This book describes persuasively and perceptively the latest thinking and theories in value creation through professional sports management and lays out a framework to fully understand the new paradigms and realities of success in this dynamic category.

The authors' research and findings provide stimulation and a framework for business leaders to understand and impact the critical success factors involved in the rapidly growing, ever more important, world of sports.

Unlike any other phenomenon, sport uniquely defines a new stakeholder model and taps into the deepest emotional feelings of the world's population regardless of geography, age or demographics.

Sport encompasses both the global and the local. Today, people define themselves by their differences and are searching to demonstrate local commitment, local tribalism and local passion whilst at the same time savouring the benefits of the global economy on their own terms. Sport is a way of demonstrating your true colours, your true passion and your deeply held instinct to compete and succeed. Supporting a club team becomes a way of defining yourself, your values and your beliefs, and of separating you from the rest. Supporting your national team allows you to express yourself on the worldwide stage. Simultaneously it provides an opportunity to create a sustainable future for everyone regardless of wealth, education or status. If you are talented enough, committed enough and lucky enough you can reach the very top of the sporting profession and be the best that you can be, irrespective of your own particular environment/background; truly an equal opportunity business.

This social phenomenon has now turned into an economic phenomenon with the sports business being one of the top ten industries in the world, and one of the fastest growing. Many commentators talk about sport as being 'big business'. They are missing the point. Sport is bigger than big business. It is as big as a conventional business, yes, but it is much more socially involving and engaging, and much more complex in its stakeholder structure. It is very much the new twenty-first century stakeholder model.

This book goes a long way to explaining exactly the depth of the new stakeholder model in sport and how it can be managed to create sustainable value over the long haul.

I am not an academic. I am a businessman who believes that sustainable growth will best be achieved through combining the best of business practice with the best of academic thinking. I'm honoured to have had the opportunity to provide a short foreword to this book which I believe will stimulate both businessmen and academics alike to think more about how sport can be developed even quicker to be the arrowhead of global sustainable enterprise development.

Kevin Roberts, President, Saatchi & Saatchi

Introduction

As an opening to the book, this introduction will address three issues:

(1) the significance of our research on sport-related phenomena;
(2) the basic approach or the common thread to/regarding their study; and
(3) the basic structure of this book.

Firstly, we refer to the significance of this research. Sport, with a capital 'S', has acquired a status in society that would have been unthinkable only twenty years ago. As a spectacle and as an activity, sport has traditionally been confined to the leisure sphere. In recent decades, however, it has become a full-blown business, one that not only stirs passions but also captures media attention around the world and generates more economic activity than even the most optimistic could have imagined.

Sport occupies an increasingly prominent place in social life, as anyone who watches the television news will know. There are endless radio and television programmes about sport, and even dedicated sports channels. The social spotlight on all things sport-related has made many sportspeople, coaches and managers famous: they have become media personalities and are often held in greater awe than politicians and other public figures.

The far-reaching transformation of the world of sport has been driven by rapid commercialization, which has reached a point where it is quite legitimate to talk of a 'sports business' (Beech and Chadwick, 2004: 496) or 'sports industry' (Foster et al., 2005: 512). Two examples of the global importance of sport are the growth of the Olympic movement and the growth of football[1] (Amara et al., 2005). To appreciate the transformation, we need only compare the budget

---

[1] Unless otherwise stated, all references to 'football' will refer to soccer.

and audience of the 1988 Olympics, just twenty years ago, with those of the recent Beijing Olympics, in which billions of dollars were in play, an entire country was brought to a halt and the host country's economy and image were transfigured.

The broadcasting of sports events, especially by television, has created revenue-generating opportunities for sports organizations through the sale of broadcasting rights, individual and team image rights, advertising, and so on. The media – television in particular – has revolutionized the world of sport, giving it a privileged status in social and economic life and making it the focus of a network of interests encompassing a variety of actors in society and the economy. The change is apparent in the expansion of the World Cup budget or the budgets of the leading European football clubs over the last two decades. The figures speak for themselves: twenty years ago Real Madrid football club had a budget of less than €60 million; today, it is €400 million.

Except for marketing, brand management and sponsorship, this phenomenon has so far received relatively little attention from management scholars and social scientists. In order to analyse what makes a club successful, we need a solid, comprehensive theoretical framework.

Sports institutions and clubs today have much in common with large or medium-sized businesses. In effect, they have become companies, creating economic value added, though with the specific characteristics of sports organizations, and so deserve to be studied on their own terms. In 2003, the Spanish sports daily newspaper *Marca* estimated that the soccer industry worldwide had a turnover of €235 billion (Agudo and Toyos, 2003: 398). It is hardly surprising, therefore, that the football industry should have become a major economic activity involving a variety of stakeholders. Linked by common interests, these stakeholders form a circular network, creating a virtuous circle of value creation.

This striking and thought-provoking development has prompted numerous intellectuals and academics to analyse and study the situation and its economic and social consequences for society, for the countries and cities that host major events, and for individual sports organizations and clubs.

No leading management education institution, faculty or business school can afford not to invest in research that will provide a conceptual basis for teaching activities directed to the world of sport. Any such teaching and research activity must be focused on the character-istics of sports organizations from the moment they stop being mere providers of entertainment to becoming a major source of economic value added. Without specific prior research covering the length and breadth of the sport business, it is impossible to provide high-quality education that adds real value to sports executives. In 2005, there-fore, IESE Business School created a dedicated research centre, the Centre for Sport Business Management (CSBM). This book presents a small sample of the centre's work in sport and other areas over the last three years.

We are convinced that this book offers a novel conceptual frame-work and provides unique theoretical and practical insights for researchers and sports organization managers. Although all types of sport are included, the emphasis is on the sports that are most popu-lar in Europe, football being the most emblematic on account of its economic structure, its fan base and its professionalization.

We now proceed to provide the reader with information about our basic approach. The common thread that runs through the chapters of this book and around which they cohere is the concept of value cre-ation. Value is destroyed or subtracted when management of the sport entities or governing bodies in their ignorance misguide the organiza-tion. On the contrary, if they get it right and guide their organization wisely, value is added.

The value creation concept in sport-related businesses has trad-itionally been understood as:

(1) narrowly related to the physical aspect as provided by coaches and trainers; and/or
(2) the management and physical aspects dealt with separately.

In this book, we focus on value creation from the perspective of man-agement. However, given its importance, reference to the physical aspect is covered among other things by the virtuous circle concept (of which more later).

Value creation from the corporate centre is the central theme in this study of corporate-level strategy. This book attempts to apply this theme to the field of sport-related businesses, in the belief that it furnishes an appropriate framework for the understanding of many phenomena in a coherent manner, since the analysis of these phenom-ena naturally becomes simpler once this framework is applied.

One caveat to note is that value created does not necessarily mean visible economic value. Notional value added also carries weight. Take the example of Real Madrid's management during the presidency of Florentino Pérez. Real Madrid centred their strategy on that of Walt Disney, which had managed to create a business independent of the success or failure of its film production. Their theme parks, such as Disneyland or Tokyo Disney Resort operating under Disney's license, are prospering thanks to the entire entertainment concept package, and not only because of Mickey Mouse, Donald Duck, or new characters created by recent films.

During Pérez's presidency, the club managed to consolidate its financial and economic base, which produced the liquidity necessary for signing excellent or high-profile players. This could be considered as an instance of value creation, albeit indirectly sport-related. Pérez's personal network, as the president of one of the largest construction companies in the world, certainly played a role: the sale of Real's training grounds must have been at least partly due to this fact.

In order to establish the dynamics for value creation, one of our first conceptual contributions was to define what we shall call the 'virtuous circle of value creation in sport'. This concept links and gives meaning to the activities of all those who participate directly or indirectly in the sports industry. The main success factor, at the centre of the 'virtuous circle', is the sports competition itself, the purpose of which is to entertain and stir passions in the target group (Miller and Letter, 2003). Entertainment is key in attracting new fans and instilling passion for the team colours, so as to create long-term associative ties or what we call the 'loyalty effect'. The initial purpose of sporting events, therefore, is to entertain and impassion. This means that the fans play a central role – they are the ones who set the circle in motion. Without fans, none of the rest would exist. So we need to understand how a sport attracts, entertains, stirs such passion and arouses such enthusiasm in its fans.

Next, we can study how a team acquires the 'magic aura' that makes its fans enduringly loyal. Why one sport is popular in one country and not in another is an interesting question that deserves sociological and historical study, but it lies beyond the scope of this book. The fact is that, while baseball is one of the top sports in the United States, it hardly exists in Europe, whereas football, the number one sport in much of the world, ranks at best fifth in popularity in the United States.

The whole sport economy clearly starts with the fans. It is the fans who open the door to other actors, who appear tentatively at first, then with increasing self-assurance. These other actors, stakeholders, or whatever one wishes to call them, add an extra sporting dimension and turn sport into a machine for generating economic value added. Finally, in the next section we outline the structure of this book.

Chapter 1 describes the virtuous circle of value creation in the world of sport and analyses each component.

Chapter 2 examines the four forms of value creation in sports organization management. Given these four forms of value creation (historical, economic, social and media capital), there is plenty of scope for diverse business models to coexist. This chapter shows that there is no one model, no 'one best way', for all sports organizations, but a whole range of aspects that help each organization choose the model that will best enable it to achieve its goals. This chapter provides tools for improving value creation in sports organizations, illustrated by case studies, including the America's Cup; the Estudiantes basketball team and temporary employment agency Adecco; the La Sexta television channel and the FIFA World Cup; and the Atlético de Madrid football club.

While accepting that diverse models of value creation are possible, Chapter 3 shows that the expansion of sports organizations is closely linked to their initial business model and the national context in which they have arisen. Studies of the revenues of Europe's largest football clubs show that there are broadly three contrasting models, based respectively on ticket sales, marketing and broadcasting rights. The ability to expand also depends on belonging to a league. For large football clubs, successful internationalization therefore does not necessarily require globalization but regionalization of their activities. A comparison with the regionalization of the auto industry indicates the real internationalization potential of sports organizations. This chapter also considers how sports organization management can become a benchmark for other industries.

Chapter 4 examines the behaviour and value creation strategy of Spain's two most respected sports organizations, Real Madrid and FC Barcelona. This comparative case study illustrates the challenge of excelling simultaneously in sport and business. Also presented in this chapter is the matrix the CSBM has developed for interpreting an organization's approach to sport and business.

Chapter 5 considers the cognitive processes of a sports organization leader based on two polar systems. The first paradigm is based on the 'profit arithmetic' approach, in which priority is given to short-term economic objectives. The second paradigm, the 'proto-image of the firm' approach, presupposes a long-term view of the organization, with more ambitious goals reaching beyond the purely economic sphere.

Chapter 6 addresses the organizational conception of an elite sports club, with special emphasis on football. In recent years the leading clubs have come increasingly to resemble conventional business enterprises. The division of functions and the coordination this requires must be founded on the structure of the organization, which must reflect all the activities a sports club must perform, given its size and objectives.

References

Agudo, A. and Toyos, F. (2003). *Marketing del fútbol*. Madrid: Pirámide.

Amara, M., Henry, I., Liang, J. and Uchiumi, K. (2005). 'The Governance of Professional Soccer – Five Case Studies: Algeria, China, England, France, and Japan', *European Journal of Sport Science*, 5(4): 189–206.

Beech, J. and Chadwick, S. (eds.) (2004). *The Business of Sport Management*. Harlow: Prentice Hall.

Foster, G., Greyser, S. and Walsh, B. (2005). *The Business of Sports: Cases and Text on Strategy and Management*. Cincinnati: South Western College Publication.

Miller, G.A. and Letter, G. (2003). 'College/University Partnerships with Sport Agencies: Evaluation of Sport Management Internships', in *National Association for Physical Education in Higher Education*. Columbus: McGraw-Hill Higher Education.

1 | *The virtuous circle of value creation in the sports industry*

1.1 Introduction

This chapter presents an exploratory discussion of the concept of the *virtuous circle*. It refers to the use of chains of reaction and interaction for the furtherance of an organization's cause. We see how the players of such chains comprise different stakeholders. The virtuous circle provides the justification for and the theoretical framework of coordinated and concerted actions on account of the synergies that they will release. Sport clubs, business entities and governmental bodies may thereby greatly enhance the effectiveness and efficiency of their tasks.

This chapter describes the virtuous circle of value creation in the world of sport and analyses each component in turn (Figure 1.1). The virtuous circle is a concept predicated on the assumption that when, in sport activities, town or regional development, for example, an appropriate measure is taken it will unleash a chain of positive reactions amongst the involved stakeholders. It implies the value creation process that reinforces itself through dynamic feedback loops.

1.2 Sports events: rivalry and competition

The main objective for the organizers of sports events and the teams or individuals who take part in them is to entertain the fans and win the competition. The basic ingredients that keep any competition alive are interest, uncertainty and a passionate involvement in the outcome. To create these ingredients, there has to be fierce competition between the teams and an enduring rivalry (Figure 1.2).

Without strong, evenly matched rivals there is no uncertainty or excitement about the outcome and the fans do not feel the need to proclaim their identification with and loyalty to their team. A

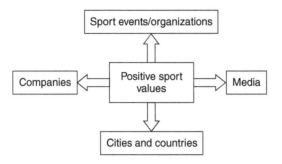

Figure 1.1 The sport virtuous circle
Source: Authors

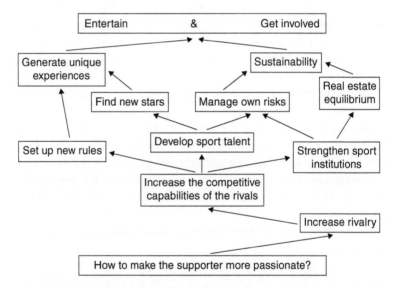

Figure 1.2 Key success factors of sports: entertain and get involved
Source: Authors

championship that is a foregone conclusion or that is always won by the same person or team (because the rivals are unevenly matched) loses its main attraction, which is the excitement of the result. When that happens, attendance at sports events plummets and the fans lose interest, at least temporarily. The more evenly matched the rivals, the greater the uncertainty and passion, which is what generates interest and economic value. The various and ongoing changes to

NBA rules reflect how important it is to maintain a balance between competing teams in order to keep the fans' passion alive. Such competitive balance is the only way to preserve the uncertainty as to the result, which is what ultimately keeps the spectators interested (Toft, 2003). Sports teams need strong rivals; otherwise they fade away.

Competition in sport is very different from competition in other areas. In sport, the aim is not to eliminate the weaker rival. The adversaries need one another and to some extent they also need the balance between them to be maintained (Elías and Dunning, 1992). The idea of a type of competition in which competitive and cooperative behaviour are not only compatible but can coexist in firm strategy is encapsulated in the concept of 'co-opetition' (Brandenburger and Nalebuff, 1996).

In the competitive models that predominate in conventional industries, profit maximization and profit appropriation are the rule, whereas in cooperative models the goal is profit generation. The fact that a football team wins the European Cup is a gain not only for the individual club but for all the clubs in the country, as it improves the country's ranking for subsequent European championships. Unlike other industries, participants enter into and maintain collaboration agreements to explore new sources of revenue and exchange ideas on best practices (Panstadia International, 2009). In any case, competition and rivalry must stay within limits, based on the values that sport promotes. 'Rivalry in sport is good provided the rivals get on with one another' (Normile, 2005).

1.3 Sports organizations

Sports organizations, as they exist today, cover a broad spectrum, so in order to study them we need to distinguish between different types. According to the Canadian author Trevor Slack, a sports organization is any social entity that participates in the sports industry, is goal-oriented, engages in a rigorously structured activity and has clear boundaries (Slack, 1997).

Given the breadth of the concept, we need to classify sports organizations according to their mission, goals and principal activity (Chelladurai, 1985; Gómez and Opazo, 2006). The mission of a 'sports governance' organization, be it a government department, a national or international federation or an Olympic committee, is to foster and develop sport at all levels in a certain geographical area. 'At all levels' means that sport is to be fostered among all categories of sportspeople (youth, amateur and professional), for both men and women, and for all age groups (children, adolescents, adults and older people). In order to 'foster sport', these bodies must start organizing sport activities at school level, in order to get people involved in sport from a young age. Child and youth championships, school tournaments and university championships all help to consolidate sporting activity among the younger generation.

Another mission these organizations have is to formulate and regularly review the rules of sports competitions and events and establish a disciplinary regime, so that the rules of fair play are respected. They must make every effort to make competitions interesting and review the rules of the game as necessary to promote an even match between teams, which is key to the rivalry and passion that attracts devoted fans. Sports governance bodies are by definition not-for-profit and obtain most of their revenues from public funds. Nowadays, however, many of them have opportunities to raise funds from the private sector, allowing them to broaden their horizons and finance a wider range of activities.

The role of the suppliers of sport activity, that is, the sports clubs and associations (ACB, LFP, ASOBAL, etc.), is different from that of sports governance bodies. Clubs and associations are private organizations that provide sports activity or produce sports events. Their aim is to supply a community with sporting activities, at both a recreational and a competitive level, and take part in national and international competitions. Also, they must defend the rights of the individuals and teams that take part in sports competitions.

Organizations with multi-million euro budgets and, in some cases, global reach and impact, obviously cannot be managed by enthusiastic amateurs who would be overwhelmed by the scale of the organizational challenge. The presidents of national and international federations, Olympic committees and large sports clubs need a different profile from that which was customary in the past. In order to manage sport institutions and companies, they need to be better trained and more specialized. As chief executives, they must be aware of the changes in recent decades and rise to the challenge. To succeed, they must be consummate professionals. Professionalism means having the necessary qualifications, commitment and concentration (enthusiasm and a love of sport are taken for granted). While respecting the peculiarities of the sport business, sports management must appropriate the latest management concepts and techniques.

In response to an increasingly demanding environment, the professionalization of sports management and organization is already well under way. Sports organizations have adapted to meet changing needs, taking on new areas of activity and coordinating them towards a common goal.

Division of labour on account of professionalization and therefore specialization requires coordination, or 'integration', to achieve the common goal. Differentiation and integration are two key processes for understanding organizational structure (Hodge *et al.*, 2003). Nowadays, depending on its size and budget, every organization or club must cover certain vital areas: corporate governance and the responsibilities and functions of governance bodies; internal organization; business and sports strategy; marketing and sponsorship policy; communication and institutional relations; financial planning and budget control; revenue development; sport and people management; and youth development. These are all part of the work of a sports organization today. How the different areas are coordinated has to do with the way roles and responsibilities are distributed and the level at which decisions are taken. The distribution of power has important consequences for decision-making, organizational performance and motivation. Much remains to be done, especially in sports organization governance and key strategic decision-making.

The transformation of sports clubs into sport companies adds a new dimension. The resulting opportunities and threats, and the repercussions in terms of company and employment law, need to be analysed in the light of events. Club owners may make decisions that take only commercial objectives into account or that jeopardize a club's future. In sport, where feelings and emotions are strong, even irrational, and forge a special bond between supporters and 'their' club, purely commercial or economically nonsensical approaches that flout the most elementary rules of good governance should be guarded against. To avoid misgovernance and bankruptcy among clubs, federations and private associations should take on a regulatory role and guarantee fair play by maintaining competition, establishing certain ground rules and overseeing financial management.

1.4 Cities and countries

National and international sports competitions create opportunities for cities and countries that should not be neglected. These opportunities have various dimensions and cannot be fully exploited without a proper business strategy.

The first dimension is purely sport-related: the goal of promoting sport among the general population and creating sports facilities and clubs to channel sport activity. Regional, national and international competitions can be organized to provide a challenge for sportspeople and teams and showcase a city or country's talent and its capacity to organize large-scale events.

The second dimension concerns the goal of making the best possible use of facilities and infrastructure built for specific events but remaining afterwards as new assets for the city or country; how such assets are to be integrated in city development, how they are to be financed and how they are to be used are issues that demand serious consideration.

The third dimension is economic. Whether in construction, infrastructure or services, sport activity and competitions attract companies which make investments, create jobs and promote economic activity in the region. The influx of fans at large events has an immediate impact on the service sector (e.g. restaurants, hotels and transportation). Indeed, major national and international competitions can have a significant impact on regional or national GDP.

Community support for sport is expressed in various ways. Sport builds a bridge between generations. It has always been considered a healthy activity, not just physically but also for the values it teaches. Attending a competition or sports event is much more than merely watching a show; it is being part of a community that shares certain values. Fans get the rest of their family involved and may even buy a family season ticket. The ability to sell these feelings and elicit an emotional commitment to sport is essential to winning local community support.

For an example of effective sports event strategy we need look no further than the city of Valencia. In the last decade, besides fostering youth sport by promoting sports centres, private clubs and regional competitions, Valencia has notched up a number of successes (for further details see Appendix 1.1): it built a motor-racing circuit in Cheste, where a large annual motorcycling championship and numerous other national and international tournaments are held; it hosted the 32nd America's Cup and is in the running to become the venue for the next America's Cup; and it built an urban circuit for the Formula 1 Grand Prix of Europe, held in August 2008. These sporting events, infrastructure projects and their subsequent operation, and the resulting business and tourist activity have had an extraordinary economic impact on the Valencia region, making Valencia one of the world's most talked about destinations.

1.5 The media

In the last two decades the world of sport has been revolutionized by the rise of free-to-air and pay television. The emergence of the Internet and mobile phones has opened up further possibilities for the future. The worldwide scope and economic scale that major sports events have acquired is largely thanks to the media.

We need to distinguish between the role of television and that of the press and radio. All media aim to boost their audience, but while television achieves this merely by showing images, radio and the press use spectacular, sometimes explosive headlines. In pursuit of economic benefit, they tend to put audience first and information second, without due concern for the consequences this may have for sport in general and sports clubs in particular. Besides information, analysis and criticism, which are their specialty, all too often the press and radio enter judgment and even impose sentence. It is becoming all too common to read and hear accusations levelled without concern for the repercussions.

At the same time, under the pressure of events and the immediacy of sports results, the analysis, reporting and criticism we expect of the press and the radio tend to be superficial and coarse, designed mainly for immediate impact on readership and circulation or audience figures. This stands in the way of objective analysis of the real causes of events.

It is important to consider the role of the media as objectively as possible, without falling into the trap of underestimating their importance.

In Spain, one of the most significant recent examples was the media campaign against the national football coach, Luis Aragonés. While television held back, the rest of the media, baying for blood, called for his dismissal, in a blatant attack on his hard-earned reputation. In the end, the chairman of the Spanish Football Federation held firm and the media did not get what they wanted. But with their aggressive campaign they undermined both the position of the national coach, who displayed admirable strength of character and endurance throughout, and the performance of the national team. And then, in June 2008, in spite of everything, the Spanish team became European champions for the first time in forty-two years. Whereupon, the very same Luis Aragonés who had been vilified by the media was suddenly a hero, an outstanding coach who deserved the highest praise and should be kept on at all costs. Incredible, but true. What happened was completely irrational.

So, knowing the power of the media, how can clubs, federations, associations and sportspeople deal with them? This is an important issue which deserves serious study and research. On the one hand, it is the managers and sportspeople in the spotlight who supply the media with the information they need. On the other hand, media appearances by managers and sportspeople give fans an insight into their club and the way it works and also attract sponsorship. The media can just as easily throw an organization off course or destroy a person's reputation as they can spread a favourable image of a sportsperson, manager or club.

How can the media be encouraged to behave more rationally? Nobody questions the crucial role they play or their influence on fans' opinions. This gives them added strength and power. But they cannot survive without the information they get from the large clubs.

The clubs need to build a balanced, independent, honest relationship with the media, in which mutual respect is guaranteed. To achieve that, there must be certain mutually accepted rules of the game, within which each medium may compete as best it can and pursue its business goals without flouting the code of conduct or the values that should govern relations in the worlds of sport and business.

1.6 Advertising and sponsorship

Attracted by audience numbers and the impact of television, press and radio, companies see sports clubs and high-profile sports events as effective means of implementing their advertising and sponsorship strategies. This interest on the part of companies is an important source of finance for clubs and sports event organizers.

This is a business transaction in which both sides stand to gain: the clubs broaden their activities and finance their budgets, which would be impossible with sports revenues alone, while the companies reach millions of people with a minimum of effort. A company may gain as much or more from the identification of its corporate values with certain social, ethical and environmental values as from an advertising campaign. Forming a strategic alliance with a team or sports tournament can help a company convey a particular image.

The growth of sports sponsorship has prompted considerable academic research into sponsor selection and assessment criteria. The recommendations to date have been aimed at enabling sports organizations to identify and satisfy their sponsors' motives, interests and wishes. The motives for sports sponsorship can range from making direct contact with a target audience to demonstrating corporate citizenship by supporting cultural and social events. This forces clubs to do what companies want, so that companies' business expectations are met. In the medium term, sports clubs can become strategic partners for their sponsors.

This commercial activity, combined with huge media exposure, poses a challenge to the way sports organizations have traditionally operated, driving them to develop marketing strategies, find new uses for sports facilities and extend their range of services (Cousens and Slack, 2005). Because attracting private sponsorship and marketing commercial products and services has become such a major success factor, it has become a primary goal for many sports organizations, federations, associations and clubs. No sport strategy or club budget is conceivable these days without private-sector support. This is one of the most important changes to have affected sports organizations in recent decades: the marketing of services and products. Companies, in turn, depending on their commercial and economic interests, invariably design their marketing and sponsorship strategies to convey a certain desired image to society, so as to reinforce the company's mission and values.

1.7 Fostering the values of sport

Besides all the issues mentioned so far, it is vital for society that its members practice sport from an early age.

The values inherent in any sporting activity deeply influence the behaviour of individuals, families and entire generations, extending to all areas of social life. These values include the pursuit of professional excellence, endurance in the pursuit of goals, strength of will, fair play, respect and consideration for rivals, team spirit, readiness to make decisions, and solidarity.

Sports idols have some of these qualities and are seen as role models by young people longing for ideals to imitate and emulate. An Olympic gold medal, a team victory or a statement by a leading sportsperson can have a huge impact on the fans' desire to follow in their footsteps. Pau Gasol in basketball, Rafael Nadal in tennis or Miguel Indurain in cycling illustrate just how much elite sportspeople can mean to a society such as Spain, emerging from its backwardness by reaffirming and symbolizing the vitality and creativity of its people.

The above-mentioned values motivate an individual, personal and unique style of behaviour or way of life and, at the same time, promote a positive attitude in society towards physical exercise and sport at all ages. Eventually, this leads to the creation of a 'social culture' in which these values are internalized and jealously preserved, so that they may be passed on to later generations.

1.8 Conclusion

We have discussed in this chapter the newly coined concept of 'virtuous circle' regarding the chain of reactions and interactions in the panorama of regional and city development as well as that of sport-related businesses.

By taking advantage of this circle the value creation process will become more efficient and effective thanks to synergies created and dynamic feedback loops.

Appendix 1.1 Virtuous circle unleashed: the case of Valencia[*]

Based on the 'virtuous circle' concept developed in Chapter 1, this appendix sheds light on the potential that the leveraging of some industries

[*] Source: Kimio Kase and CSBM.

(in this case sport activities) has for the development of a region or a city on the basis of the successful example of Valencia city and region, a Mediterranean region in Spain with 518 km of Mediterranean coastline, covering 23,259 km² of land with 4.8 million inhabitants (2005).

Starting point

With 3.99 trillion Pesetas (at 1986 prices) Valencia region (la Comunidad Valenciana) represented 10 per cent of Spain's total GDP in 1991; only a little over half of Catalonia's contribution in the same year at 19 per cent. What's worse it shrank by 0.6 per cent in 1992 whereas Spain's total GDP grew by 0.7 per cent.[1]

Against this backdrop, the region's traditional industries were agriculture, especially horticulture, textiles dating back from the fourteenth century, ceramics, furniture making, automobiles and tourism.[2] Except for the last two industries, much growth in the economy was not to be expected.

The incumbents in the regional government and town-planners saw a chance to spur the economic development in the promotion of tourism and sport-related events. Several factors were in its favour such as a mild climate ranging from 7 degrees centigrade in January to 21 degrees centigrade in August;[3] forty-four days of rain per year;[4] gastronomy; access by road (A-3 from Madrid, A-7 from Barcelona), airplane and railway; cultural tradition; relatively high living standard with per capita GDP at 93.9 per cent of EU in 2003 in terms of the purchasing power parity,[5] and so on.

The development plan sought the enhancement of the city's and region's standing, first and foremost. The transport infrastructure was improved at the same time.

Urban development plan in the 1990s

Valencia city hall and the Generalitat (the regional government) jointly initiated the development 'campaign' by means of a tourism

---

[1] Instituto Nacional de Estadistica: Contabilidad Regional de España: Base 1986 – Serie (1980–1996).
[2] Data drawn from http://es.wikipedia.org/wiki/ Econom%C3%ADa_de_Valencia_(ciudad).
[3] Instituto Nacional de Meteorologia: www.inm.es (accessed on 2 April 2009).
[4] Instituto Nacional de Meteorologia: www.inm.es (accessed on 2 April 2009).
[5] Eurostat news release 23/2007 dated 19 February 2007.

promotion in the early 1990s.[6] This focused on the region's cultural heritage – the city has such monuments as the Lonja de la Seda (1482–1498), declared a World Heritage Site in 1996, the Central Market, the church of Santos Juanes, the church of San Juan del Hospital, the quarter of l'Eixample with art nouveau buildings, the Cathedral where they believe the Holy Grail is kept, and many others.

To implement the development plan, the Valencia Congress Centre (1993–1998) and L'Hemisféric (1996–2009) were constructed, designed by Norman Foster and Santiago Calatrava, respectively. The unique design of these buildings portended the change in the city administration, and its urban outlook convinced people that something innovative was in the air; much the same as the Guggenheim Museum designed by Frank O. Gehry achieved in Bilbao.

The riverbed through which the River Turia used to run was converted into a 110-hectare garden, greatly enhancing the city's beauty.

To support the tourism promotion, access to the region and the city was improved. One such project was the A3 motorway connecting Madrid and Valencia, along which 70,000 vehicles passed every day in 2008, of which 25 per cent were heavy vehicles.[7]

The number of tourists visiting the city increased from 372,205 per year to 600,000 between 1991 and 1998.[8]

Sport-related activities

This effort to promote tourism was paralleled by the organization of sport-related activities, which had mutual synergy effects.

Formula 1 racing

In 1999 the Generalitat inaugurated the racing circuit Ricardo Tormo, located in Cheste, accommodating 120,000 spectators with seating for 65,000. Its most important events to date are:[9]

[6] Eduardo Zaplana (president of the Generalitat between 1995 and 2002) promoted 'during his presidency the image of the region by means of publicity campaign including the collaboration with Julio Igesias as the ambassador of Valencian products in the world ... carried out the construction of the theme park Terra Mítica' (adapted from http://es.wikipedia.org/wiki/Zaplana).
[7] www.eleconomista.es/economia/noticias/643592/07/08/Economia-Transporte-Valencia-plantea-una-autopista-hasta-Madrid-paralela-al-AVE-con-un-limite-de-velocidad-superior.html (accessed on 2 April 2008).
[8] www.turisvalencia.es (accessed on 2 April 2009).
[9] www.circuitvalencia.com (accessed on 2 April 2008).

- Grand Prix of la Comunidad Valenciana (MotoGP, 250cc and 125cc)
- Grand Prix of Spain, part of the World Superbike Championship
- Test track for Formula 1
- GP2 Series
- World tourism championship
- Formula 3 Spain

The European Formula 1 Grand Prix was held on the streets of Valencia in 2008. The track, designed by Hermann-Tilke, chose a course around the city's Americas Cup port, following a seven-year deal with Bernie Ecclestone.[10]

Some estimates place the economic impact of Formula 1 Grand Prix at €70 million. Furthermore, the publicity obtained from the event is immense if we take into account the fact that television broadcasting is covered by 147 channels (eighty-six European, forty-six Asian, eleven American and four South African channels) for 597 million viewers.[11]

America's Cup

According to Wikipedia:[12]

the America's Cup is the most prestigious regatta and match race in the sport of sailing, and the oldest active trophy in international sport, predating the Modern Olympics by 45 years. The sport attracts top sailors and yacht designers because of its long history and prestige. Although the most salient aspect of the regatta is its yacht races, it is also a test of boat design, sail design, fundraising, and management skills.

In November 2002 efforts to present Valencia's candidacy in February 2003 to host the America's Cup were begun, in competition with sixty-four other cities. The stable climate conditions in Valencia worked in favour of the city, and on 26 November 2003 it was elected to be the host of the 32nd America's Cup.

The infrastructure development and the influx of tourists to the region and the city were two of the most positive effects. For example,

---

[10] www.f1fanatic.co.uk/2007/05/10/valencia-to-be-second-f1-street-track-in-2008 (accessed on 1 April 2009).
[11] www.f1fanatic.co.uk/f1-information/statistics (accessed on 2 April 2009).
[12] http://en.wikipedia.org/wiki/America%27s_cup (accessed on 2 April 2009).

the Valencia Convention Bureau estimated that the direct and indirect economic impact of tourism was €1,300 million in 2007, in comparison with €1,000 million in 2006, with the difference of €300 million being attributed to the America's Cup. The visitors to the city on account of the Cup tended to spend €170 per person per day (on lodging, meals, etc.), which is 30 to 40 per cent more than other tourists.[13]

Other events organized in Valencia, city and region

Other events taking place in the city and/or the region include:

(1) La Mostra de Valencia: cinema festival
(2) Cortocuito: short film festival
(3) Cinema Joya: cinema festival for young film directors
(4) Valencia Escena Oberta: theatre festival
(5) Encuentro Internacional de Performance: theatre event festival
(6) Certamen Internacional de Bandas de Música Ciudad de Valencia: music festival

Conclusion

Valencia, the city and the region, nicely illustrates how a virtuous circle can be created through taking imaginative action. Aware of the fact that its industry infrastructure is not strong apart from car and its auxiliary industries, the city and the region took advantage of their location on the coast of the Mediterranean Sea, the benign climate and the historical heritage. They were capable of undertaking such dynamic changes by focusing on two specific industries, namely, the tourism and sport-related industries, both of which could benefit from each other thanks to the synergies created. Frequency of mention in the media was another change factor for the conversion of Valencia. The city and the region are the paradigm of the virtuous circle effect, i.e. the initiative to realize the dynamic power of change by choosing a limited number of industries, taking advantage of its strengths (e.g.

[13] www.reporterodigital.com/valencia/post.php/2007/01/26/el_impacto_ turistico_por_la_copa_america (accessed on 2 April 2009).

the climate, location and tradition), and effective coordination among incumbent organizations.

References

Brandenburger, A.M. and Nalebuff, B.J. (1996). *Co-opetition*. New York: Doubleday.

Chelladurai, P. (1985). *Sport Management: Macro Perspectives*. London: Sport Dynamics.

Cousens, L. and Slack, T. (2005). 'Field-level Change: The Case of North American Major League Professional Sport', *European Journal for Sport Management*, 3(1): 48–69.

Elías, N. and Dunning, E. (1992). *Deporte y Ocio en el Proceso de Civilización*. Madrid: Fondo de Cultura Económica.

Gómez, S. and Opazo, M. (2006). 'Sport Organizations Structure: Trends and Evolution in the Research Field'. Paper presented at the 14th EASM Congress (European Association of Sport Management), Nicosia, Cyprus.

Hodge, B.J., Anthony, W.P. and Lawrence, M.G. (2003). *Teoría de la Organización: Un Enfoque Estratégico*, 6th edn. Madrid: Pearson Prentice Hall.

Normile, D. (2005). 'The Strategic Art of International Site Location', *Electronic Business*, 31 (October supplement): 14–18.

Panstadia International (2009). Panstadia International Quarterly Report, 9(2): 20–32.

Slack, T. (1997). *Understanding Sport Organizations: The Application of Organization Theory*. Champaign, IL: Human Kinetics.

Toft, T. (2003). 'TV Rights of Sport Events', *European Sport Management Quarterly*, 4: 95–115.

2 | Value creation and performance criteria for sport entities

TANGUY JACOPIN, KIMIO KASE AND
IGNACIO URRUTIA

2.1 Introduction

Approached from the viewpoint of value creation two questions are addressed in this chapter:

(1) are sport-related businesses different from others?
(2) if so, how and in what way are they different?

To answer these questions we focus on the different dimensions inherent in sport-related business including historical, economic and social capitals. Different business models are analysed, and different football clubs are compared on the basis of different indicators. Stakeholder model is evaluated. Wrapping up the chapter we assess the way sport entities create value.

If generic business is about the capture and retention of customers, sport business is more difficult to define due to the different dimensions that coexist. Indeed, on top of selling season tickets, merchandising products or television rights, the sport entity has to face other dimensions that are not capitalistic activities (Shulman and Bowen, 2001).

In that sense, it is interesting to figure out if the development of sport activities has emerged as a consequence of professional underdevelopment or the emergence of a new performance model. The answer to this question is fundamental to determine how and where the creation of value comes from in sport activities.

2.2 Selling a product called sport

The creation of value in a sport entity is based on the different dimensions that the product of football has; specifically we can define four dimensions that increase the value of clubs (Figure 2.1).

How can we define the value creation for a sport entity?

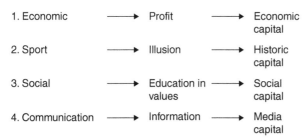

Figure 2.1 Selling a product called sport
Source: Kimio Kase and Ignacio Urrutia

The different dimensions have not been developed on the same basis and all of them offer a wide potential. Being the core business of this activity, historic capital was the first to be enhanced, either by winning sport titles or by hiring talented players without considering their impact on the budget.[1] Until 2000, however, football was above all a European and Latin American sport despite the United States hosting the World Cup in 1994. The development of football occurred in other continents thanks to the occurrence of the World Cup in countries from these areas. Indeed, the 2002 World Cup in Korea and Japan boosted the practice of this sport in Asia; in China in 2005, for the first time ever, a football match commanded a larger audience than a table tennis match. The political decision of the FIFA (International Federation of Association Football) to hold the 2010 World Cup in South Africa is supposed to give another dimension to football in that continent as well. On top of the opportunity to attend the most important football tournament, the decision of the main clubs to have international tours during the off-league season, instigated by Manchester United touring the United States, has given the emerging football markets the opportunity to regularly experience top football teams

---

[1] Many clubs managed to have successful results for a few years but the signing of expensive players without the expected return on investment led them, first, to financial trouble, and then to a deterioration of the sport dimension.

and footballers. Indeed, Milan, Real Madrid, FC Barcelona and Olympique Lyon, among others, have regular international tours abroad. In this dimension, the enthusiasm and excitement of the fans is fundamental, and one of the factors in keeping it at a high level is the previous track record. Indeed, 'famous clubs never die' because, thanks to their previous history, their future is almost ensured.

The second dimension to be developed was the economic capital. Indeed, football-club owners soon realized that their capacity to hire the best players depended on their financial situation. In that sense, maximizing income soon became a priority even if leverage (until the 1960s) was limited. Indeed, the capacity of the stadium was the most relevant variable, and explains why Real Madrid and FC Barcelona were fighting to have the biggest stadium (or even changing stadium and destroying part of the myth of the club). Hence, Real Madrid moved from Chamartín to Bernabéu and FC Barcelona moved from Els Corts to the Camp Nou. Further on, the development of merchandising and the explosion of television rights in the 1990s with the privatization of public television and the internationalization of football gave far more options to the clubs' presidents to manage their club's success thanks to their finances. The search for profits has become so important that consulting firm Deloitte undertakes a yearly survey of the top twenty richest football clubs. A good yearly result will have a positive impact on the inflows. Nevertheless, the importance of a good track record – and the consequent higher importance of stock – is demonstrated again. Referring back to 'famous clubs never die', the best example is perhaps Liverpool FC. After the Heysel stadium disaster in 1985, where rioting fans caused the collapse of a wall that killed thirty-nine people (thirty-two Italian, four Belgian, two French and one Irish), Liverpool was officially blamed and banned from all international competitions despite being, at that time, the best team in Europe. After many difficult years, including the Hillsborough disaster where a poor logistic decision (allowing hundreds of fans to enter through an inappropriate gate without turnstiles) led to ninety-six people dying after being crushed by the sheer weight of the crowd behind them, they managed to win the Champions League again in 2005, more than twenty years after their previous victory.

The third option is linked to social capital. Basically, it has two sub-dimensions: firstly, the practice of sport at a lower level and, secondly, the social activities of the club through foundations or any other social umbrella. While the first sub-dimension has been developed historically, and favours youth integration into society in such a way that some social recognition is given to the club for its work, the correlation between the second sub-dimension is, by contrast, scarcely developed. A notable exception to this is UNICEF's appearance on FC Barcelona's shirt; a unique sponsorship agreement in the world because, instead of receiving money directly from the corporate sponsor, the team pays $1.5 million to UNICEF. The benefit for FC Barcelona is clearly derived from the favourable publicity it receives from this unusual action.

The last dimension is bound up with the role of the media capital. The expression 'no event without the media' indicates the power of these institutions. Sport entities have managed to create an ongoing information flow, almost regardless of their actual sporting results. Positive news can create a sort of 'alchemy' where the fans are willing to pay for good news but, even in the case of poor results, there is first a public debate on the origin of the crisis, followed by the possible solutions, all attended by and contributed to by pundits, experts, ex-players, and a whole host of others. In that sense, sport constitutes an amazing opportunity for the media, and it is not surprising to find sports papers among the best-selling in various countries, such as *Marca* in Spain, *La Gazetta dello Sport* in Italy or *L'Equipe* in France. Having said that, however, a victory is obviously preferred every time, and not only for its impact on sales.

As we shall see, the capability to 'sell a product called football' has changed according to the dimension of the performance, evolving from a single- towards a treble-dimensional model.

2.3 Selling the football product in a renewed perspective of performance

Until the recent 'professionalization' of sport entities (that is, turning them into businesses rather than sporting clubs), the actual sport result was almost the unique criterion of performance for these organ-izations. Since then, some management issues have arisen, and the clubs increasingly focus on expansion in such terms as sport revenues and international fan base, among others. In that sense, major sport institutions seem to be driven by two variables: sport and financial performance.

Nevertheless, while taking into consideration the case of the most awarded football club in the twentieth century, Real Madrid CF, the measurement of performance according to the sport and financial results do not provide a convincing explanation of the re-election of President Florentino Pérez after his first mandate between 2000 and 2004, and the non-re-election of Lorenzo Sanz, former president be-tween 1995 and 2000. Indeed, a benchmark study of their sport and financial results shows no major differences between them. Therefore, another set of explanations has to be found to justify Florentino Pérez's re-election.

It is therefore logical to consider that sport entities have entered a third-generation business model, based not only on sport and finan-cial criteria performance but based on the value creation of virtuous circles for the stakeholders[2] of the clubs as well. The necessity to move towards such a model of performance is logical when the different dimensions of sport capital are considered, although it was not the case until now. Therefore, the inclusion of the stakeholders as a per-formance criterion closes an existing gap, i.e. the lack of explanation on the return in sport entities.

In the current case, the owners, the fans, the customers, the media, the competitors, the sponsors, the sport players and the city will all be considered as stakeholders of the club, and three sport business models will be contemplated over time for football entities. The first model considers one single dimension based on sporting perform-ance. The second model takes into account sport and financial issues, while the third model is a variation of the second with the incorp-oration of the creation of virtuous circles for the stakeholders of the clubs.

---

[2] The stakeholders of a corporation are defined as 'any group or individual who can affect or is affected by the achievement of the organization's objectives' (Freeman, 1984).

Real Madrid CF is a paradigmatic case as a sector leader,[3] and we analyse its results throughout its history and, particularly, under the rise and fall of President Florentino Pérez. A brief description of the evolution from a single- to a three-dimensional model of Real Madrid will be realized first and then we will turn our attention to asking why, despite his similar performance in the sport and the financial areas, Florentino Pérez was re-elected using a multi-stakeholder management model, whereas Lorenzo Sanz, his opponent during the election for his first mandate as president, was not.[4] Finally, we highlight that Florentino Pérez was obliged to resign due to his lack of performance according to the stakeholder criteria. Indeed, as Parker and Stone (2003) have shown, 'stakeholders can exert an obvious and powerful measure when business decisions are not to their liking'. In that sense, several dimensions of value creation can be combined in sport management (Figure 2.2).

2.4 The evolution of the sport entities business model

Until the 1950s, football competitions, amateur and professional, were led by the challenge of managing sport performance. In that sense, the first dimension of a football entity has been set historically by its sport performance.

In the 1950s, Santiago Bernabéu, then president of Real Madrid, understood that the competitiveness of a club was directly related to its capacity to sign the most important players. It was fundamental to increase income streams and, therefore, to have the biggest stadium in order to capture more value from fans. Consequently, Real Madrid first increased the size of its stadium

---

[3] The study of the Real Madrid case is relevant for its award as 'Club of the Twentieth Century', for its global and continued performances in Europe, winning nine Champions League titles, two UEFA Cups and the '*Liga*' or Spanish Championship.

[4] It has to be noted that the *socios* (season-ticket holders) elect the president (the same applies to FC Barcelona and Athletic Bilbao). This may seem democratic, but being a *socio* is a privilege that cannot be withdrawn and the waiting list to become a *socio* can be around 2–3 years. On top of that, not every *socio* can present himself or herself as a candidate, because a deposit is required of several million euros. Nevertheless, it would appear to still be a better system than when multi-millionaires simply buy clubs (such as Chelsea, AC Milan or Manchester United).

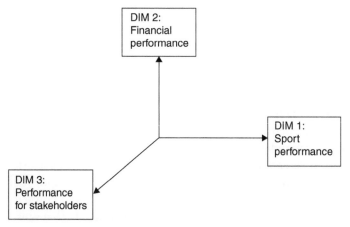

Figure 2.2 The different sport business models
Source: Tanguy Jacopin

in Chamartín (in the north of Madrid) and later created a new stadium (later named Santiago Bernabéu after the president). This period heralded what can be called the 'dual model' of sport entities, where the emphasis had to be given to both sport and financial performance.

The further development of income, from television rights, merchandising or the internationalization of the club, has until recently only complicated and refined the second-generation model with new tools available to manage different streams of income. Indeed, the philosophy of these clubs has not apparently changed; their aim remains to win titles, and to achieve that by purchasing the most expensive players in the market. Indeed, Ferrán Soriano (2007), current Vice President of Finance at FC Barcelona, confirmed the validity of this hypothesis in a study of Premier League players that showed that the correlation between the ROI provided by the most expensive players and their wages was highly positive in the long run, despite seasonal changes. This specific phenomenon has been seen in European tournaments such as the Champions League, where apparently low-profile squads such as FC Porto and FC Villarreal featured strongly.

The study of the sport and financial performance, done by comparing two elections – Real Madrid CF in 1996 and 2000 – shows

Table **2.1** *Titles won by Real Madrid between 1991 and 2004*

	Mendoza	Sanz	Pérez
Period studied	1991/1995	1996/2000	2000/2004
Liga	1	1	2
Copa	1	0	0
Champions League	0	2	1
Intercontinental	0	1	1
Total number of titles	2	4	4

Source: Authors (data from www.realmadrid.com, accessed on 1 April 2005).

different outcomes for the re-election of the president of the club, despite similar sport and financial results. Real Madrid is a paradigmatic case of new evolution, because it was awarded 'club of the twentieth century' and because its management was the first to use stakeholder management ... and the first to forget the fundamental rules.

2.4.1 *Sport results*

The difference in the sport performance between Sanz and Pérez was, on the surface, minor – both of them managed four major titles. It has to be noted though that, despite the aim of Real Madrid to become the 'best club in the world' through its use of superstar players ('Galácticos'), Pérez's management was only able to win the most prestigious and lucrative title, the Champions League, once (comparison is offered in Table 2.1). This somewhat justified the comments of former Chelsea coach, José Mourinho, when he stressed that all teams in Europe should focus on winning their own national league. The Champions League requires other systems and concepts that do not usually fit with any team's normal activities (Murillo and Murillo, 2005). It explains as well why less prestigious teams such as FC Porto, Monaco or Villarreal have performed so well in the recent past. This uncertainty explains as well, to a degree, the high level of entertainment for the spectators.

Moreover, the expectations linked with the success (or failure) of the previous managing team was another factor to be taken into consideration – the poorer the previous results, the easier to leverage the expectations. As the results obtained by Mendoza were quite poor, Sanz was able to use this as a variable for his election. Nevertheless, despite winning three major titles, compared to only one for Mendoza, he did not manage to get re-elected.

Indeed, Florentino Pérez managed to establish a new set of priorities and therefore expectations. Real Madrid obviously had to win titles but, above all, had to consider first the Liga, after FC Barcelona won four times in a row. Besides, they felt that the 'nice game' should not be exclusive to FC Barcelona. Last, but not least, the ACS CEO highlighted the importance that should be given to the financial criteria. By considering the frustration of Real Madrid's owners and fans, Florentino Pérez set new expectations.

2.4.2 *Financial results*

Before continuing the example of Real Madrid, some insights have to be given to understand why the club of the twentieth century did not put so much emphasis on financial results. Indeed, it has to be noted that the spectrum of income streams in football increased indirectly because of the tragedy that hit the Heysel stadium. The Union of European Football Associations (UEFA), despite there having been no enquiry, decided that it was Liverpool FC's fault and decided to ban all English clubs from international competitions until the fans could be kept under control. This obviously forced many clubs to develop alternative sources of income, such as merchandising through branding programmes, tours of the United States and Asia, and floating on the stock exchange (Manchester United were successful in all these examples).

Teams in continental Europe followed suit (Real Madrid most notably and successfully) and, as a result, this sector has seen an impressive growth in the last decade mainly due to the pursuit of income diversification and internationalization (see Figure 2.3).

The unique issue here, however, is that the football clubs apparently 'forget' to compare their results with their competitors. Real Madrid under Florentino Pérez apparently performed well because he doubled the club's income, while Lorenzo Sanz only increased them by 30 per cent. Nevertheless, an analysis of Deloitte and Touche's 20 Richest Football Clubs (2005) chart demonstrates that the financial

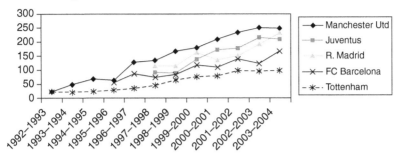

Figure 2.3 The growth of the football sector
Source: Soriano (2007)

position of Real Madrid has not substantially improved compared to its competitors. Table 2.2 highlights this paradigm.

Indeed, a different analysis of the four years of each presidency, using the total yearly rankings divided by term, shows a clear advantage in favour of Sanz against Pérez (10/4 = 2.5 vs. 18/4 = 4.5) even if Pérez's reign showed steady evolution in terms of progression vis-à-vis the competitors. In that sense, it is possible to say *ex post* that the international positioning was on the verge of providing an interesting ROI. Nonetheless, these variables were still only estimates at the time and were not valued as a main factor of differentiation during the elections.

One of Pérez's first actions in office was to build brand equity through brand valuation programmes. Indeed, the Interbrand Foundation has valued Real Madrid as the tenth most valuable Spanish brand in terms of equity and recognition (2005). In 2006, the brand equity of Real Madrid was valued at 292 million euros. Nevertheless, the lack of tracking related to the previous period prevents the authors from including this variable in this comparison.

Despite what has been said in the media, there is a lack of insight to explain the owners' behaviour concerning Pérez's re-election and Sanz's defeat using the sport and financial criteria exclusively. These facts suggest the emergence of a third-generation performance model for sport entities, where the social and media dimensions of sport capital are involved as well.

Table 2.2 *The richest football clubs in the world*[a]

Position	Club	Lorenzo Sanz				Florentino Pérez			
		1996/19997	1997/1998	1998/1999	1999/2000	2000/2001	2001/2002	2002/2003	2003/2004
1	Manchester Utd	1	1	1	1	1	1	1	1
2	Juventus	4	4	5	5	2	2	2	5
3	Bayern Munich	5	3	2	3	3	3	5	9
4	Real Madrid	3	2	3	2	6	6	4	2
5	AC Milan	6	7	7	4	4	4	3	3
6	FC Barcelona	2	6	6	8	11	12	6	7
7	Inter Milan	10	8	9	9	11	12	6	8
8	Chelsea		9	4	7	10	12	6	4
9	Liverpool	9	10	11	19	7	5	8	10
10	Newcastle Utd	8	5	12	20	14	13	9	11

Notes: [a] Explanation of the chart: the richest club is ranked 1 on the chart, the second 2 and so on.
Source: Deloitte and Touche (various reports from 1996 to 2005).

2.4.3 *The emergence of a third-generation business model for sport entities*

Sport entities have usually been slow in adopting successful perform-ing criteria and, while the recent 'professionalization' has enabled these institutions to reduce the gap with other sectors, it does still exist. Although all sectors have been engaged in corporate governance since the mid-1990s, with strong emphasis given by the shareholders to finance and ROI, the situation is completely different for European sport entities, and football clubs particularly.[5] Indeed, in contrast to the majority of the sectors, sport entities – such as Real Madrid – are often owned by their fans. The priority of these fans is obviously their team winning a good match, rather than the club's ROI. They will still prefer a healthy finance structure, if only to avoid paying for more expensive season tickets, but the priority clearly remains the sporting activity.

Therefore, the duties of the president of a football club are different from those of companies. While the aim is to satisfy the shareholders in both cases, companies want to increase profit and ROI, while sport entities want to win titles. However, football presidents still often try to behave as they did in the economic context that existed up until the 1970s, when they were managing the companies while reporting as little as possible to their shareholders.

The recent shift towards civil society governance, with an increased priority given to environmental, ethical and social criteria, has given rise to an increasingly complex system of governance, where stake-holders are fundamental in leading companies and sport entities. In that sense, the management of football entities has evolved towards a much more complex model, going beyond the sport and the financial criteria, as we will see further on.

---

[5] In contrast to European sport entities, American teams are run as franchises and have an obligation to try to make a profit. On the same basis, the shareholders are not large numbers of fans, but rather businessmen searching for high ROI. Nevertheless, although many clubs have been floated on the Stock Exchange, such as Manchester United, Juventus Torino, Lazio Roma, it still has to be noted that the shareholders will not be able to impose their will on the fans and, instead, in most matters they will have to try to win them over.

2.5 Towards a third-generation business model for sport entities

As the two first dimensions of the current business model in football organization cannot explain the re-election of Florentino Pérez and the non-re-election of Lorenzo Sanz, then stakeholder management can. More precisely, the establishment of winning relationships with the stakeholders, whatever the driving factor, is fundamental to understanding the 90 per cent supporting vote that Florentino Pérez had in the 2004 elections against Lorenzo Sanz.

2.5.1 Successful stakeholder management

The shift from corporate governance to civil society governance has occurred because the stakeholders can create some value for the company, and can provide a more important return on investment by working with them, rather than ignoring them. Indeed, some companies such as Iberdrola in the electricity sector have created a competitive advantage based on renewable energies and their dialogue with the stakeholders, including NGOs, customer associations and regulatory entities (Jacopin *et al.*, 2008).

In the case of the sport industry, there are some clear benefits to be gained from the integration of the stakeholders. The awareness of the stakeholder issue has continuously increased in sport literature (Mahony *et al.*, 2005; Mason and Slack, 2001; Mason *et al.*, 2006; Trail and Chelladurai, 2000; Wenner, 2006) but still remains low in practice in sport events, even though the 2000 Olympic Games Committee in Sydney and the 2006 Football World Cup in Germany have created processes to encourage sustainability.

These elements are far more correlated with the economic, social, historic and media capitals and, therefore, should facilitate a holistic view of the sport reality.

Concerning the situation in Real Madrid, the fans, customers, owners, media, competition organizers, competitors, sponsors, sport players and the city will all be considered as stakeholders of the club. The sport entity stakeholder model considered will be the one presented in Figure 2.4.

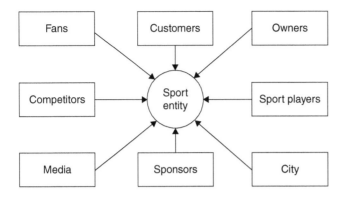

Figure 2.4 Sport entity stakeholder model
Source: Authors

The media

Because of the exponential development of the Internet in recent years, it is difficult to make fair comparisons between both presidencies. For this reason, attention has been paid exclusively to the traditional media, i.e. newspapers, radio and television. In this light, it is considered that Florentino Pérez received more support than Lorenzo Sanz, because the former created more value for the different stakeholders than the latter. Becoming a new area of interest in the business and social press was not obvious at first glance but, in fact, Real Madrid managed to do just that; creating high awareness in many areas other than traditional sporting channels, and thus getting closer to all consumers.

In fact, the media model of the Galácticos has been selling more news. Therefore, the media as stakeholder became one of the key elements of Florentino Pérez's leadership, because the media gave their support to the sport entity and actors that provided them with more coverage. Some evidence can be found in the press, as we will now consider in Table 2.3.

The same phenomenon happened with the sales of Madrid newspapers. As opposed to what happens with most events, good news in sport sells more than bad news, because fans want to be associated with the success of their team – there is a very strong emotional connection. Of course, this can also mean a lack of results can cool

Table 2.3 Number of articles dedicated to Real Madrid CF

Period studied	Lorenzo Sanz				Florentino Pérez			
	1996/1997	1997/1998	1998/1999	1999/2000	2000/2001	2001/2002	2002/2003	2003/2004
CincoDías	3	10	16	13	13	15	26	47
Expansión	6	5	12	12	22	29	31	32

Source: Author (*CincoDías* and *Expansión*).

the 'relationship' where the fan ceases to care or, worse, cares about another team. In such a case, the newspaper is forced to introduce some controversies, however contrived, to keep the sales at a minimum level.

Florentino Pérez's arrival constituted an event in itself, accompanied as it was by the promise of Luis Figo, one of the icons of rival FC Barcelona. Managing such a move was a key moment in his successful relationship with the media during his early presidency. Moreover, the promise of the arrival of a superstar every year maintained this high level of expectation. 'Every summer, a Galáctico is signed thanks to our beloved President', and the media sales and audience numbers rocket. In that sense, Figo, Zidane, Ronaldo and, above all, Beckham were the annual 'summer gifts'. The presentation of the players became so successful that they became international events; indeed, the official presentation of Beckham was attended by 499 journalists.[6]

Moreover, all the Galácticos were supposed to represent a specific target group and to give the media a fantastic platform between the club and the consumers. Zidane was the Real Madrid ambassador in French-speaking and Muslim countries. Beckham was the icon for the English-speaking and Asian publics, as well, of course, for women in general. Ronaldo, Figo and Roberto Carlos represented the Portuguese-speaking markets, and Raúl the Spanish. The appeal of these players in the media is then clearly easy to promote.

Pérez's successes are even more notable when compared to the stars signed by Sanz where the exclusive criterion taken into consideration was the sport performance. Indeed, Suker, Redondo, Karembeu or Seedorf could not be considered anywhere near as glamorous and iconic as the Galácticos.

Last but not least, the aftermath of this move increased international coverage to more than forty-five countries throughout the world. Although the Spanish Liga is a long way from the world viewing figures attained by the English Premier League, broadcast in almost ninety countries, the importance to consumers of Real Madrid as a club is beyond question, as we will see when we analyse the relationship the club maintains with its consumers, fans and owners ('*socios*').

[6] www.realmadrid.com (accessed on 2 May 2008).

Consumers, fans and *socios*

In contrast to the majority of major football clubs in Europe, Real Madrid's owners are not successful businessmen such as Glazer or Abramovich, but rather '*socios*' – fans of Real Madrid[7] who buy season tickets. Therefore the club is the property of the *socios* and thus the vote for the president can be truly split. It also explains why being a *socio* of Real Madrid is so cherished, and why the average waiting time is about two years. In this, one of Florentino Pérez's great virtues was to make it such a thrill for the average fan to become a *socio*, even bringing a certain prestige to the status.

Above all, the success of the former president of Real Madrid was to increase the fan base by selling them the idea that they had the right to see the best players because they were backing the best team in the world. It is therefore important to realize that football is more about satisfying needs than about pure sporting or financial performance. Indeed, the arrival of Zidane, soon called 'the Magician', clearly boosted attendance at Real Madrid games and this, among other such phenomena, has strengthened the feeling of being a part of an exclusive club, while the increasing internationalization of the club has only deepened this sensation.

Also thanks to their internationalization, Real Madrid has managed to convert fans with a strong interest in soccer, or with a strong interest in Real Madrid's superstar players, into Real Madrid customers, as the Landor Associates survey demonstrated in 2002 (Table 2.4).

Average attendance by game by season since 1996
(Liga exclusively)

International coverage supposes international spectators and a more important customer/fan base. The playing skills and manner have to be attractive and, of course, goals scored, in order to appeal to the recently converted 'football nations' such as the United States and Asia, since they do not have the same emotional, historical or cultural ties as Europe. In that sense, the legacy of Florentino Pérez cannot yet be completely understood because the international advances during his

---

[7] Also the case for FC Barcelona and Athletic Bilbao.

Table 2.4 *Leading soccer clubs, as per survey of soccer fans in selected countries (2001)*

Rank	Latin America	United States	Japan	England	France	Germany	Italy	Spain
1	**Real Madrid**	Man. Utd	Parma	Man. Utd	**Real Madrid**	Bayern Munich	**Real Madrid**	**Real Madrid**
2	Corinthians	**Real Madrid**	Milan	Liverpool	Man. Utd	**Real Madrid**	Juventus	Barcelona
3	FC Barcelona	DC United	**Real Madrid**	**Real Madrid**	Juventus	Man. Utd	Man. Utd	Man. Utd

Source: Taken from the Real Madrid HBS Case, Quelch and Nueno (2004) and adapted from Landor Associates (2002).

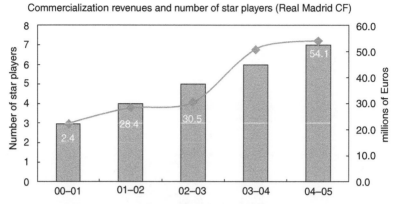

Figure 2.5 Income according to number of Galácticos
Source: Kase, Opazo & Urrutia CSBM, IESE (2006)

presidency do not yet appear in the statistics. Longitudinal studies are therefore necessary.

Sport players

Until Florentino Pérez became the president of Real Madrid, the common thinking was to consider the best player as a liability and not an asset. Whereas the wages of the football players and their playing style were the two single variables previously considered, Pérez managed to get these players wide international coverage thanks to the development of a huge programme of communication and sponsorship. A clear demonstration of the power of this communication was the arrival of David Beckham, where all the shirts with his number 23 were sold out even before his official presentation to the fans. The income relative to the number of Galácticos is thus impressive (Figure 2.5).

A virtuous circle happens when some charismatic players are signed by a club: the attractiveness of the club increases in line with the expectation that the player will increase the club's performance. Moreover, the ability to sign new players is linked to financial and emotional benefits – Florentino Pérez was able to hire the future Galácticos because they were willing to be part of the best team in the world. Their egos are flattered and, besides, they were able to manage their own financial virtuous circle by increasing their wages and their brand revenue by being Real Madrid 'ambassadors' to their respective geographical areas. With such benefits on offer, the Galácticos were clearly going to back the Pérez management.

Spanish and foreign competitors

Their competitors' income streams also benefit from the celebrity of Real Madrid. Unlike most activities, soccer clubs may benefit from people's attitudes towards another club. Indeed, Spanish clubs in general will benefit from the victories of Real Madrid in UEFA tournaments, because country indices determine the number of clubs that have access to the Champions League and the UEFA Cup, and so are more likely be involved in European tournaments in following years. In that sense, Pérez promoted the Spanish Liga as well as his own team, by attracting the most famous players in the world, and simultaneously decreased the attractiveness of other European championships in exactly the same way as he did with Figo – weakening his opponent by strengthening his own team.

Nevertheless, this logic does have some limits, because television rights are paid to the clubs according to their attractiveness for television viewers and the rank in the championship. The fact that only two Spanish clubs are attractive at an international level weakens the Spanish Liga in the long run. International football competitors understood this and were thus willing to increase their cooperation (through the former G14[8]) because, united, they could be stronger against other sports such as baseball, basketball or American football.

City

The brand name of Real Madrid has enabled Madrid to compete for the Olympic Games, and to put Madrid on the map at the same level as London, Paris, New York and Beijing. The Olympic Games in Barcelona and the America's Cup in Valencia had the same results.

---

[8] The G14, created to provide a unified voice in negotiations with UEFA and FIFA, comprised the most powerful European clubs: Ajax, Arsenal, FC Barcelona, Bayer Leverkusen, Bayern Munich, Borussia Dortmund, PSV Eindhoven, Internazionale, Juventus, Liverpool, Manchester United, Milan, Lyon, Marseille, Paris Saint-Germain, FC Porto, Real Madrid and Valencia. It was disbanded in 2008, amid accusations that it was 'elitist', after new reforms were introduced by UEFA and FIFA that effectively rendered the G14 obsolete.

In that sense, it is interesting to find articles such as 'Spain gets serious on hosting' (Carey and Ledwith, 2006) but, above all, it has to be noted that Real Madrid is a team that makes the city of Madrid a more attractive location, just as the White Sox do for Chicago (Hille, 2006). Hence, cities are more entitled to favour such entities because the ROI is far higher for the cities in terms of city brand, communication and mass support.

Sponsors

Sport sponsorship motives have been reported to range from establishing direct communications with a specific target market to demonstrating 'good citizenship' by supporting civic-oriented events. Empirical evidence has suggested that the traditional primary motive was to enhance the company image. However, as sport sponsorship acquisition and retention has become increasingly competitive, a greater focus has been directed towards a measurable impact on business. Thus, the evolutionary nature of sport sponsorship warrants a contemporary analysis of the motives for sport sponsorship engagement to assess the significant changes that reflect a shift towards result-driven outputs.

The results of the study realized by Lough *et al.* (2000) indicated measurable outcomes such as 'increase in market share' and 'sales' as those most desired by respondents. Interestingly, the comparative analysis found limited differences between companies operating in the United States and Canada regarding motives for sport sponsorship. These findings support the notion that those sponsorships considered most appealing to corporate clients will include business-building opportunities ranging from point-of-purchase promotional tie-ins to client entertainment.

The success of a sport entity has a direct correlation with the number of sponsors that are willing to get involved with this entity, thanks to the greater awareness of the company it provides. The cost of being the main sponsor may have doubled from six to twelve million euros between the presidencies of Sanz and Pérez, but the fact that the exposure of the Real Madrid brand has more than doubled in that same time ensures the continued backing from the sponsors.

Real Madrid and its stadium have become a convenient place to do business. Therefore, sponsors are desperate to be involved, and only a lack of results over several years would change that.

2.5.2 The fall of Florentino Pérez at Real Madrid

The fall of Pérez two years after his triumphal re-election cannot be completely understood without referring to the third-generation business model. The vast majority of clubs could have survived a third consecutive elimination in the quarter-finals of the Champions League, especially given that the opponents included two future finalists of the competition, Monaco and Arsenal, and the respectable Juventus. Moreover, achieving second place in the Spanish Liga, behind FC Barcelona, was an honest sport result. Furthermore, financial results could not have been better – in 2005, Real Madrid had managed to become, for the first time, the richest club in the world thanks to an aggressive commercial strategy led at a worldwide scale (Deloitte, 2006).

Therefore, the explanation surely has to come from the deterioration of relationships with the stakeholders: in short, Pérez dug his own grave by failing to properly manage the expectations of the stakeholders.

Fans, customers and socios

Florentino Pérez was elected President of Real Madrid because he correctly understood the *socios'* and fans' desire for their team to win the national Liga, and built upon the idea of 'the best players can play the best game in a fair spirit'. The difficulty of winning one title per season – always in the last game and in adverse conditions (Zidane's all-but-impossible goal in the Champions League, or winning the last game of the Liga against Real Sociedad, top of the league table until that last game) did not make Florentino Pérez change his approach and, of course, helped to reinforce the uncertainty of football.

Rather than change his approach, he went one further; he claimed that Real Madrid could win 'the triple' (Champions League, National League and Cup) and increased the expectations of the fans. However, by making such a bold statement, he reduced his room to manoeuvre and, as a result, put Real Madrid in danger.

Finally, and perhaps worst, he admitted setting almost all of his expectations on the financial field and that he was not able to manage the team. In doing so, he lost his credibility in front of players, fans and *socios*.

Leading a sport entity supposes respecting the wishes and criteria of the owners or *socios* and not imposing one's own, just as the CEO of a company needs to satisfy the wishes of shareholders and investors. On top of that, Pérez did not realize the specificities of leading sport entities. Indeed, in contrast to companies, sport entities do not respond to their president but to their *socios*. Indeed, corporate governance is characterized by shareholder influence. In that sense, the shareholders – i.e. the *socios* – had given a mandate to Pérez to:

(1) win football titles (and above all Ligas); and
(2) to improve Real Madrid's finances.

Instead he focused almost exclusively on finance, and gave priority to the Champions League instead of the Liga ... even if this was arguably the better bet.

Media

Media can easily turn against the sport entity if their interests are not fulfilled. Unlike most non-sporting events, a good piece of sporting news sells more than a negative one because of the emotional ties and sense of belonging. This means that any lack of sport results is a problem throughout the media and, sure enough, sales went down as a result of Real Madrid failing to win titles and thrill their fans. Elimination from the Champions League in the early rounds or a bad position in the Liga constitutes a strong negative impact in media sales during the last weeks or months of the competition. Consequently, the recent contracts signed by Media Pro with Real Madrid and FC Barcelona (for 1,050 million euros and almost 1,000 million euros, respectively) for the television rights for the 2008–2013 period is almost certainly going to exert huge pressure on the sport entities if they do not fulfil the television expectations. The sport war that was initiated at the beginning of the 2007/2008 Liga is an aftermath of the willingness of media to broadcast sports.

Sport players

Management of the players themselves is one of the most difficult tasks in sport management. The acquisition that occurred, for most of the Real Madrid players, at the most promising moment of their careers supposes that their operability remains high for a four-year

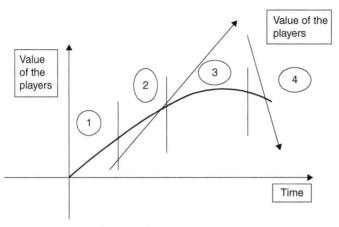

Figure 2.6 Sport-player cycle

mandate, but actually prevents the team from being competitive in the long run. Indeed, these players do not usually accept being replaced or having their wages lowered.

Moreover, as most Real Madrid players are international icons, all their difficulties can be analysed from the sport, the economic and the 'people' media. The risks of entering a vicious circle are high when results do not follow or when the dream fulfilment is declining, as we can see taking into consideration the sport-player cycle (Figure 2.6).

Different phases of the sport-player cycle:

(1) emerging player
(2) maximizing value of the player
(3) saturation of the player
(4) going towards the end of the player's career and its residual value[9]

This was clearly seen at Real Madrid where the ability to score went down when the players' average age exceeded twenty-nine, as shown in Figure 2.7 where the ratio between the age, the goals and the games in which these players were involved shows a clear decrease in the performance.

[9] Source: Tanguy Jacopin.

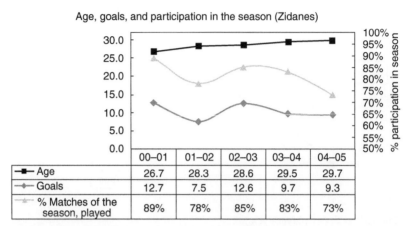

Figure 2.7 Age, goals and games per season (Zidanes)
Source: Kase, Opazo & Urrutia, CSBM, IESE, (2006)

The decrease in efficiency is particularly important for this squad because most of the signings were made with attacking players ('forwards') and, above all, because it was around -20 per cent between 2002/2003 and -10 per cent in the following year. The lack of sport results did not affect their wages, and the personal economic rewards obtained through sponsorship were greatly increasing. Therefore, with pay apparently not linked to performance, the players did not seem to have any interest in changing their behaviour.

City

Sport entities and sport events can put a city on the map, but poor results or reputation can just as easily do damage. While inconclusive, it is interesting to note that the failure of Madrid in its bid for the Olympic Games occurred when Real Madrid had already entered its decline and that Paris' failure for the same bid was followed by strong resentment from the French people regarding the perceived decadence of their capital and of their country. An explanation of the rise and the fall of Florentino Pérez at Real Madrid thanks to the stakeholder performance model is full of such insights (Table 2.5).

The evolution of the sport business sector towards a treble-dimension model for performance leads to a major contradiction for sport managers. Their leverages are not proportional with their businesses.

Table **2.5** *Rise and fall of Florentino Pérez according to the stakeholder performance model*

Effect on stakeholder	Rise	Fall
Owners, fans and consumers	Raise the expectations taking into account the sport priority of the owners and fans Focusing on the weak point of his challengers: win Ligas Attracting best stars in order to play best football	Incapacity to fulfil expectations No more titles Stars unable to play the best football Expectations always increasing, despite the fact sport results did not match initial target Lack of respect for fans (preference to business press rather than sport press)
Management	Professionalize the financial and marketing departments	Unable to manage priorities of owners (first attain sports result then financial income) or at least to explain his management style
Media	Strong support because of new audience (women and business through the respective niche publications)	Lack of results causes strong prejudice to media because the sales go down due to the lack of excitement and resulting impact on several weeks' sales
Sport players	Galácticos as assets All players in the world are willing to join Real Madrid to increase their status, earnings and reputation	Galácticos as liabilities (i.e. the price to pay for a top player is offering astronomical wages) Unable to make the players play as a team Reputation of the players goes down and thus their ad/promo/merch income as well

Table 2.5 (*cont.*)

Effect on stakeholder	Rise	Fall
City	Puts Madrid back on the map and enables, among other things, the participation in the Olympic Games bidding	Madrid loses bid and is unable to attract major sport events, the infrastructure works are not well perceived by Madrid inhabitants and electors
Sponsors	Increase worldwide exposure with strong values (being number one; fair spirit)	Unwillingness to be associated with a losing team
Competitors	Benefit from new interest for soccer. Possibilities, among others, to target female audience	Better for them for the sport criteria but their 'kudos' decreases as well. FC Barcelona is nothing without Real Madrid, etc.

Source: Jacopin.

Indeed, their management will be approved by the stakeholders if they have good results in the sport dimension, an area where their influence is quite limited, whereas their options to improve the finance of the clubs and to effectively manage their stakeholders are far greater but less relevant in terms of management success. Figure 2.8 shows the difficulty of the task of the sport managers. Indeed, the key successes of performance offer low sport-management leverages.

That is the reason why the management of all the dimensions of sport capital requires the professionalization of the sport entities, in order to ensure its maximization under the three dimensions of performance.

2.6 Value creation and dimension of performance

Any entity needs to create value to remain sustainable in the long run. As has been seen, the existence of various capitals in the sport entity,

Key success of performance

Sport management leverages

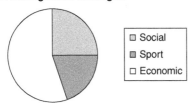

Figure 2.8 Key successes of performance vs. sport management leverages
Source: Tanguy Jacopin

whether sport, economic, social or the communication results, and the shift towards ever-more complex performance models, force the club's management to position itself in terms of what value creation is needed. Indeed, several emphases are possible from the sport or the company point of view.

It has to be noted that the vast majority of professional football clubs competing in European competitions, on a regular basis, try to maximize both sport and economic results. Nevertheless, the ability to improve both dimensions at the same time is almost impossible, and clubs are repeatedly forced to choose just one of the dimensions, at least in the short term. Real Madrid first prioritized the sport variable, with the incorporation of Figo and Makelele, and then went to the economic variable by placing strong emphasis on marketing development (while, to a degree, even going so far as to forget the sport performance). On the other hand, FC Barcelona under Laporta's presidency placed the emphasis on the re-negotiation of debt, and then moved quickly to sport performance by signing Ronaldinho and Eto'o, which eventually increased the income of the Catalan club. The key issue for sport management consists of improving the simultaneous emphasis on sport and business, without creating a strong distortion towards one of these two variables and thereby losing sight of the

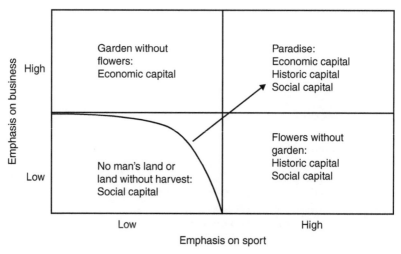

Figure 2.9 Business/sport emphasis
Source: Kimio Kase and Ignacio Urrutia

other. Another way of looking at these two scenarios is the 'garden without flowers' in cases of abundant cash but low fan appeal, or 'flowers without the garden' in cases of extensive fan appeal but poor business results (Figure 2.9).

Nevertheless, the creation of value should necessarily move from the 'indefinition zone' (see Low and Low quadrant) towards either of these two variables simply by forecasting the next move towards the other variable. The lack of ability to manage the second stage is the main difficulty of sport entities. The incapacity of any football club since the 1980s to win the Champions League in Europe during two consecutive years would seem to clearly demonstrate some weakness in strategic planning.

That said, the uniqueness of sport business models is not offered as a cause of this phenomenon. On the contrary, the assumption taken here is that several sustainable paradigms coexist. Indeed, some sport teams base their identity on political and regional differences; Athletic Bilbao, for example, exclusively hires Basque players. Others are more obsessed by the P&L of the club than by their sport results. The most famous example illustrating this case comes from an English club that remains in the second division, despite its flotation on the stock exchange. The matrix on the sport and business emphasis can be exploited in Figure 2.10.

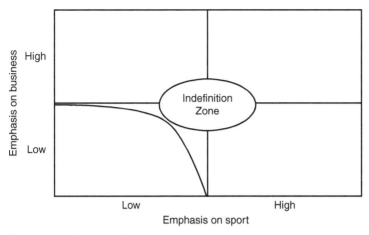

Figure 2.10 The sport/business emphasis
Source: Kimio Kase and Ignacio Urrutia

Nevertheless, when the priorities have been established, the means have to be determined to reach them. In order to proceed, various cases will be studied using a reduced model of stakeholders (fans, companies/sponsors, city, owners and media) trying to highlight virtuous circles leading to value creation. It is worth highlighting the existence of various business models for the sport entities on the one hand, and the difficulty of maximizing value creation with all the stakeholders on the other hand. In that sense, the move towards value creation for sport entities becomes much wider than for other sectors.

The existence of different ways to value creation, through the creation of virtuous circles involving the fans, the companies, the cities, the media and the owners, will be illustrated by the cases of Real Madrid, Atlético Madrid and the basketball team of Adecco Estudiantes.

2.6.1 *Real Madrid, or how the appeal through purchasing the Galácticos can initiate a virtuous circle*

The value-creation model of Real Madrid is based on the following axes. On the one hand, there is an input stemming from the owners of the club who buy their season tickets every year in order

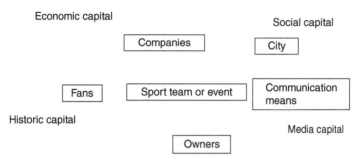

Figure 2.11 Do sport entities create value?
Source: Authors

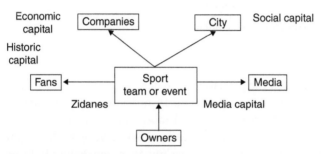

Figure 2.12 The Real Madrid case
Source: Kimio Kase and Ignacio Urrutia

to obtain titles, success, awareness and identity with the winner. On the other hand, there are several outputs of value generation from the clubs. Indeed, hiring high-performing players such as the Galácticos increases the satisfaction of the fans. The sponsors benefit from the recognition of the Real Madrid brand name. The elements provide the news contents to the media that put Madrid on the map as a successful place to live or an interesting place to visit (Figure 2.12).

In fact, such a model is very complex and difficult to maintain at high performance because it requires feedback at all levels in order to satisfy the different stakeholders – the decline of 'old' stars, and the high level of expectation from the fans and the *socios* are current examples.

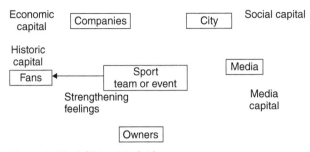

Figure 2.13 Atlético Madrid
Source: Ignacio Urrutia

2.6.2 *Atlético Madrid, or how historic membership feelings can initiate a virtuous circle*

While Real Madrid tries to create value for all its stakeholders, the situation is quite different for the 'second club' of Madrid. Indeed, instead of being led by the *socios* of this club, all the shares of the club are held by its president, Enrique Cerezo. Until now, he has had to invest in his club without having any return on investment. This situation can be explained by the historically poor track record compared to Real Madrid, and the fact that the Atlético fans are more deeply involved with their club, independent of the results; their fans are more loyal than those of Real Madrid, and thus it is not surprising that the value creation occurs far more in the club–fan relationship. When Atlético was relegated to the Spanish second division in 2002, they had more fans attending the games in that season than when they were playing in the first division. Taking into consideration these elements, it is not surprising that the media receives far less content from this club and that the city of Madrid cannot significantly increase awareness of it.

Although Atlético Madrid has managed to design a successful model of value creation with its fans, the results with its other stakeholders are far from being optimal, according to their management (Figure 2.13). Nevertheless, the sustainability of the club is practically ensured by those exceptional ties existing between the team and its fans.

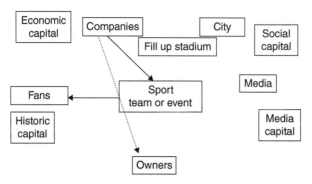

Figure 2.14 Adecco Estudiantes
Source: Ignacio Urrutia

2.6.3 *The Adecco Estudiantes basketball team, or how the sponsor initiates the virtuous circle*

Moving away from football to study the case of the Adecco Estudiantes Basketball team, we can see how the sponsor, Adecco, managed to redesign the strategy of the club without being its owner, and invested in some player hiring when the team stopped being as competitive as it had been in the past. The intervention of the sponsor, in this case Adecco, substituting for the 'town hall' interest present in the majority of the clubs, reactivated the fans' passion (Figure 2.14).

2.6.4 *The America's Cup, or how a city can shape a virtuous circle*

The America's Cup is not just a sailing competition – it also has the surprising distinction of being the third most important world sport event after the football World Cup and the Olympic Games.

The winning team traditionally organizes the following competition so, when Alinghi, the Swiss team, won the America's Cup in 2002 in Auckland, nobody knew where the next competition would be, due to Switzerland's famous lack of sea borders. Alinghi launched a bidding process to select the next city to host the next America's Cup. The competition was won by Valencia, Spain, despite it not

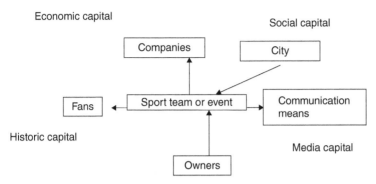

Figure 2.15 The city of Valencia and the America's Cup
Source: Jacopin and Urrutia (2006)

being the favourite. Thanks to this event, Valencia was put on the map at an international level, and has been able to remodel itself (with Santiago Calatrava as the driving architect) with a greater focus on the sea, despite being historically oriented towards agriculture (and, of course, the famous oranges).

The involvement of the city was a key aspect in launching the America's Cup because it mobilized the sponsors (the utilities group Iberdrola with the 'Desafío Español' team), the media and the fans (Figure 2.15).

2.6.5 *The Football World Cup, Germany 2006, or how the media – i.e. La Sexta – can create a virtuous circle*

The multiplication of television channels always makes it more difficult for new channels to achieve some awareness in their target group. Nevertheless, a new Spanish television channel, La Sexta ('the sixth'), was able to profit hugely from, and publicize its existence through, its 100 million euro bid for exclusive television rights to the football World Cup in Germany, 2006. This decision was motivated by the fact that although La Sexta was not a paid subscriber channel, potential viewers had to invest in new technology to be able to receive the broadcasts (Figure 2.16).

This decision was a success because the channel decided to go for strong support by the Spanish fans by creating some re-transmission

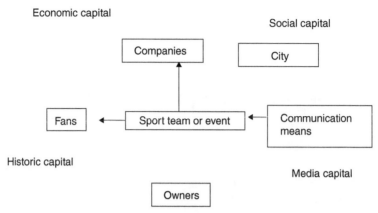

Figure 2.16 La Sexta and the 2006 World Cup
Source: Tanguy Jacopin

events in many Spanish cities, including Madrid and Barcelona. The mass following this generated (despite the elimination of the Spanish team in the quarter-finals) a huge success for the World Cup and, of course, for La Sexta in terms of brand awareness among the same population. The recognition of this virtuous circle by the managers of La Sexta apparently didn't go unnoticed – the same campaign was used for the 2006 Basketball World Cup which, this time, Spain won.

2.7 Conclusion

The different cases that have been developed show the absence of a single best way for sport entities to create value. Indeed, the possibility to perform well in any one of the different key dimensions of sport performance always provides more options for the sport entities to be competitive, whether at a local or at an international level.

Special emphasis has to be given to the emerging dimensions. The financial dimension in the sport activity became important quite some time after corporate governance had been standardized in public companies. However, this gap has decreased with the third-dimension model of performance, with the inclusion of stakeholders as key factors to create value.

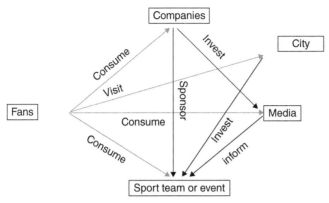

Figure 2.17 Value creation under the third dimension of performance for sport entities
Source: Authors

The thrill and excitement to give the fans the victories the team can attain, the brand identity that can be returned to companies via sponsorship programmes, the content generated for the media, the social projects with the city, and the return on investment for the owners, whether they be fans or investors; these are all variables to consider in order to create a sustainable value creation programme as Figure 2.17 shows.

Thus we can see that value creation for the sport entities is engaged when one of the stakeholders initiates the virtuous circle of the sport entity; the key variable being the involvement of the fans and their conversion into consumers (Figure 2.11). The maximization of the value creation is related to the acceptance of the role of the stakeholder. Indeed, a lack of involvement or, conversely, too much involvement, can lead to inefficient processes and could even lead to value destruction.

References

Carey, R. and Ledwith, D. (2006). 'Spain gets Serious in Hosting', *Sportbusiness International*, **December/January**: 38–40.
Deloitte (2004, 2005 and 2006). The Top 20 Richest Football Clubs.
Freeman, R.E. (1984). *Strategic Management: A Stakeholder Approach*. Boston: Pitman.

Hille, B. (2006). 'The Best Sport Cities', *Sporting News*, **230**(32): 22.

Interbrand (2005). *Best Global Brands*. Online, available at: www.interbrand.com (last accessed 21 February 2008).

Jacopin, T. and Urrutia, I. (2006). 'The NGO as Stakeholder of the America's Cup'. Paper presented at the Major Sport Events as Opportunity for Development: The International Promotion of the City, Valencia.

Jacopin, T., Poisson, S. and Fontrodona, J. (2008). 'Iberdrola: A Utility's Approach to Sustainability and Stakeholder Management', *Journal of Business Ethics and Education*, **8**: 30–5.

Kase, K., Gómez, S., Urrutia, I., Opazo, M. and Martí, C. (2006). 'Real Madrid CF-Barcelona: análisis de las estrategias económica y deportiva del período 2000–2006', Occasional Paper OP 06/12, IESE Business School, Barcelona.

Landor Associates (2002). 'Energizing the Brand through the Image Power of Football: Scoring with Sponsorship'. Online, available at: www. landor.com (last accessed 2 February 2008).

Lough, N.L., Irwin, R.L. and Short, G. (2000). 'Corporate Sponsorship Motives among North American Companies: A Contemporary Analysis', *International Journal of Sport Management*, **1**(4): 283–95.

Mahony, D.F., Hums, M.A. and Riemer, H.A. (2005). 'Bases for Determining Need: Perspectives of Intercollegiate Board Athletic Directors and Athletic Board Chairs', *Journal of Sport Management*, **19**: 170–92.

Mason, D.S. and Slack, T. (2001). 'Evaluating Monitoring Mechanisms as a Solution to Opportunism by Professional Hockey Agents', *Journal of Sport Management*, **15**(2): 107–34.

Mason, D.S., Thibault, L. and Misener, L. (2006). 'Reconfiguring the Rings? A Perspective on Corruption in the Bidding Process for the Olympic Games', *Journal of Sport Management*, **20**: 52–73.

Murillo, E. and Murillo, C. (2005). *El Nuevo Barça: contado por sus protagonistas*. Madrid: Peninsula.

Parker, C. and Stone, B. (2003). *Developing Management Skills for Leadership*. Harlow: Financial Times.

Quelch, J. and Nueno, J.L. (2004). The Real Madrid Club de Fútbol, Harvard Business School Case n. 504063.

Shulman, J.L. and Bowen, W.G. (2001). *The Game of Life: College Sports and Educational Values*. Princeton: Princeton University Press.

Soriano, F. (2007). 'The Governance in Big Soccer Clubs', in P. Rodriguez, S. Kesenne and J. Garcia (eds.), *Governance and Competition in Professional Sports Leagues*. Oviedo: University of Oviedo.

Trail, G. and Chelladurai, P. (2000). 'Perceptions of Goals and Processes of Intercollegiate Athletics: A Case Study', *Journal of Sport Management*, **14**(2): 154–78.

3 National context and profit strategy of the sport entity: how to overcome the national borders of the sport entities?

TANGUY JACOPIN

3.1 Introduction

Can sport entities move away from their national context? If so, how? If not, why not? In the first step, based on football, this chapter answers those questions and contends that sport clubs are conditioned by their national context. This contention is later tested by extrapolating the argument to other sports and to a non-European context. In the light of the prevalence of the national context in the management of sport entities, another question is raised about whether to push forward the internationalization or regionalization in future. The similarities between sports and other industries, such as the automotive and entertainment industries, are discussed.

In the absence of one best way for sport entities to expand and, its corollary, the existence of different ways to create value thanks to the sport, financial and stakeholder dimensions, always provide more opportunities to perform successfully on a national and international basis. Moreover, expansion opportunities are increased through the possibility of generating a virtuous circle among the fans, the city, the media, the sponsor and the sport team or sport event, in relation to the different forms of sport capitals, whether historic, social, economic or media.

Nevertheless, the scope of influence of the sport entities is still far more limited than it looks. In this chapter, the focus will be to demonstrate that sport entities still currently depend too much on their country of origin. Indeed, the income of the clubs is bound to the structure of the national league and to their relationships with their stakeholders. Moreover, the search for efficiency in Europe is linked to the impetus of the national league, which necessarily limits the deficiencies of the sport entity due to the priority given to the sport results, whereas sport entities in the United States mainly have to be profitable.

Thus, after developing a parallel with the automotive industry, we will show that, whether in Europe or in America, a strong emphasis has to be given to the maximization of opportunities linked with the specificities of the national context, which is in contrast to profit strategies of companies. Only when this condition has been fulfilled can the sport entity analyse how it can overcome national limits and properly foster profit strategies in an international mindset.

The comparison with the automotive industry, through some of the most prominent international research networks on this topic – IMVP[1] of MIT and, above all, GERPISA (Groupe d'Étude et de Recherche Permanent sur l'Industrie et les Salariés de l'Automobile) – reveals some key insights for the future of the development of sport entities based on the management of the duality existing between the growth mode of national income and the profit strategy of the sport entity.

The structure of this chapter will underscore the veracity of this problem by comparing, in a second stage, the situation of the sport entities in the US system (closed league, financial-results driven) and in the European case (open league, sporting-results driven) in various sports. Third, a transversal study among the five main European football powers (England, Spain, Italy, Germany and France) will examine the importance of the national context for the sport entities of these different countries.

Once these aspects have been assumed, the emphasis will be given to the internationalization of sport entities and, more specifically, to the means of managing it in the most successful way. While its justification is beyond doubt, taking into consideration the magnitude of this phenomenon, the key question is whether sport clubs should prioritize either globalization or regionalization, in order to maximize opportunities for profit strategies. Indeed, although the vast majority of football clubs have opted for growing and non-saturated markets, such as China, Japan and the United States, the lessons learnt from the automotive sector and the Walt Disney Corporation (a reference we will return to later) suggest that the answer lies in both globalization and regionalization.

3.2 Comparisons with the automotive industry: national context versus profit strategies of the firm

The use of a comparison between the sport and automotive industries is relevant for several reasons. First, benchmarking the most paradigmatic industry that pioneered, among other things, mass production,

[1] International Motor Vehicle Program.

volume and diversity strategies, and constant cost reduction, can definitely offer key insights to sport entities on how to broaden their activity through the twenty-first century. Second, and even more interestingly, the two industries have recently faced the same questions – although in different proportions – about the existence of one or several performance models, and on the debate over regionalization versus globalization. Reflection on these points leads us in both cases to the conflict between the national context of a firm and the profit strategy of the firm. In that sense, this debate relates to the variety of capitalism, to the possibility of replicating a business model independently of the national context, and to the limits of globalization at a time when all renowned sport entities are constantly evoking their internationalization and copying the model of Manchester United's expansion following the 1985 Heysel disaster (as mentioned in Chapter 2).

The study of the automotive industry can provide valuable insights into the sport industry by examining what happened in this sector in the 1990s when MIT's International Motor Vehicle Program (IMVP), led by Womack and Jones, considered the existence of a 'single best way' pursued by all manufacturers as a solution to favour the growth of this industry. By contrast, GERPISA, led by Boyer and Freyssenet, focused on the absence of a 'single best way' and on the importance of the national context for the carmaker strategies. Empirical evidence demonstrated the veracity of the GERPISA model. It has to be noted that the results of our previous chapter highlighted the same scenario for the sport industry due to the possibility of initiating a virtuous circle from different stakeholders, even if the reference of the sport entities is to maximize their professionalism.

While the GERPISA framework focused on the importance of the national context in the automotive industry and on the national growth regime, we can note that many scientific publications considered that the twentieth century was divided into three major productive paradigms. The first phase involved, as Freyssenet *et al.* (2003) explained, 'semi-craft production, characterized by a wide variety of goods made by self-organized professional workers seeking to satisfy a demand that emanated from the upper social categories, these being the only persons who could access such custom-made items'. If we adapt these conclusions to the sport industry, this phase corresponds to the amateurism of the majority of the European sport entities until the 1970s.

The second paradigm was mass production. Its main characteristics were linked with the manufacturing of large, standardized goods by unskilled workers performing precise tasks. The scope of this paradigm was to position the companies as the nations' best, and illustrated at this time by the success of US, French and Italian companies. From the 1970s to the mid-1980s, the professionalization of the sport entities led to the pursuit of sporting results on a much more structured basis, but without considering internationalization at this stage.

Lastly, 'lean production' appeared in the 1990s; first in Japan and then worldwide. This system was supposed to have enabled the manufacturing of diversified, high-quality and competitively priced goods, thanks to employees' and suppliers' effort towards a continuous improvement in performance. The MIT researchers instituted an International Motor Vehicle Program (IMVP) to direct research into automobile manufacturers and variations within their levels of productivity. This research revealed some mechanisms that these researchers considered as 'single best way' tactics. The third phase in the sport industry can be likened to the 'lean production' in the sense that there existed a 'single best way' based on the financial performance. This can be considered as a result of the development of the movement in favour of corporate governance. Compared with the evolution of sport entities, this poses the question of the existence of one or several business models among sport entities. As many sport teams viewed Manchester United as the leading institution focusing on the diversification of income streams (by examining the positioning of the Walt Disney company), the question was whether to copy Manchester United's business model or to adapt it to their specific backgrounds.

In contrast to the MIT research group, GERPISA, another group of researchers, mainly Europeans but including some Japanese and Americans, claimed that there was an underlying confusion behind the concept of lean production, citing the examples of two different business models, 'Toyotism'[2] and 'Hondism'.[3] The existence of

---

[2] 'Toyotism' refers to the model that was created by Ono in Toyota. It 'stems from a process that makes it possible to resolve the contradiction between a production system whose organization had been entirely based on the reduction of costs, and an employment relationships that guaranteed jobs and career development' (Shimizu, 1999).

[3] 'Hondism' refers to the model that was created by Honda and that 'implements an innovation and flexibility strategy which is particularly relevant in growth modes where national income distribution is competitive' (Freyssenet *et al.*, 2003).

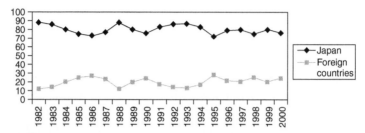

Figure 3.1 Japan's and foreign countries' contribution to Toyota's global net profit, 1982–2000
Source: Jetin (2003)

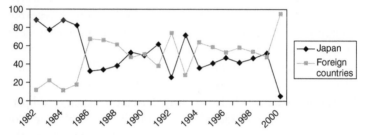

Figure 3.2 Japan's and foreign countries' contribution to Honda's global net profit, 1982–2000
Source: Jetin (2003)

the diversity of the business models in the automotive industry could mainly be explained by the correlation between the profit strategies of the companies and the national growth modes where these companies operated. In that sense, this approach, when transferred to sport entities, offers a more holistic approach involving all their stakeholders and enabling the national growth models.

Japanese carmakers such as Honda and Toyota did manage to consolidate their activities, both in their country of origin and abroad.[4] In the case of these two companies, there was coherence between national and international expansion. Nevertheless, as shown in the following two graphs, the business models were radically different in both cases – Toyota first implemented its success on a more national basis as Figure 3.1 shows, while Honda (see Figure 3.2) went for international profit from the competitive growth required to sustain innovative cars.

---

[4] As it is not the topic of the book, we will not focus on Japanese companies, such as Nissan, Isuzu or Mazda, that had the same difficulties as US ones.

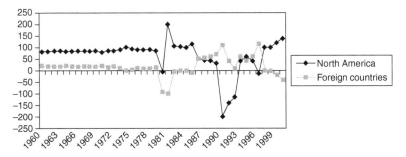

Figure 3.3 North America's and foreign countries' contribution to GM's global net profit, 1960–2000
Source: Jetin (2003)

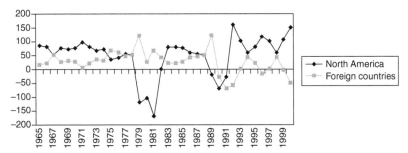

Figure 3.4 North America's and foreign countries' contribution to Ford's global net profit, 1965–2000
Source: Jetin (2003)

Adopting a model without understanding its key parameters can be a problem for companies that do not have the same profile as the inventors of the business models – indeed, we can go so far as to say that blind imitation is usually disastrous. Besides, when the internationalization of a firm begins, the mistakes become cumulative on national and international scales – or can cause the opposite results in the country of origin and the remaining countries where these companies operate. For instance, GM and Ford – which are represented respectively in Figure 3.3 and Figure 3.4 – are clear examples of this trend in the last forty years. Indeed, the evolution of the American automotive companies depicted in the following tables highlights the opposite performance to that obtained into the home country and in foreign offices. This is one of the reasons why companies have had to tend towards 'multi-local' strategies and to fit to their environment.

This situation has to be taken into consideration to analyse the future development of sport entities. In that sense, it has to be remembered that UNCTAD[5] studies (2000) have demonstrated that commercial internationalization has only recently developed. For instance, in 1993, the top 100 multinational companies (MNCs), all sectors of activities considered, still relied on their national market for 57 per cent of their business. Commercial internationalization evolved at a faster pace than international assets or international workforce because foreign markets reached a proportion of 52 per cent in 1997/1998. Jetin (2003) demonstrated that the automotive industry is far above the average with more than 57 per cent of international commercialization (Table 3.1).

The global synthetical average is an average of commercial revenues, production, total assets and workforce indexes, while the UNCTAD's synthetical index is an average of commercial revenues, workforce and total assets indexes.

Although expansion abroad is usually viewed as mandatory for expansion, Jetin's study pointed out first the limits of internationalization, because it can be a source of substantial losses, and second that these entities are still dependent on their country of origin for their production, as the following graphs show. The interest to compare the sport entities with the automotive industry comes here from the fact that the production of contents, i.e. the games, and the players act mainly in the team's country of origin. Figure 3.5 presents the production share of the automotive manufacturers outside the country of origin.

It should be noted that only Daimler Chrysler, VW, Scania and Volvo had more than 50 per cent of their production share outside of their country of origin, and Daimler Chrysler was the only company to have 50 per cent of its production share outside of its region of origin. If this situation seems surprising, it should be remembered that 'most competitive advantages based on economies of scale are found in local and niche markets, where either geographical or product spaces are limited and fixed costs remain proportionally substantial' (Greenwald and Kahn, 2005). This trend is illustrated by PSA, Renault,[6] BMW and Volvo, all of whom had a production share outside their region of origin of under 10 per cent until 1999 (Figure 3.6).

[5] United Nations Conference on Trade and Development.
[6] The merger between Renault and Nissan is contemplated as two separate entities.

Table 3.1 *The internationalization of the automotive industry*

Firms	Degree of internationalization of automobile firms, 1995–1999					Synthetical index internationalization	
	Commercial revenues	Productive revenues	Production	Workforce	Total assets	Global	UNCTAD
American companies							
Chrysler (1995–1997)	13	nd	38	17	15	21	15
Ford (1995–1997)	34	nd	46	48	26	39	36
GM (1995–1996)	30	nd	45	33	27	34	30
Average	26	nd	43	32	23	31	27
European companies							
BMW (1995–1999)	72	nd	49	41	62	56	58
Daimler-Benz (1995–1997)	61	48	47	23	38	42	41
Fiat Auto (1995–1999)	59	nd	41	34	42	44	45
PSA (1995–1999)	61	51	23	24	39	37	41
Renault (1995–1999)	58	46	27	31	49	41	46
Scania (1995–1999)	90	nd	74	50	nd	nd	nd
VW (1995–1999)	65	36	53	47	58	56	57
Volvo (1995–1999)	90	nd	68	44	nd	nd	nd
Average	63	44	45	38	54	51	52

Table 3.1 (*cont.*)

| Firms | Degree of internationalization of automobile firms, 1995–1999 | | | | | Synthetical index internationalization | |
	Commercial revenues	Productive revenues	Production	Workforce	Total assets	Global	UNCTAD
Japanese companies							
Honda (1995–1999)	69	65	47	73	54	61	65
Isuzu (1996–1999)	60	36	42	56	10	42	42
Mazda (1995–1999)	61	37	18	24	17	30	34
Mitsubishi (1995–1999)	53	33	30	30	30	36	38
Nissan (1995–1999)	56	52	40	71	38	51	55
Subaru (1995–1999)	52	39	17	35	26	32	38
Suzuki (1995–1999)	52	23	37	nd	18	nd	nd
Toyota (1995–1999)	54	43	31	60	43	47	52
Average	57	41	31	49	30	43	46

Source: Jetin (2003).

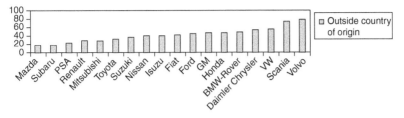

Figure 3.5 Production share outside the country of origin, 1995/1999 (%)
Source: Jetin (2003)

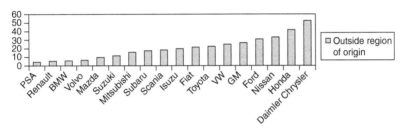

Figure 3.6 Production share outside the region of origin, 1995/1999 (%)
Source: Jetin (2003)

Although carmakers have recently attained a fast pace of internationalization through mergers and acquisitions, the carmakers are still not global – at best they are regional players. In all cases, the national and the regional paths still play a fundamental role in the development of this industry and, by the same token, the study of recent developments of sport entities has to take this into account.

3.3 Two different approaches of sport business: the US way versus the European way

Before focusing on the importance given to the national context at the moment of designing the sport entity's profit strategy over time, an historic perspective will be given to show the dichotomy among the sport entities in Europe and the United States. Indeed, the United States initiated sport as a professional activity with training of their elite at sport colleges in the second half of the 1950s, while Europe was developing free and subsidized mass sports, with an attendant under-development of professional sports. The concerns in the United States centred around antitrust, the formation of a labour market, racial

Table 3.2 *Common areas of specialization in sport economics*

Areas	Topics
Pricing	Inelastic pricing and demand for spectator sports, attendance, pricing the uses of sport facilities and recreation parks, sports services as collective goods or merit wants
Mega sport events, sport facilities	Economic impact (multipliers), cost–benefit analysis, externalities, use and non-use values, willingness to pay with information asymmetry (different methodologies)
Investment	Local government subsidies and regional (urban) economic development, sport and leisure economics
Financing	Overall sport finance, financing, professional team sports, financing sport facilities and events
By-products	Sport broadcasting, sponsorship, gambling
National sport wins	Economic determinants of medals (Olympics), comparative advantage of nations
Designing contests	Theory of tournaments and the design of sporting contests, optimal prize structure and balanced contests in professional individualistic and team sports

Source: Andreff (2006).

discrimination and making money, whereas the concerns in Europe were for inclusive sport participation, amateur sport and accounting, public governance and non-profit associations (Andreff, 2006).

Nevertheless, sport entities from both sides of the Atlantic did actually begin to find common areas of specialization due to the progressive professionalization of sport in Europe and the development of amateur sport in the United States, as Table 3.2 suggests. This suggests that sport entities realized the limits they had in their own system, and indicates their willingness to look for an optimal situation.

However, their cultural backgrounds often prevent them from moving ahead. The principal sports remain different on each side of the Atlantic, with football (American football), basketball, baseball, ice hockey and Indy cars being preferred in the United States, and football (soccer), basketball, rugby, cycling, Formula 1 and a whole host of amateur sports in Europe.

Table 3.3 *Professional sport focus in the United States and in Europe*

	America	Europe
Leagues	Closed	Open
Teams	Profit maximizing	Win maximizing
Team mobility	Horizontal: franchise relocation	Vertical: promotion and relegation system
Labour market	Regulated	Deregulated (Bosman)
Financing	Naming, merchandising, antitrust, law exemption	Television rights, stock flotation, European competition rules

Source: Andreff (2006).

The main differences are linked to the priorities of the groups involved in the sports, and the possibilities of change are quite limited (Mondello and Pedersen, 2003). Indeed, there are still some major divergent aspects about the two regions' respective sport businesses and economics, as Andreff (2006) demonstrated in Table 3.3.

These opposite approaches to these leagues, namely open versus closed, have a direct impact on the sport perspective. Indeed, in the first case, a sport entity without victories may be relegated, in which case the focus cannot remain exclusively on making profit and has to turn to sport success. For this reason, the search for equality among teams will never happen, as it does with the NFL. Nevertheless, one can easily argue that the most powerful sport entities in Europe will never renounce their budgets, which are far higher than that of their most humble adversaries at national or European levels. They prefer the current system because the risk of poor results is far lower than in the NFL system. Ferran Soriano demonstrated there was a correlation between the budget of the European football clubs in the Premier League in England and their results (Murillo and Murillo, 2004).

3.4 The prevalence of the national context upon the development of European and US sports

While there have been several attempts to broaden the impact of European and US sports beyond their home markets, all such initiatives to escape the national context have been doomed to failure, at least from an economic viewpoint. Indeed, the expansion of a sport activity can be judged by its take-up by children or teenagers, in the ability to create or draft star players, in its broadcasting on television and its coverage compared to the national sports, and in its ability to reduce dependency on income generated in the country or region of origin.

Leaving aside basketball, played on both sides of the Atlantic, it has to be noted that soccer and rugby on one side and American football, baseball or ice hockey on the other side have all increased their practice in the other continent, to the point where players have to choose in which discipline they can become professionals because only major continental sports provide this option. Nevertheless, if we consider football, it has to be noted that, despite being the fastest growing sport in the United States, there are still only fifteen million participants in this country (Soccer Nova, 2003). Comparing this figure with the one billion participants or the 320 million fans watching the Champions League football games every week (UEFA, 2005) clearly shows the limits of the phenomena. Detractors will highlight the emergence of a new business niche with nine million girls playing football, of which 90 per cent are under the age of eighteen (SGMA, 2007). The main weakness, however, deals with the lack of 'history, tradition or respect of all these other leagues' (Pastorino quoted in Pons and Standifird, 2007).

The arrival of worldwide stars, such as Beckham at LA Galaxy, can bring a new legacy to the imported sports but the results are far from always successful. Indeed, European football tried to expand in the United States in the 1970s with the incorporation of worldwide stars such as Pele, Cruyff or Beckenbauer in Cosmos New York at the end of their career, but the implant of these relatively 'old' stars failed at that time.

Soccer in the United States is currently most popular with girls, Latin Americans and college students and this lack of wider popularity in American society prevents this sport from being more successful in terms of merchandising and broadcasting, despite the annual tours of major European football clubs such as Manchester United, Real Madrid and FC Barcelona.

The situation is even worse for American football, baseball, ice hockey or rugby. The exception might be basketball, where each continent is able to generate its own talent, as Spain, Greece and Argentina demonstrated in the last World Cup. Nevertheless, cannibalization exists among the NBA and its European equivalents; the best talents are invariably poached by the NBA. A positive aspect comes from the NBA broadcasting in Europe, with a fairly constant viewing public despite the small target group that has satellite television.

Nevertheless, this success is limited by the difficulties faced by European basketball teams wishing to upgrade their contracts and to increase their visibility in their country, their continent, and abroad. Thus it may be more appropriate to move back to the benchmark of the automotive industry and to consider the example of Toyota, who first managed its success on a national scale before focusing on its regionalization and internationalization. In that context, the different cases of the main European football leagues will be studied as a survey to examine the dichotomy sport entities face between their national context and their own profit strategy.

3.5 Pan-European football study: the prevalence of national context upon the design of sport entities' profit strategies

The pan-European study on football presents several assets for its generalization to other sport entities. First, this sport is the most representative in terms of participants and viewers, and currently the most capitalized in Europe. Moreover, the richest clubs in Europe have contemplated their internationalization and, in some cases, their globalization, while trying to rid themselves of the national context in order to acquire new dimensions. Nevertheless, some clubs seem to forget that their international success will be linked to their ability to develop their national core competences at an international level. Therefore, an analysis of the relationship between the entity path and its national context is needed to find out the best opportunities for growth for sport entities. The advice for major entities willing to increase their sphere of influence can be useful at a lower scale for regional entities wishing to implement themselves at a national level.

In this survey, attention will be set first on the study of the richest clubs in the world. The immediate correlation between the number of clubs and their country of origin indicates a clear pattern where the national context prevails upon each sport entity's progress. Further on, the different national modes of income will be detailed and will provide the same correlation between growing sources of revenues and country.

3.5.1 *Exploring the European football landscape*

The annual survey of the richest football clubs, conducted by the consulting firm Deloitte, provides insights concerning the different business models existing in that sport. Only thirty-one different clubs have been included in the top-twenty ranking in the last ten years, which suggests a certain maturity in the sector. The individual positions in the charts indicate some consolidation in the sector – twelve clubs have featured every year since the creation of this index in 1996. Nevertheless, it has to be noted that, after these top twelve entities, the fight among the best in class depends in a large measure on the year's sport results (in the Champions League, UEFA Cup or national league) and therefore the continuity of their economic situation is not ensured unless the club attains good results several years in a row.[7] Simply throwing money at a club in an attempt at ensuring better sport returns is by no means a safe bet, at least at a European level if not the national level, as some clubs found to their cost and ended up in bankruptcy – Leeds, Parma or Borussia Dortmund, for example.[8]

As can be seen from this chart, in the last ten years, thirty-one teams have featured in the Cumulative Deloitte Richest Football Club ranking featured in the Table 3.4, and the teams are from the following countries:

- England (11)
- Italy (6)
- Germany (4)
- Spain (3)
- France (3)
- Scotland (2)
- Portugal (1)
- Brazil (1)

---

[7] In some cases, the presence of the clubs can be due to strategic reasons as well. For instance, Manchester City's new stadium enabled the club to increase its income by 36 per cent since the opening of the stadium in 2003.

[8] Desbordes (2007) illustrated the differences bound with the French model of regulation that fixed some strict financial rules following the financial scandals in Girondins Bordeaux in the 1980s and in Olympique Marseille in the 1990s.

Table 3.4 *Cumulative Deloitte richest football clubs, 1996/2006*

Position	Club	1996/ 1997	1997/ 1998	1998/ 1999	1999/ 2000	2000/ 2001	2001/ 2002	2002/ 2003	2003/ 2004	2004/ 2005	2005/ 2006	Cumulative points
1	Manchester Utd	1	1	1	1	1	1	1	1	2	4	14
2	Real Madrid	3	2	3	2	6	4	2	2	1	1	30
3	Juventus	4	4	5	5	2	2	2	5	4	3	36
4	AC Milan	6	7	7	4	4	4	3	3	3	5	46
5	Bayern Munich	5	3	2	3	3	3	5	9	7	8	48
6	FC Barcelona	2	6	6	8	11	12	6	7	6	2	66
7	Inter Milan	10	8	9	9	11	12	6	8	9	7	89
8	Liverpool	9	10	11	19	7	5	8	10	8	10	97
9	Arsenal	20	13	10	11	13	8	7	6	10	9	107
10	Newcastle Utd	8	5	12	20	14	13	9	11	12	13	117
11	AS Roma	15	19	16	10	9	10	11	12	11	12	124
12	Tottenham HS	16	18	15	17	16	16	15	14	13	15	155
13	Chelsea		9	4	7	10	12	6	4	5	6	NREY
14	SS Lazio	19	12	8	6	8	14	17	15	20		NREY
15	Glasgow Rangers	14	16	18	15	17			19		18	NREY
16	Leed Utd		20	17	13	5	11	16				NREY
17	Borussia Dortmund	7	11	14	12	15	15	12				NREY
18	Parma	18	14	13	18	18	18					NREY
23	Paris SG	13	15									NREY
31	Flamengo	11										NREY

Table 3.4 (*cont.*)

Position	Club	1996/ 1997	1997/ 1998	1998/ 1999	1999/ 2000	2000/ 2001	2001/ 2002	2002/ 2003	2003/ 2004	2004/ 2005	2005/ 2006	Cumulative points
21	O. Lyonnais									15	11	NREY
30	O. Marseille								18			NREY
19	Schalke 04								17	14	14	NREY
24	Hambourg SV										16	NREY
20	Manchester C.								16	17	17	NREY
25	West Ham										19	NREY
26	Benfica										20	NREY
22	Celtic								13	16		NREY
28	Valencia									19		NREY
27	Everton									18		NREY
29	Aston Villa								20			NREY

Notes: Eleven English teams; six Italian teams; four Spanish teams; three French teams; three Scottish teams; two Portuguese teams; one Brazilian team.

NREY = not ranked every year.

Source: Author, from Deloitte.

Table 3.5 *Winners of the Champions League, 1996–2006*

• 2005–2006 Barcelona	• Four Champions Leagues won by Spanish teams
• 2004–2005 Liverpool	
• 2003–2004 Porto	• Two Champions Leagues won by English teams
• 2002–2003 Milan	
• 2001–2002 Real Madrid	• Two Champions Leagues won by German teams
• 2000–2001 Bayern	
• 1999–2000 Real Madrid	• One Champions League won by an Italian team
• 1998–1999 Man. United	
• 1997–1998 Real Madrid	• One Champions League won by a Portuguese team
• 1996–1997 Dortmund	

Source: L'Equipe, 2 April 2006.

In the last ten years, only twelve teams have managed to appear in the table every year, and if we consider the last four years, two more were added (Chelsea and Schalke 04) but none disappeared; this suggests, firstly, that the industry is fairly consolidated and, secondly, that the English model is superior to that of their European counterparts. This becomes even clearer when the sport results of the English teams are analysed taking into consideration the most attractive tournament in Europe, namely the Champions League. As can be seen in Table 3.5, it transpires that the performances of the English teams are not superior to their European counterparts, and this tournament provides the highest return on investment. As we mentioned in the previous chapter, it seems that the few Spanish teams represented in the Deloitte charts focus more on the sport aspect than on the financial, or perhaps the results in the Champions League lead to financial results because the financial results constitute one of the core competences.

Concerning the teams that manage to be part of the Champions League on a recurrent basis, they have succeeded in creating an elite division that keeps this competition under control. Moreover, the qualification for the Champions League provides extra revenues that widen the gap from the national competitors. The resources that are distributed to these teams are likely to be used to invest in talent in order to dominate the competition in the future. For example, a modest Champions League run to the quarter-finals for Manchester United is likely to generate income in the region of around €45 million (about €30 million in broadcast fees and €15 million in ticket sales), while more than half of the Premier League has a total annual income of less than €75 million. It is hard to see how the smaller teams could generate the financial resources to compete effectively in the domestic league. It would appear that the Champions League has created a chronic imbalance both inside the competition itself and outside in the domestic league championships (Szymanski, 2006b). In that sense, regular participation in the Champions League consolidates the financial activity of the sport entity.

It is not hard to see how the Champions League added to the level of competitive imbalance. Champions League revenues derive principally from gate receipts and from the distribution of television revenues. Each team retains the gate revenues from its home matches. While in the 2003/2004 season around £280 million was distributed between the thirty-two teams that participated in the group stages, exactly half of these teams came from the big five television markets (England, France, Germany, Italy and Spain) and these teams received over 70 per cent of the money distributed (Szymanski, 2006a). Partly this reflected the greater success of the clubs from these countries, since the payments are partly based on results, but in part it reflected pure pulling power. To restore football's competitive balance, the UEFA decided to force teams to include at least four players in the squad that have been trained by the club, and another four players that have been trained in the national association. However, this balance has been distorted by sport agents and teams drafting players at an ever-younger age and preventing the development of a local squad, which was one of the initial aims of the UEFA proposal.

While the creation of the Champions League by the UEFA can be seen as a 'monster that has produced this unequal struggle between haves and have-nots in countries across Europe' (Johannsen, former UEFA President, 2005, quoted in Szymanski, 2006b), England is the only country in Europe that has managed to place more than four clubs in the Deloitte charts, four clubs being the maximum number of clubs a country may have engaged in each Champions League tournament. Therefore, some other factors are needed to explain this situation. The phenomenon in England demonstrates to the contrary that sport entities in the other countries do not manage to set aside the national constraint because their main preoccupation remains the qualification for the next Champions League.

3.5.2 *The existence of profit strategies based on the national contexts*

Following the data provided by the Deloitte ranking of the richest football clubs, an analysis was performed to determine the existence of the variable of the national growth models in the five main countries in Europe (UK, Spain, Italy, Germany and France).

If the sport entities' income is divided into three main categories (Stadia, Commercial and Broadcasting), it has to be noted that the models vary completely from one country to another, and not from one club to another. Indeed, the stadium incomes – which are country-based by definition – represent from 20 per cent (in the case of Italian football clubs) to 40 per cent (in the case of some English clubs). Moreover, an impressive part of the merchandising and of the broadcasting still depends on the national market and its development. For instance, English fans are much more concerned with showing their interest for the club than Italian or French fans. Expenses for football will be radically different and will provide, in the long run, a competitive advantage to the English clubs in terms of assets, of evolution of football fans, of drafting players. Indeed, the Premier League generated €2 billion; over €600 million more than the Italian Calcio and €1.1 billion more than the French Ligue in 2005/2006 (Deloitte, 2007).

Besides, the clear distinction appearing between the countries leads the authors to evoke several growth modes of national incomes, as in the automotive industry. In the following pages, the examples of the most distinguished football nations will be studied.

As can be seen in Table 3.6, in England (specifically Manchester United, Chelsea and Newcastle) and Scotland (Glasgow Rangers and Celtic), the emphasis is on match day. The use of a new stadium and the practice of selling half of the season tickets to the fans are common policies in the UK to maximize the income. This situation presents several advantages. First, a capacity crowd is always a guarantee for television broadcasting. Moreover, as the system of broadcast sharing is fair, it increases the visibility and awareness of the main sport entities that benefit from the sheer number of popular games. Given that eleven English clubs are among the thirty richest football institutions, there is a reasonable guarantee of high interest in 110 games (11 x 10), even without considering all those games where one of the top eleven plays against a lower profile team. This situation has to be

Table 3.6 *Income breakdown of the football clubs, 2004/2005*

	Commercial (millions)	Match day (millions)	Broadcasting (millions)	Total (millions)
Real Madrid	124	63	88	275
Manchester Utd	72	102	72	246
AC Milan	58	38	138	234
Juventus	82	23	124	229
Chelsea	55	84	82	221
FC Barcelona	63	66	79	208
Bayern	117	36	36	189
Liverpool	56	49	75	180
Inter Milan	38	36	103	177
Arsenal	44	55	72	171
Roma	27	28	77	132
Newcastle	35	52	41	128
Tottenham	36	31	38	105
Schalke 04	58	23	16	97
O. Lyonnais	27	20	46	93
Celtic	21	47	25	93
Manchester City	29	22	39	90
Everton	17	28	44	89
Valencia	16	24	44	84
Lazio	24	15	44	83

Source: Elaborated by Jacopin from Deloitte (2006).

contrasted with the Spanish case, for instance, where only two teams have international visibility; Real Madrid and FC Barcelona.

Measuring the income breakdown of the major football entities in 2004/2005 and in 2005/2006 as reflected in Tables 3.6 and 3.7, it appears that Italian teams place strong emphasis on national broadcasting. Indeed, Italians usually do not go to their local stadium, as they are usually fans of one of the major teams, mainly Juventus, Torino or AC Milan. This inability to fill up the stadium constitutes without any doubt the most important failure while contemplating the situation of the main European competitors. In the case of Juventus, it represents only 20 per cent of the match-day income of Manchester United and 25 per cent of Real Madrid's. The expansion therefore can only be driven by commercial growth (such as merchandising, Internet and so on) even if the value creation by the stadium

Table 3.7 *Income breakdown of the football clubs, 2005/2006*

	Commercial (millions)	Match day (millions)	Broadcasting (millions)	Total (millions)
Real Madrid	126	76	91	292
FC Barcelona	88	78	93	259
Juventus	63	18	171	251
Manchester Utd	73	104	65	242
Milan	52	31	155	238
Chelsea	62	84	75	221
Inter Milan	46	29	130	207
Bayern Munich	111	51	43	205
Arsenal	50	63	79	192
Liverpool	56	48	72	176
O. Lyonnais	32	24	72	128
AS Roma	29	22	76	127
Newcastle	40	46	38	124
Schake 04	55	30	38	123
Tottenham	40	26	42	107
Hambourg	47	37	18	102
Manchester City	32	22	15	89
Rangers	33	40	15	88
West Ham	23	23	41	87
Benfica	30	38	17	85

Source: Elaborated by Jacopin from Deloitte (2007).

constitutes a bottleneck. On the contrary, the ability of Italian clubs to obtain good broadcasting contracts constitutes the counterpart of the lack of supporters in the stadia. With the internationalization of the clubs, and if Italian clubs manage to eradicate corruption in their sport, they should benefit from newer opportunities thanks to the capabilities acquired to broadcast football games. The expansion of football incomes in that country still depends on stakeholders and, if their interest varies, it may happen as in the United States[9] where television sponsorship went down after many years of strong support (Baran, 2004).

---

[9]   The Super Bowl is still the favourite sport event for sponsoring but it 'remains a television anomaly, unique as a television and cultural event. Rating for individual television sports programs generally continue to decline' (Baran, 2004).

With the problems linked to the Kirch network crisis in 2002 (Woratschek *et al.*, 2007), the German Bundesliga has evolved towards a new model based on the development of commercials. The leading position of the German clubs in this area should pave the way to the most impressive growth for these clubs against their competitors, providing as well the necessary independence that the majority of football clubs miss today. Indeed, copying the positioning of the German clubs should not enable an automatic gap reduction with the German clubs due to the first-mover advantage managed by the German clubs. The unique difficulty German clubs suffer is in attracting worldwide superstars. Nevertheless, the drafting of Ribery and Toni to Bayern Munich may mark the start of a new era.

If all the three previous models have had some Champions League success, the most efficient model in terms of sport results should come from Spain with four Champions League wins (three for Real Madrid and one for FC Barcelona). However, there is no Spanish model. Real Madrid adopted the commercial model when Florentino Pérez was the president, drafting the biggest football stars to join the 'Galácticos' and developing commercial revenues above all. In contrast, FC Barcelona focused on broadcasting, with the support of the Catalan network. Until now, the main liability of the Spanish Liga comes from the lack of competitors to ensure a wide broadcast of their games. Indeed, only three and sometimes four teams – Real Madrid CF, FC Barcelona, FC Valencia and, more recently, FC Sevilla – attract international public broadcasting compared to the ten or so English teams.

This situation can be summed up as follows in Figure 3.7 with the emergence of several polar national models.

The opportunities and risks that these entities might face, first at a national scale and then at an international one, are, therefore, completely different. While broadcasting rights depend on the ability of each league to negotiate increasing fees, the stadia and the commercial revenues bring more opportunities for the profit strategies of the firms, even if dependency on the national context remains. Table 3.8 sums up the profit strategies based on the national context.

3.5.3 Restrictions bound to the national leagues

The restrictions that have appeared concerning the most performing entities in the big five European leagues are confirmed when analysing

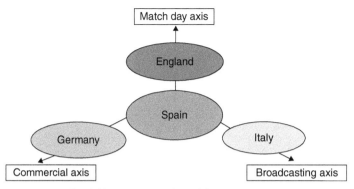

Figure 3.7 The different national models

the structured revenues and profits of these leagues. Each national championship is characterized by its own productive resources (players, teams, facilities and team budgets) and inner regulations that favour the attitudes towards change concerning the evolution of the competition and the income fees. International relationships develop at the initiative of private actors as a response to the structural differences among the different national championships. The international relationships reflect the differences among the national championships. Nevertheless, as in the economic field, the nature of the international regime is linked to the dynamics of the leading national championship which sets the trend in income innovation, whether in merchandising, broadcasting or in the training of new players. The leading championship brings new opportunities of growth to the other championships at the same time as it adds new constraints to these leagues.

Although the differences between the five major leagues were not substantial at the end of the 1990s, the competitiveness of the English Premier League against its main competitors has increased greatly in the last years – as shown in Figures 3.8 and 3.9 – because they initiated the diversification of income streams far before their continental counterparts. The gap should continue to widen in future years even though the main teams of the four other leagues look to Manchester United in order to replicate their strategy.

The competitiveness of a national championship is based on its ability to transform its own national structure to the international

Table 3.8 *Profit strategies based on the national context: opportunities, risks and solutions to risks*

	Commercial dependency	Stadium dependency	Broadcasting dependency
Opportunities	(1) Unique option to grow independently. (2) Through the development of good practices, the commercial income may open new perspectives to the clubs.	A lively experience that can be spread out to the other sources of income.	If the national basis is strong enough to generate sufficiently interesting games for an international public, it constitutes a real asset.
Risks	(1) The natural area of influence of the clubs will be distorted because several clubs will compete for the same fans. (2) Economic mistakes that endanger the finance of the club.	(1) When the stadium is full, impossible to increase this income. (2) If football fans' interest decreases, then the sport entities might face a major crisis.	(1) External source of income. (2) Fatigue of the television companies to sponsor the football clubs. (3) If the basis of the national league is constituted by few clubs, any crisis of these entities might weaken all the sport entities.
Solution to the risks	(1) Increase loyalty and retention policy. (2) Prudential policy to minimize the risk.	(1) Build a new stadium and develop alternative funding. (2) Ensure the experience is a differentiating factor and insist on the sustainability of the practices of the sport.	(1, 2) Find alternative sources of income. (3) Teamwork to sustain the national championship.

Source: Jacopin (2007)

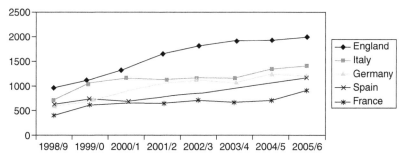

Figure 3.8 Revenue growth of the big five European leagues, 1998/2006
Source: Deloitte (2007)

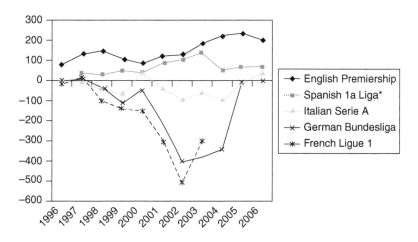

Figure 3.9 Profits of the big five European leagues, 1998/2006
Source: Szymanski, Deloitte (2003 and 2005), LFP (France), Calcio, DFL

standard, while taking into consideration new trends and keeping control of the national market. Globally, all leagues have increased their competitiveness through the construction of new stadia, increased broadcasting, the consequent increase of commerce, measures to stop expense increases (such as salary caps negotiated in the G14), the introduction of variables into the wages of the players[10] (Soriano, 2007) or new sources of financing such as flotation on the stock exchange (Appendix 3.1).

---

[10] The intention is to move from a 5–10 per cent variable wage to a 20–30 per cent.

Table 3.9 *Cumulative income of the richest football clubs, 2001/2006 (in millions)*

Club	2001/ 2002	2002/ 2003	2003/ 2004	2004/ 2005	2005/ 2006	Cumulative income for the period
Manchester Utd	229	251	259	246	243	1,228
Real Madrid	152	193	236	276	292	1,149
Juventus	177	218	215	229	251	1,090
AC Milan	159	200	222	234	239	1,054
Bayern Munich	176	163	166	190	205	900
FC Barcelona	139	123	169	208	259	898
Inter Milan	124	162	167	177	207	837
Liverpool	154	149	140	181	176	800
Arsenal	141	150	174	171	192	828
Newcastle Utd	109	139	137	129	124	638
AS Roma	136	132	109	132	127	636
Tottenham HS	100	96	100	105	107	508
Chelsea	143	134	217	221	221	936
CUMULATE TOP 13	1,939	2,110	2,311	2,499	2,643	11,502

Source: Elaborated by Jacopin.

Indeed, Table 3.9, showing the cumulative income of the richest clubs in Europe from 2001 to 2006, confirms the previous data, in that the top thirteen entities have managed to grow by an average of 30 per cent in five years (2001–2006), and the most competitive ones, such as Real Madrid, doubled their income in this period. By contrast, the entities between the ranks of fourteenth and twenty-ninth have a strong standard deviation of 20 per cent minimum of their income every consecutive year. Therefore, the financial planning of the club and the evolution of the sport entity itself suppose too many uncertainties to maximize the management of these entities.

However, with the exception of FC Barcelona and Real Madrid, the other clubs remain under the spell of the national specialization

Table 3.10 *Stadia income of the fourteen richest football clubs,*
2002/2006

Club	2002/ 2003	2003/ 2004	2004/ 2005	2005/ 2006	Evolution (%)
Real Madrid	58	62	63	76	31.03
Barcelona	43	58	66	78	81.40
Manchester Utd	101	95	102	104	2.97
Chelsea	44	81	84	84	90.91
Arsenal	40	51	55	63	57.50
Liverpool	41	40	49	48	17.07
Newcastle	47	52	52	46	−2.13
Tottenham	37	30	31	46	24.32
Milan	32	28	38	31	−3.13
Juventus	23	17	23	18	−21.74
Inter Milan	33	29	36	29	−12.12
AS Roma	41	24	28	22	−46.34
Bayern Munich	45	41	36	51	13.33
Schalke	32	28	23	30	−6.25

Source: Jacopin (2007) from Deloitte (2007).

of their league. Considering the top fourteen institutions since 2002, we can deduce from the relative evolution of the main income streams that English teams outpace their European competitors in stadia rights and experiential football (which can be defined as a variation of experiential marketing that encompasses senses and live experiences to relate to customers (Schmitt, 1999)). Table 3.10 shows, apart from the stadia rights, the exceptional growth potential acquired by FC Barcelona, Arsenal, Chelsea and Real Madrid.

The know-how acquired by English teams has enabled them to integrate an obvious learning curve, first in filling the football stadia and, second, in improving the commercial streams – Figure 3.11 – at such a pace that their growth is superior to the German teams, which had been the most efficient teams in that field in past years.

For their part, the Italian clubs have managed to compensate for the strong reduction in attendance by focusing on broadcasting rights – Table 3.12 – and by increasing their concentration in that area at the expense of other income streams. If Italians are eager to boost their

Table 3.11 *Commercial income of the fourteen richest football clubs,*
2002/2006

Commercial	2002/ 2003	2003/ 2004	2004/ 2005	2005/ 2006	Evolution (%)
Real Madrid	68	86	124	126	85.29
Barcelona	39	45	63	88	125.64
Manchester Utd	66	92	72	73	10.61
Chelsea	47	51	55	62	31.91
Arsenal	35	32	56	50	42.86
Liverpool	43	49	44	56	30.23
Newcastle	32	35	35	40	25.00
Tottenham	23	34	36	40	73.91
Milan	58	60	58	52	−10.34
Juventus	79	67	82	63	−20.25
Inter Milan	37	35	38	46	24.32
AS Roma	29	34	27	29	0.00
Bayern Munich	98	105	117	111	13.27
Schalke	49	47	58	55	12.24

Source: Jacopin (2007) from Deloitte (2007).

internationalization through broadcasting, no doubt they will be in a
favourable position to earn market share abroad.

The only clubs that have managed to create superior room to manoeuvre in their national context are the leading Spanish teams, FC
Barcelona and Real Madrid, who outperform their competitors in
almost all the income streams. Moreover, they used the real-estate
boom to increase their financial capabilities by more than €1 billion
in less than five years (*El País*, 13 November 2006). Understanding
the Spanish teams' ability to unlock their own national context will
be one of the main drivers of the next section, where the emphasis will
be given to the internationalization of the football clubs.

Success story: how can Newcastle and Tottenham be part of
the top 14 clubs between 2002 and 2006, despite not playing
in the Champions League?

Some key success factors can influence the performance of these
institutions.

- Demographics enable them to have a sufficient customer base. Indeed, all the clubs in the top fourteen, with the exception of Schalke, are in cities with multi-million populations. Nevertheless, the German club is surrounded by the Ruhr cities, which gives the required potential to be present at this level.
- Newcastle and Tottenham are playing in an attractive league confirming the evidence of the agglomeration of the investments. The purchase of several teams by multi-millionaires has increased the economic potential of the Premier League.
- Both teams have accepted the Premier League specialization in filling up stadia and have maximized that particular income stream; they can concentrate on the commercial streams in the future.
- Last but not least, while Tottenham and Newcastle have not managed to reach the UEFA Champions League, they have managed to deliver consistent performances and frequently reached the last rounds of the UEFA Cup which, unlike the risky Champions League and despite its less glamorous side, offers regular income. Thus the clubs constitute good investments for investors.
- While these clubs have been floated on the stock exchange, it has to be taken into consideration that for the year 2006, the capitalization evolution was slightly negative for both of them.

3.6 How can the profit strategies of sport entities survive their national constraints when becoming international?

The design of profit strategies is becoming more exacting for football clubs because trade-off issues arise concerning the necessary expansion that they should have. Currently, the vast majority have chosen globalization with a strong emphasis on Asia and the United States, but lessons learnt from the automotive sector indicate that the national constraint remains strong and can even prevent internationalization from being successful, or to focus on the right topic, i.e. globalization versus regionalization. In that context, and without supposing to provide a unique solution for all football clubs, some insights will be provided to choose the strategy that best fits each organization, while taking into consideration the attractiveness of each option at three levels: national, regional (i.e. European Union) and global, as shown in Figure 3.10.

Table 3.12 *Brodcasting income of the fourteen richest football clubs,*
2002/2006

Broadcasting	2002/ 2003	2003/ 2004	2004/ 2005	2005/ 2006	Evolution (%)
Real Madrid	66	88	88	91	37.88
Barcelona	43	66	79	93	116.28
Manchester Utd	84	72	72	65	−22.62
Chelsea	43	85	82	75	74.42
Arsenal	75	90	72	79	5.33
Liverpool	66	51	75	72	9.09
Newcastle	60	50	41	38	−36.67
Tottenham	36	36	38	38	5.56
Milan	110	134	138	155	40.91
Juventus	117	130	124	171	46.15
Inter Milan	93	102	103	130	39.78
AS Roma	62	51	77	76	22.58
Bayern Munich	20	25	36	43	115.00
Schalke	37	16	16	38	2.70

Source: Jacopin (2007) from Deloitte (2007).

Before looking at the three possible strategies, a few considerations
need to be taken into account. First, the number of national key players (i.e. the teams regularly present in Deloitte's list of richest clubs)
provides some indication of the potential revenues and potential profits that teams may have in the future. Indeed, the more clubs there are,
the more attractive the league is for national and international customers willing to purchase the television rights. Moreover, in case of future
concentration, this situation implies 'pockets of growth' for the most
competitive team set up in the country. For instance, Real Madrid and
FC Barcelona accumulated 46 per cent of all revenues from the Liga
Profesional de Fútbol (LFP). As standard industrial organization models explain, the reduction of the number of the competitors implies an
increase of profit for the existing entities but, in the case of football,
an increase in their domination of the Spanish Liga will decrease the
attractiveness of this product because the uncertainty of sport results
will reduce and therefore the interest of fans will decrease as well.

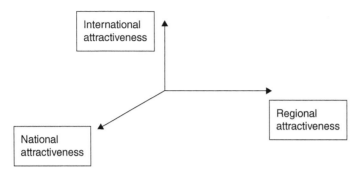

Figure 3.10 Measuring the football club attractiveness
Source: Elaborated by Jacopin from Deloitte (2004, 2005 and 2006)

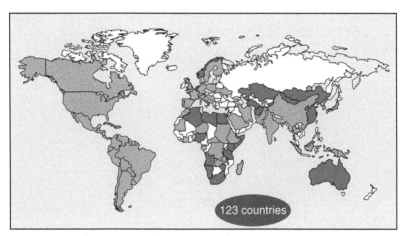

Figure 3.11 Television distribution: English Premier League
Source: Muñoa (2005)

In the long run, their ability to extend their national market is far more reduced owing to the lack of the global broadcasting penetration of the Spanish Liga (nineteen countries) compared to the Premier League (123 countries) (Muñoa, 2005) as shown in Figures 3.11 and 3.12.

The vitality of the Premier League is expressed by the number of teams currently in the Deloitte chart. Such a figure demonstrates that football is more than a mere competition and requires cooperation among the clubs in order to provide a win-win framework to all the clubs, or at least the majority.

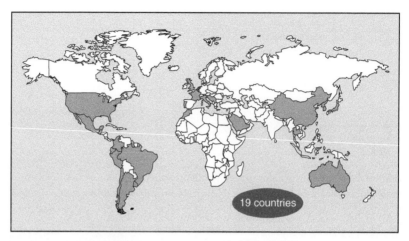

Figure 3.12 Television distribution: Spanish LFP League
Source: Muñoa (2005)

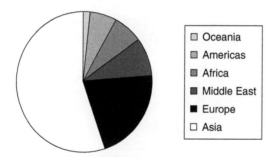

Figure 3.13 Premier League: international broadcast rights fees by region, 2007/2010
Note: broadcasting right fees for Europe exclude the UK and Ireland.
Source: Deloitte (2007)

Assuming that increasing the capacity of the existing stadia is impossible, broadcasting and commerce constitute the two main opportunities for expansion. International broadcasting has become a strategic issue because it constitutes an opening towards emerging football countries in Asia and the United States. In fact, as the Deloitte analysis shows in Figure 3.13, 55 per cent of the international broadcast right fees come from Asia for the Premier League, and the rising interest in football there, seen during the recent World Cups, has led to international tours organized by all the major clubs and the creation of football schools in all continents.

Nevertheless, broadcasting at the international level supposes solving several issues. First, time differences constitute a geographical barrier to watching games. While the Premier League and the Bundesliga do not suffer too much from this problem by scheduling the games on Saturday afternoons, it is far more problematic for the Spanish Liga, the Italian Calcio and the French Ligue. Second, the games broadcast can be only be national-league matches because the UEFA Championship matches are held on Tuesdays and Wednesdays; this explains why television rights outside Europe are so low compared to European television rights: €28 million versus €454 million. Third, loyalty mechanisms are different in Europe than in emerging countries. In Europe, fan loyalty is practically ensured whereas, in emerging countries, loyalty is given to individual players and winning teams. The cyclical factor bound to the football activity implies some difficulties in anchoring the positioning in these countries. Last but not least, while the international tours enable fans' exposure to the stars on a once-a-year basis, the lack of continuity can be problematic as the fans may have greater exposure to national sports, and this alone can prevent the commercial revenue streams from increasing.

3.6.1 Global expansion through the entertainment model

The Walt Disney Corporation has constituted the main source of inspiration for improving the internationalization of the most successful clubs, i.e. Manchester United, Real Madrid and FC Barcelona (who we will use for our illustration). However, it has to be noted that this process is far from being achieved with all these entities – even Disney continues to have a national context dependency, with a large proportion of its revenues and profit achieved in the United States.

Disney focuses on a mixture of cartoons that enable the company to create and capture value through multipliers involving movies, videos, theme parks, merchandising, and so on (see Figure 3.14), and has been able to constantly acquire new customers since its creation. Furthermore, the company has managed to design new strategies to capture family and adult consumers.

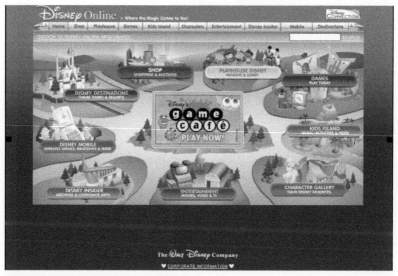

Figure 3.14 Disney website in 2006
Source: http://disney.go.com (accessed 2 February 2006).

The model followed by FC Barcelona rests on the assumption that football is an entertainment industry providing entertainment (the game) on an irregular (but constant) basis with stars (the players). They play around twenty-five games in the home stadium and one game in China. The Catalan executives consider their games on the same basis as Disney movies – kids expect a new Disney movie at Christmas and, similarly, Chinese fans await the annual FC Barcelona game in August. In addition, instead of having 'flat' characters, such as Disney's Mickey Mouse and Donald Duck, FC Barcelona offers a mix of local stars, such as Xavi and Pujol, and international ones, such as Ronaldinho and Eto'o (Jacopin and Murillo, 2005).

At the same time, the Spanish club has moved from a regional and national customer target to a much more universal one using its social mass – 140,000 fans worldwide are registered to FC Barcelona – as a competitive advantage to acquire critical size independent of the sport and financial results of the entity.

Opening new markets must be carefully managed to retain the approval of fans and *socios*. In that sense, sport entities cannot afford to lose sight of their main stakeholders, i.e. their local fans, who are often also the owners. The emergence of a radically new income stream will be hard to manage unless the clubs are managed by shareholders

Table 3.13 *Setting up a hierarchy of supporting teams*

Level of team supported	Example: French case
1st level – near home town	Brest (French 2nd Division)
2nd level – one of the top national clubs	Olympique Marseille (French 1st Division and sometimes Champions League)
3rd level – one of the top international clubs	FC Barcelona (Spanish Liga and frequent participant in Champions League)

Source: Jacopin (2007).

whose aims are financially-oriented instead of sport-oriented and the influence of national stakeholders (such as the national fans and the media) is reduced.

3.6.2 Regional expansion

While global expansion presents some attractive features for sport entities, the race for the Asian and US markets presents some incompatibilities for some of the football entities, even the richest ones. First, football is a European game and therefore the ability to increase awareness, perceived quality, and preference for the football product is far higher in Europe than elsewhere. Just as sports clubs manage to reach national fans beyond the club's hometown, they can also adopt the same policy at a regional scale. Fans may have a 'hierarchy' of clubs they support, as shown in Table 3.13. For instance, they could have three levels of teams that they support.

The ability to set up this kind of strategy offers several advantages. First, the geographical issue bound to the time differences disappears and the fan is much more involved with the team. Travelling around Europe with low-cost airlines is much cheaper and tour operators increasingly bundle tourism with sport/leisure activities. Second, broadcasting rights are far more interesting and the option to leverage the pay-per-view games or the fees for the UEFA Champions League is far more interesting than the rights obtained for the national league. The description of the fees earned by the UEFA Champions League in Figure 3.15 is eloquent on this front.

Moreover, fan loyalty is earned in Europe because loyalty goes to teams, not individual players or only leading teams. Therefore, the need to capture value in Europe in the short run is more urgent than expansion in Asia, where hiring stars can always leverage some advantage over competitors. The first-mover advantage is key in Europe.

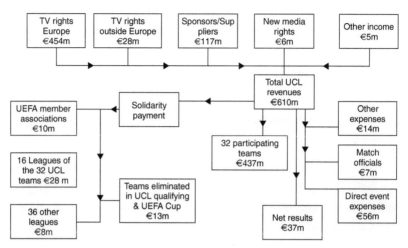

Note: UCL designs UEFA Champions League

Figure 3.15 UEFA Champions League income sources and distribution of funds, 2005/2006
Note: UCL designs UEFA Champions League.
Source: Deloitte (2007)

Lastly, activity in Europe provides a better correlation with the national context of the club and, through the selection of the country in which the club is going to operate over time, this situation ensures income streams on a continuous basis with the incorporation of the emerging stars of that country.

3.6.3 *Players, teams, championships and broadcasting for the purpose of internationalization*

As Dobson and Goddard highlighted in their *Economics of Football* (2001), 'broadcasting companies tend to act increasingly as a conduit through which revenues are channelled from the public as final consumers to the football clubs ... (using) players as the ultimate monopoly suppliers of the performing services the public wishes to view'. This situation provides two benefits to the players. First, they accumulate income corresponding to the increasing packages paid by television networks capturing spectators who are willing to pay to watch football, because the players' wages increase in line with the income received by the clubs. Second, they become a key success factor in the internationalization of a club or a championship abroad because they are intangible assets representing their own country.

As an example, Platini created a trend when he was signed to Juventus in the 1980s. All his games were broadcast in France, Juventus merchandising increased in France, and a bond was formed between France and Italy in the 1980s (*L'Equipe*, 5 April 1985). Nakata, Cantona and Matthaeus in their time, and now Torres, have managed to leverage the passion for their new team in their native country and facilitate their club's positioning in their native country. The systematization of this system was fully realized by Florentino Pérez signing specific players from different geographic areas to Real Madrid – Figo, Zidane, Ronaldo and Beckham represented respectively the Portuguese market, the Francophone market, the Latin American market and the English-speaking market. However, the marketing should not eclipse the sport, as happened at Real Madrid and culminated in Pérez's downfall in 2006.

The match between these icons and their own team provides short-term benefits such as awareness for the team, opportunities to increase the television rights, and international tours. However, the maximization of this positioning will be most effective when the team systematically signs players from the same location. A good example is Juventus, probably the most popular international club in France for sport and marketing reasons (Landor Associates, 2002) thanks to players such as Platini, Deschamps, Zidane, Henry, Thuram, Trezeguet, Zebina and Boumsong. More recently, Arsenal and Liverpool have adopted the same approach, attracting French and Spanish players and benefiting from both their football and merchandizing value.[11] In that sense, players constitute key elements in the internationalization of the clubs.

Although salary caps have limited the 1990s wage inflation that so benefited the players, their bargaining power is still high thanks to the internationalization of the clubs. However, the control of broadcasting might move from television networks to Internet or cellular companies in the future. In this, sport entities have already protected themselves by signing joint-ventures with these emerging companies

[11] Other entities have had a long tradition of hiring players from the same country, such as FC Barcelona with the Dutch players, and Olympique Lyon with Brazilian players.

and, therefore, the impact of the players in the internationalization of the clubs should decrease in the near future to being exclusively mere intangible assets. Even though Manchester United have two star players (Ronaldo 2003–2008 and Rooney 2004–), they and other clubs have started this trend of focusing more on the team than on the players. The advantage of this positioning is increasing the brand value of the team regardless of the possible departure of any player, thus consolidating the sustainability of the club.

3.7 Conclusions

Sport entities follow their convergence towards standard sectors of the economy at an accelerated pace. Therefore, the lessons offered by the automotive industry could be adapted to the sport entities in the sense that there is no single best way to be competitive and to win sport titles. Indeed, the national context is a key element for sport entities to take into consideration before contemplating internationalization. After examining the five major football leagues, three polar models have emerged based on stadium incomes (the English model), on commercial incomes (the Italian model) and broadcasting incomes (the German model). There is no Spanish model because the dichotomy between its two main powers, Real Madrid and FC Barcelona, highlights a dual-class model where the two trendsetters have been the best in class at the European level by dragging themselves out of the national context by improving their different incomes through globalization. However, as is the case in the automotive industry, regionalization should not be eliminated as an option of internationalization.

If this chapter points out lessons from other industries such as the automotive sector, the most interesting feature of the evolution of sport management comes from its nature, i.e. the necessity to have a competitive balance among the teams. Indeed, the maximization of benefits implies the design of a strategy that benefits all engaged teams, as is the case in the American National Football League (NFL), for instance. As the global economy has entered into the dynamics of 'sharing' and win-win, lessons and mechanisms applied in the sport industry will be developed to the rest of the economy. The concept of 'co-opetition' developed by Brandenburger and Nalebuff (1996) is quite new for standard companies because the expression was only coined relatively recently, whereas sport sectors conceptualized competitive balance in the 1960s (Dobson and Goddard, 2001). Therefore, the ability to create a virtuous circle using different forms of value has been far from realizing its full potential until now.

Appendix 3.1 Twenty-eight teams listed on the stock exchange

Table A3.1 *Twenty-eight teams listed on the stock exchange (Cinco Días, 22–23 April 2006)*

Country[a]	Team listed	Capitali-zation € m	Income € m	Profit/loss € m	Evolution capitaliza-tion (%)
UK (11)[b]	Tottenham	49	101	6	−7
	Aston Villa	67	74	−2	−14
	Newcastle	86	124	0	−5
	Southampton	21	64	0	47
	Preston	5	11	−3	32
	Birmingham City	18	61	2	−6
	Sheffield	42	19	−2	16
	Millwall	4	10	−4	−17
	Charlton	34	58	1.9	32
	Watford	18	12	−3	−18
	Celtic Glasgow	14	89	−11	−25
Denmark (6)	Aalborg	8	9.3	−1	−4
	Aarhaus	15	6	−3	−39
	Brondby	42	n/a	6	14
	Kopenhaven	298	n/a	6	79
	Schaumann	4	1	−30	48
	Silkeborg	4	4	0	53
Turkey (4)	Besiktas	146	30	−9	−11
	Fenerbahce	330	30	32	4
	Galatasaray	164	23	18	13
	Trabonzspor	93	1	0	21
Italy (3)	Juventus	243	n/a	n/a	46
	Lazio	31	73	24	48
	Roma	71	133	10	5
Portugal (2)	Oporto	40	47	24	2
	Sporting	29	24	−9	2

Table A3.1 (*cont.*)

Country[a]	Team listed	Capitali-zation € m	Income € m	Profit/loss € m	Evolution capitaliza-tion (%)
Germany (1)	Borussia	67	75	–79	–10
Holland (1)	Ajax Amsterdam	156	67	3	–3

Notes: [a] Olympique Lyonnais joined the stock exchange in 2007 and was the first French football club to finance through financial markets.
[b] Manchester United and Chelsea withdrew from the stock exchange after the take-overs by Glazer and Abramovich, respectively.

References

Andreff, W. (2006). 'International Trade in Sporting Goods', in W. Andreff and S. Szymanski (eds.), *The Handbook on the Economics of Sport*. Northampton, MA: Edward Elgar.

Baran, S.J. (2004). 'Sports and Television', in S. Rosner and K. Shropshire (eds.), *The Business of Sports*. Sudbury, MA: Jones and Bartlett, pp. 143–7.

Brandenburger, A.M. and Nalebuff, B.J. (1996). *Co-opetition*. New York: Doubleday.

Deloitte (1996–2006) *The Top 20 Richest Football Clubs*. London: Deloitte Touche Tohmatsu.

Deloitte (2005). *Annual Review of Football Finance 2004*. London: Deloitte Touche Tohmatsu.

  (2006). *Annual Review of Football Finance 2005*. London: Deloitte Touche Tohmatsu.

  (2007). *Annual Review of Football Finance 2006*. London: Deloitte Touche Tohmatsu.

Desbordes, M. (ed.) (2007). *Marketing and Football: An International Perspective*. Oxford: Butterworth-Heinemann, p. 518.

Dobson, S. and Goddard, J. (2001). *The Economics of Football*. Cambridge: Cambridge University Press, p. 458.

Freyssenet, M., Shimizu, K. and Volpato, G. (2003). *Globalization or Regionalization of the European Car Industry*. London: Palgrave.

Greenwald, B. and Kahn, J. (2005). *Competition Demystified: A Radically Simplified Approach to Business Strategy*. New York: Portfolio.

Jacopin, T. and Murillo, C. (2005). *The Internationalization of the FC Barcelona*. Barcelona: University Pompeu Fabra.

Jetin, B. (2003). 'The Internationalization of American and Asian Automobile Firms: A Statistical Comparison with the European Companies', in M. Freyssenet, Y. Lung, K. Shimizu and G. Volpato (eds.), *Globalization or Regionalization of the American and Asian Car Industry*. London: Palgrave Macmillan, pp. 9–52.

Landor Associates (2002). 'Energizing the Brand through the Image Power of Football: Scoring with Sponsorship'. Online, available at: www.landor.com (last accessed 3 March 2008).

Mondello, M. and Pedersen, P.M. (2003). 'Investigating the Body of Knowledge: A Content Analysis of the Journal of Sports Economics', *Journal of Sports Economics*, 4(1): 64–73.

Muñoa, J. (2005). 'Internationalization of the FC Barcelona'. Unpublished PowerPoint presentation.

Murillo, C. and Murillo, E. (2004). *El Nuevo Barça: contado por sus protagonistas*. Barcelona: Peninsula.

Pons, F. and Standifird, S. (2007). 'Marketing of Professional Soccer in the US: The Successes and Failures of MLS and WUSA', in M. Desbordes (ed.), *Marketing and Football: An International Perspective*. Oxford: Butterworth-Heinemann, pp. 366–94.

Rosner, S. and Shropshire, K.L. (2004). *The Business of Sports*. Sudbury, MA: Jones & Bartlett.

Schmitt, B. (1999). *The Experiential Marketing*. New York: The Free Press, p. 280.

SGMA (2007). *Sport Participation in America in 2007*. Online, available at: www.sgma.com (last accessed 3 March 2008).

Shimizu, K. (1999). *Le Toyotisme*. Paris: La Découverte.

Soccer Nova (2003). *History and Statistics about US Soccer*. Online, available at: www.soccernova.com (last accessed 2 December 2005).

Soriano, F. (2007). 'The Governance in Big Soccer Clubs', in P. Rodriguez, S. Kesenne and J. Garcia (eds.), *Governance and Competition in Professional Sports Leagues*. Oviedo: University of Oviedo.

Szymanski, S. (2006a). 'Tilting the Playing Field: Why a Sports League Planner would Choose Less, not More, Competitive Balance'. Working Papers 0620, International Association of Sports Economists.

(2006b). 'The Champions League and the Coase Theorem'. Working Paper 0617, International Association of Sports Economists.

UEFA (2005). *Champions League Technical Report 2004/2005*. Geneva.

UNCTAD (2000, 2001, 2002, 2003, 2004 and 2005), *World Investment Report*. New York and Geneva: United Nations.

Warfield, T. (2005). 'Playing to Win', *Sport Business Journal*, 7(45): 17.
Woratschek, H., Schafmeister, G. and Ströbel, T. (2007). 'A New Paradigm for Sport Management in the German Football Market', in M. Desbordes (ed.), *Marketing and Football: An International Perspective*. Oxford: Butterworth-Heinemann, pp. 163–85.

4 Value creation in two of the most prestigious Spanish football clubs: Real Madrid CF and FC Barcelona, 2000–2006

KIMIO KASE, SANDALIO GÓMEZ, IGNACIO URRUTIA, CARLOS MARTÍ, MAGDALENA OPAZO AND TANGUY JACOPIN

4.1 Introduction

An in-depth analysis of the value-creation models used by Spain's leading football clubs is conducted in contrast to those of other European clubs. Assessment is made of the results brought about by these models. Using the sport-emphasis and business-emphasis matrix, an explanation of the context in which the models are positioned is provided in an effort to generalize the findings from the analysis.

In contrast to the English, German and Italian football championships, Spain does not have its own value creation model. Yet despite this, Real Madrid and FC Barcelona are, without doubt, two of the European clubs that have generated the most income in 2006, and, moreover, that have shown consistent progression in their results over the last two years (Deloitte, 2008). Nevertheless, throughout the period 2000–2006, Real Madrid CF and FC Barcelona have used different strategies, with different results. The former, despite some triumphant years in the sporting world, has failed to achieve any important win in the last three years at all. Yet it has been recognized as the world's richest football club.[1] As for FC Barcelona, following the difficult presidency of Joan Gaspart (2000–2003) – memorable for both his sporting and financial failures – the Catalan club, under the leadership of President Laporta, has taken back the sporting lead. Over the past two years FC Barcelona has won the UEFA Champions League once and the Spanish national premiership ('La Liga') two years in a row, initiating a return to financial health at the same time.

---

[1] According to the latest Deloitte report, *Football Money League*, from 2006.

Analysis of the strategies of Real Madrid CF and FC Barcelona during this period, along with the economic and sports results obtained, allows us to get a clearer idea of the different ways in which a sports entity can achieve success and how this can be measured.

This chapter will look in detail at the special features of the world of sports activities, focusing on these two football clubs which, despite their similarities (in line with the purpose of sports clubs defined the Spanish Sports Act 1990[2]), have taken very different routes; routes, notwithstanding their differences, that were both indicative of the way each club has built its success. From a time perspective, the trajectories of each club can be analysed by distinguishing the different periods in terms of strategies and results, in the sporting and financial fields.

As such, in the 2000–2003 period, Real Madrid CF started in a delicate financial position, which Florentino Pérez, as the new president, was able to resolve by balancing the budget and reorganizing the structure of the balance sheet, thanks, in the most part, to the income from the sale of the club's training ground. On the other hand, the sports status of the club, inherited from predecessor Lorenzo Sanz, was much healthier since, during the four years of his presidency, the club managed to win the Champions League twice and La Liga once. In fact, Pérez managed to maintain Real Madrid's impressive sports trajectory, taking them to victory in La Liga twice on a national level, and winning one Champions League and an Intercontinental Cup on an international level.

In the same period, 2000–2003, FC Barcelona incurred a significant budget deficit, further aggravating the already-difficult financial situation of the club. During this time FC Barcelona didn't manage to achieve any sporting success at all and, inevitably, the downward spiral on the sports side began to leech economic resources.

In the period 2003–2006, Real Madrid managed to keep their financial situation healthy. They even became top of the list of European football clubs in terms of turnover, being crowned 'the richest football club in the world'.[3] However, in terms of sport over these years, the club did not enjoy any success worth mentioning.

---

[2] 'Promote one or more categories of sport, the practice of such sports by their associates, in addition to the participation in sports activities and competitions' (Sports Act 1990 'Ley del Deporte, 1990').

[3] Thursday 16 February 2006. *El País*, *Marca*, *El Mundo*.

FC Barcelona, by contrast, with Joan Laporta as president from 2003, opted for 'revolution' to put this club back on top in both financial and sporting terms. Firstly, the club experienced a significant improvement in the balance of the annual budget[4] thanks to the syndication of the club's debts to eighteen banks (Murillo and Murillo, 2005) aiming to renovate the first team and emphasizing a priority on sport. This strategy allowed the club to achieve significant sporting success: winning La Liga twice and the UEFA Champions League once.

The burning questions raised here are as follows: what types of strategies have Real Madrid CF and FC Barcelona followed in order to reverse the success and failure of both teams in so few years? What variables help us to explain this difference? Is there a difference perhaps between their corporate[5] and sporting strategies?

This chapter will analyse and compare the strategies followed by two emblematic clubs over a specific time period, with the aim of finding out how we can explain the differences observed between them.[6] To do this, the financial and sports data of each club will be analysed for the period 2000 to 2006.

This chapter is divided into three parts. The first explains the clubs' financial strategy with regard to their profit and loss (P&L) and balance sheets; the second looks at the sports strategy applied through the measures adopted and the results obtained; and the final section considers the synthesis of both strategies and their results, proposing a more generalized interpretation through a matrix created by the CSBM[7] which allows the strategy of one sports entity to be related to another, in a financial and corporate field as well as a sports one.

It should be highlighted that part of the difference between the P&L and the balance sheets of Real Madrid and FC Barcelona comes from Real Madrid's sale of their training ground for 500 million

---

[4] However, they had still not been able to find a solution to the complicated status of their balance sheet.

[5] Corporate strategy is understood as that equivalent to the strategy of a conventional company managed and organized with professional criteria in order to achieve specific objectives.

[6] In order to compare the positioning of the clubs with different combinations of corporate and sporting emphasis, a matrix (to be described later) designed by IESE's Center for Sport Business Management was used.

[7] CSBM (Center for Sport Business Management) research centre at IESE Business School.

euros.[8] Meanwhile FC Barcelona have still not sold their training ground, although they did get rid of some land assets such as Can Rigalt I and II for approximately ten million euros.

4.2 Financial and corporate strategy

Before sports competitions were broadcast by television and the evolution of all the commercial mechanisms surrounding the events, the main source of income in the football business came from ticket sales. The fans bought season tickets and match tickets, so clubs focused their efforts on finding ways to gain their loyalty and commitment, thereby encouraging them to come to the stadia en masse.

Today, it is clear that a club's income does not just come from ticket sales. Other sources of income are becoming increasingly important, such as television rights, sponsorship, merchandising, distribution and licensing. According to the Deloitte report, *Football Money League*, published in 2007 the 'richest [football] club in the world' is Real Madrid CF, while FC Barcelona comes in at number six, with a difference of seventy million euros between the two clubs. However, the most interesting thing about this report is what can be seen when the income is separated into three categories (income from commercial activities, income from the match day, and income from broadcasting rights). The results can be seen in Table 4.1.

If we look at the amount of income per type for each country, we can see that, in the case of German clubs, the greatest share of income comes from commercial activities (German model). Whereas, the Italian clubs tend to gain most of their income through the sale of television rights (Italian model). As far as the English clubs are concerned, their income structure relies more on their capability to fill the stadia and sell experiential marketing[9] to their fans (English model).[10]

---

[8] *El País*, 13 November 2006.
[9] Referential marketing was an idea developed by professors at Columbia University (Holbrook and Lehman *et al.*) in the 1970s. Schmitt from the same university has successfully brought the idea up-to-date. Experiential marketing refers to the need to get close to the customer through experience of their feelings.
[10] Elaboration of the table and German, Italian and English business models by Tanguy Jacopin, Research Fellow CSBM.

Table 4.1 *Income breakdown of the richest football clubs, 2005/2006*

		Commercial	Match day	Broadcasting	Total
2005/2006	Real Madrid	126	76	91	292
	FC Barcelona	88	78	93	259
	Juventus	63	18	171	251
	Manchester Utd	73	104	65	242
	Milan	52	31	155	238
	Chelsea	62	84	75	221
	Inter Milan	46	29	130	207
	Bayern Munich	111	51	43	205
	Arsenal	50	63	79	192
	Liverpool	56	48	72	176
	O. Lyonnais	32	24	72	128
	AS Roma	29	22	76	127
	Newcastle	40	46	38	124
	Schalke 04	55	30	38	123
	Tottenham	40	26	42	107
	Hambourg	47	37	18	102
	Manchester City	32	22	35	89
	Rangers	33	40	15	88
	West Ham	23	23	41	87
	Benfica	30	38	17	85

Source: Jacopin, from Deloitte (2007).

The Spanish clubs can't be grouped into a particular model like the German, Italian and English clubs. As can be seen from the data, Real Madrid CF's main source of income is its commercial activities (German model), where FC Barcelona's income sources seem to be balanced between commercial activities, match-day income and television rights (English model). The general belief that Real Madrid CF and Manchester United share a similar business model is not supported by comparing this data. In fact, Real Madrid CF's model is more similar to that of the German clubs than that of the English ones.

The report shows that the sources of revenue of Real Madrid CF and of FC Barcelona are not the same, and that this is mostly due to the difference between the strategic focus of the two clubs. We can also see that the traditional association of Real Madrid CF with the English business model cannot be empirically corroborated.

To compare the financial strategy of Real Madrid CF with that of FC Barcelona, we will look at the financial data of both sports entities, analysing the balance sheets and P&L of each club respectively (Appendix 4.1). In order to understand the path that these two clubs have followed over the 2000–2006 period, we will consider the financial and sports data for two periods. The first period, from 2000 to 2003, was when Joan Gaspart took the helm at FC Barcelona following the resignation of José Luis Nuñez and Real Madrid CF was in the middle of Florentino Pérez's two terms of running the club. The second period, from 2003 to 2005, was when Florentino Pérez resigned and elections were called at Real Madrid CF, while Joan Laporta was in the middle of his presidential phase at FC Barcelona.

4.2.1 First period (2000–2003)

In the 2003 P&L of both clubs we can see that a significant proportion of income was spent on personnel expenses. At Real Madrid CF, 72 per cent of the income went on personnel expenses (sports and non-sports), while FC Barcelona spent 83 per cent. This probably explains why the results of both clubs were negative: minus twenty-two million euros and minus twenty-six million euros respectively. Nevertheless, 2003 saw a return to health at Real Madrid CF, thanks to the extraordinary results. The sale of real estate (Real Madrid CF's training ground) meant a considerable increase in extraordinary income (500 million euros[11]) which in turn led to the club registering a small, but positive, profit by the end of the financial year. In contrast, FC Barcelona's extraordinarily low income, combined with extraordinarily high expenses, contributed to the club's negative results. So much so that, on an operations level, the P&L showed that FC Barcelona had made a loss of 164 million euros. It is worth pointing out, however, that the Catalan club hadn't – and still hasn't – sold off their training ground and, as such, no matter how bad their position

---

[11] *El País*, 13 November 2006.

may have seemed, the club's managers still had room to manoeuvre. Bearing in mind the huge amounts of money we are dealing with, it's important to consider this fact in order to carry out a fair comparative analysis of the clubs.

In terms of the 2003 balance sheets (Appendix 4.1) for both clubs, Real Madrid CF had positive equity and positive working capital, although it also had significant amounts relating to short-term liabilities (mainly pending remuneration) and long-term liabilities (relating to deferred tax[12]). At that time, the club's intentions to improve their financial situation could be seen mainly at a P&L level, since the balance sheet still contained a number of prior expenses.

The situation of FC Barcelona was more complicated, to such an extent that it registered negative equity of seventy-five million euros, a loss for the period of 164 million euros and negative working capital. If FC Barcelona were a conventional limited liability company, the negative working capital would have resulted in the club being technically insolvent; however, this precarious situation can't come about in a football club. The 137 million euros in short-term credits were mainly associated with other creditor clubs for player transfers. The situation which can be seen in FC Barcelona's 2003 financial data was public knowledge at the time.[13] In fact, it provoked a veritable crisis in the club, provoking Gaspart's resignation and the lack of club leadership until the electoral process brought in Laporta in 2003.

In terms of assets, in 2003 Real Madrid CF showed greater liquidity than FC Barcelona, thanks to the 140 million euros held in temporary financial investments, in contrast to the three million euros held by FC Barcelona in the same year.

4.2.2 Second period (2003–2006)

In 2005 the position of both clubs improved along the same lines. That is to say, Real Madrid CF consolidated their balance model,

---

[12] Deferred tax as a result of the fiscal treatment granted to the capital gains obtained from specific assignment of federative rights of players, merchandising, Internet, image broadcast and distribution, as well as part of the land of the old training ground.

[13] 'The very same week the Financial Services Consumers Association placed Barcelona as the most indebted Spanish club, owing some 230 million Euros', www.elmundo.es, 7 February 2003.

while FC Barcelona, although improving, was still exhibiting the same weaknesses it had in 2003.

When we look at the P&L for 2005 (Appendix 4.1), we can see that both Real Madrid CF and FC Barcelona have managed to achieve an acceptable level of operating results (11% and 9%, respectively). For Real Madrid the net finance charges were nil, as it had no bank debt, whereas Barcelona had net finance charge equal to 18% of revenue. Real Madrid achieved a lower net profit[14] than FC Barcelona due to the allocation of a higher value to anticipated depreciation.[15]

Table A4.5 of Appendix 4.1 includes the 2005 balance sheet of both clubs (liabilities). Once again, FC Barcelona has negative equity, which, though less than the previous period (thirty-seven million euros), means it would still be in the same technically insolvent position we noted for 2003, if it were a conventional limited liability company. This position explains why the 'distributable income in other tax years'[16] and the 'risk and expense provisions'[17] are also classed as debt, contributing to the increase in liabilities.[18] Since Real Madrid CF has positive equity, it has no solvency issues.

A difference can also be seen in the credits and in the amount of total debt. While FC Barcelona has an outstanding debt of sixty-four million euros with various credit entities, Real Madrid FC's balance sheet shows no debt of this type. Further, FC Barcelona has non-commercial debts of 123 million euros, and Real Madrid CF has only sixteen million euros of this kind of debt.

Table A4.6 of Appendix 4.1 compares the state of the assets of the two clubs. Here we can see that the 157 million euros allocated to temporary financial investment has kept Real Madrid CF's liquidity high, in relation to FC Barcelona's 6 million euros. Moreover, it is

---

[14] After tax.

[15] The club depreciates the players as soon as it buys them.

[16] According to the 2004/2005 annual report this income may not be freely distributed because it is related to an amount pertaining to the bank guarantee pursuant to Spanish Royal Decree 449/1995.

[17] According to note 13.a of the 2006 annual report, these provisions are linked to the amount corresponding to inspections by the tax authorities from previous years.

[18] Although it's also clear that the assets are undervalued: the club has failed to include any increase in player values, which if included would cover the negative equity.

significant that FC Barcelona's working capital is negative by forty-nine million euros,[19] while that of Real Madrid CF is positive by nine million euros. Thus, although FC Barcelona's working capital has improved with respect to 2003 – reducing the amount outstanding – it continues to be negative.

In summary, the financial weakness of FC Barcelona is sustained in the economic data from 2005. Despite exhibiting a certain improvement on 2003, the same areas continue to determine the club's difficult financial situation: negative equity, negative working capital and lack of liquidity. Nevertheless, radical change is needed in the management of both clubs since the results of 2000–2003 were more the consequence of erratic economic and financial management. The arrival of Laporta and Soriano heralded a commitment to an emphasis on sport, deferring the payment of accumulated debt and holding the sport itself as a key competence in the sector. The sports and financial results that followed have proved FC Barcelona's new management team were right, since their income went from 123 million euros in 2003 to 259 million euros in 2006 (Deloitte, 2005 and 2008), moving up from the sixth to the second richest football entity in Europe.

In the same vein, Real Madrid CF showed signs of recovery in their 2003 P&L, and went on to confirm this trend in 2005, achieving positive operating results. Both the P&L and the balance sheet reflect a concerted effort to maintain healthy results and an orthodox approach to business strategy in the management of income and expenditure and the structure of the balance sheets.

If we analyse the status of operating income and expenditure over the five-year period (Figure 4.1) we are looking at, FC Barcelona's situation can be seen to be improving. The following figures allow us to compare this data, for both clubs over the last five years.

Figure 4.1 shows that FC Barcelona have kept their income and expenditure balanced. Although their profit margin has not been very high, the trend has meant that the operating income was higher than the operating expenditure (except in the periods 2000–2001 and 2002–2003). Real Madrid's graph, in contrast, shows a sharp

[19] This situation probably isn't as bad as it looks, since the highest proportion of these current liabilities is represented by the 123 million euros of other non-commercial debts, probably associated with the transfer of players and the deferral of payments to other clubs.

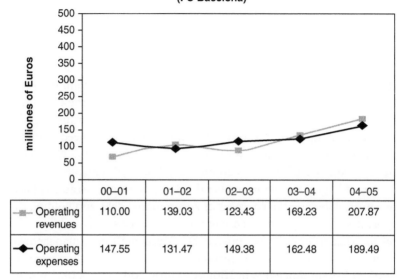

	00–01	01–02	02–03	03–04	04–05
Operating revenues	110.00	139.03	123.43	169.23	207.87
Operating expenses	147.55	131.47	149.38	162.48	189.49

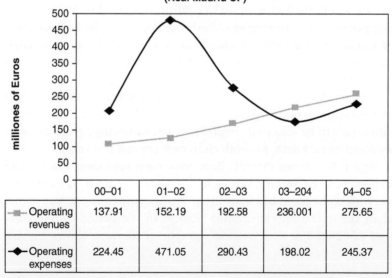

	00–01	01–02	02–03	03–204	04–05
Operating revenues	137.91	152.19	192.58	236.001	275.65
Operating expenses	224.45	471.05	290.43	198.02	245.37

Figure 4.1 Operating income and expenditure (2000–2005)
Source: Annual reports of Real Madrid CF and FC Barcelona
* Adjustment for the anticipated depreciation costs of the players.

Table 4.2 *Footballers' income (2002)*

Footballer	Income (in millions of euros)
1. David Beckham	15
2. Zinedine Zidane	14
3. Ronaldo	11.7
4. Rio Ferdinand	9.62
5. Alessandro Del Piero	9.55
6. Hidetoshi Nakata	9.36
7. Raul Gonzalez	9.3
8. Patrick Vieira	9.28
9. Michael Owen	8.9
10. Roy Keane	8.65

Source: European Football Statistics (2002), available at: www.european-football-statistics.co.uk/special/old/0305highestpaidplayer.htm (accessed 5 May 2003).

increase in the operating expenditure in 2001–2002 – caused by the sale of their training ground – which is later kept under control in the periods 2003–2004 and 2004–2005. From this we can once again see the business emphasis which characterizes the club throughout the period, in as much as the sudden increase in expenses is associated with a keen interest in improving the club's financial situation as quickly as possible, through the sale of real estate between 2000 and 2003; a decision which allowed the club to go on to achieve the economic prosperity it enjoys today.

A final observation to bear in mind is the comparison between the clubs' financial strategy and their expenditure on personnel. Table 4.2 allows us to get an idea of what it means to buy star players at the level that Real Madrid CF has, and keep them on the team. We can see that, of the ten players on the highest incomes, five of them have played for Real Madrid in at least one of the seasons in the period 2000–2003, while none played for FC Barcelona throughout this period.

However, the situation had changed substantially between 2003 and 2006 (after the World Cup in Germany) since Owen and Zidane had left Real Madrid CF, while Ronaldinho, recruited by FC Barcelona,

Table 4.3 *Footballers' income (2006)*

Footballer	Income (in millions of euros)
1. Ronaldinho	29.2
2. Beckham	22.9
3. Ronaldo (ex Madrid)	22.1
4. Rooney	20.4
5. Zidane (ex Madrid)	19,1
6. Del Piero	14.6
7. Lampard	12.4
8. Henry	12.4
9. Terry	12.3
10. Gerrard	11.3

Source: *Business Week* (2006) from France Football.

began to appear as the highest paid footballer in the world, with an annual salary of some thirty million euros. With the imminent departure of Ronaldo and Beckham, the issue of shortages linked to the player-management system established by Florentino Pérez arose.

With players of this type on the payroll, as described in Table 4.3, this expense as a proportion of the club's income is significant. If we analyse the relationship between personnel income and expenditure, it can be seen that both clubs try to maintain a similar proportion of around 50 per cent; that is to say, the personnel costs do not exceed 50 per cent of the income. Having said that, FC Barcelona experienced a period of increase in personnel expenditures, with respect to their income until 2003, the last period under Gaspart's management, as described in Figure 4.2. Then the change in the board of directors marked a clear focus on the reduction of personnel costs, allowing the club to pass the crucial 50 per cent mark in 2004/2005.

In conclusion, FC Barcelona's financial situation is more difficult on the static side – which includes the balance sheet – but the club has managed to achieve a healthier situation on the dynamic side, that is, the P&L. In terms of Real Madrid CF, the data and graphs show a clear business emphasis, allowing the club to achieve positive and balanced accounts, which they have been able to improve over the years.

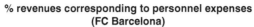

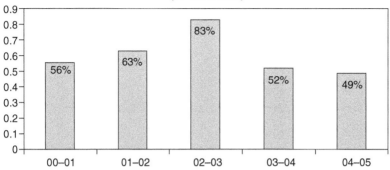

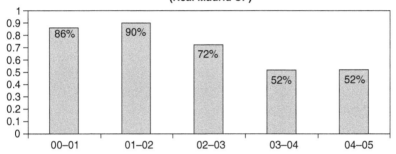

Figure 4.2 Proportion of personnel expenditure in relation to income (2000–2005)

Source: Annual reports of Real Madrid CF and FC Barcelona 2000 to 2006

Despite FC Barcelona's (very) relative financial weakness – having still not sold their training ground – and Real Madrid CF's relative strength in business and financial management – given that a large proportion of the income raised by the sale of the training ground has been invested in signings – why are the fans of the former club currently happier than those of the latter? The answers may be as follows.

The difficult financial situation doesn't seem to affect the mood or emotions of football fans, proving that finance is not the most important area for this type of entity. In short, the variables affecting the popular success of a football club are not financial.

Sports results always deal with a short period of time and are achieved almost independently of the financial results. Nevertheless, in the long term, the clubs' survival depends on their financial results.

This analysis of the financial strategy of the clubs has allowed us to see the difference between Real Madrid CF and FC Barcelona in terms of financial results. However, these are certainly not the only results which can be evaluated in a football club and, with this in mind, the next section will analyse the comparative sports strategy applied by each club.

4.3 Sports strategy: different models, different results

In the analysis of the sports strategy of both clubs, we focus on four variables relating to the sports side of a football club. These are:

(1) the sports managers, including coaches on the payroll;
(2) the composition of the playing staff (signing policy);
(3) players' participation in the season; and
(4) sports results.

Similar to the approach taken in the financial strategy analysis above, we will again analyse the period in two parts, corresponding to stages which characterize the evolution of both clubs: 2000 to 2003 and 2003 to 2006.

4.3.1 *Sports managers*

Real Madrid CF
The organization and delegation of duties and responsibilities in the technical area of the sport is key for a club, particularly in the medium- to long-term. Not only as far as the formal structure is concerned, but also in terms of the choice of action plans, which, though most of the time not expressed explicitly, can be deduced from an analysis of the facts. This dimension shows the clubs' internal coherence, since it establishes a logical relationship between the clubs' decisions, organizational structure and delegation of sports duties and responsibilities. Therefore there should be a link between management and performance, which explains Table 4.4 created to analyse the performance of each coach of FC Barcelona and Real Madrid.

In 2000 Florentino Pérez took over as chairman of Real Madrid CF, establishing a sports policy which began to take shape over time. During this period, the formal responsibility for the sports side fell to the Sports Director, Jorge Valdano, and his assistant, Emilio

Table 4.4 *List of coaches and wins*

Real Madrid CF			FC Barcelona		
Coach	Year	Wins	Coach	Year	Wins
Del Bosque (Spanish)	1999–2003	2 European Cups; 1 Intercontinental Cup; European Cup-winners' Cup; 2 Ligas; 1 Spanish Cup-winners' Cup	L. Van Gaal (Dutch)	1997–2000	2 Ligas, 1 Cup
C. Queiroz (Portuguese)	2003	1 Spanish Cup-winners' Cup	Ll. Serra Ferrer (Spanish)	2000–2001	
J.A. Camacho (Spanish)	2004		C. Rexach (Spanish)	2001–2002	
M. García Remón (Spanish)	2004		L. Van Gaal	2002–2003	
V. Luxemburgo (Brazilian)	2004		F. Rijkaard (Dutch)	2003 –	2 Ligas; 1 Spanish Cup-winners' Cup; 1 European Cup
J.R. Lopez Caro (Spanish)	2005–				

Source: www.realmadrid.com; www.fcbarcelona.com; www.realmadrid.com and www.fcbarcelona.com (accessed 6 April 2006).

Butragueño, with Vicente del Bosque kept on as the first-team coach for three more seasons. Thus, the most significant characteristic of this era was the continuity of the organizational staff, the action plans, and the people in charge and, therefore, continuity in the sports strategy was achieved. At this stage, significant sports results were obtained; winning La Liga twice and the UEFA Champions League once.

In the second phase of Florentino Pérez's leadership, the opposite situation can been seen: there is a constant turnover of coaches, who in many cases didn't even finish the season, along with a change in the sports management model, creating a Vice Chairman, Emilio Butragueño, and a succession of sports managers: Emilio Butragueño himself, Arrigo Sacchi and Benito Floro successively. This instability in the technical sports management of the club happened at the same time as the club achieved very few sporting triumphs, allowing us to conclude that management stability is associated with attainment of sports results.

FC Barcelona

In 2000, Joan Gaspart made his debut as the new chairman of FC Barcelona, seen by a few as something of 'a fan who became chairman of his club'.[20] He aimed to appoint most of the candidates who ran with him for the chairmanship of the club to the board of directors, yet he failed to bring the actions and decisions of the club under this umbrella. He allowed himself to be governed by his feelings rather than a coherent and developed strategy, a fact reflected in the increased expenditure in signings (more than 180 million euros) and in the financial problems which led to FC Barcelona being considered 'one of the Spanish clubs most in debt'.[21]

During this phase there was little continuity in the management of the sports side of the club, highlighted by the constant turnover of coaches (Serra Ferrer, Carlos Rexach and Van Gaal). Moreover, a prolonged absence of sporting success ensued, with the ongoing crisis exploited by the media, finally bringing about Gaspart's resignation.

In 2003 Joan Laporta took over as Chairman of FC Barcelona. Following the instability in the sport management and lack of success between 2000 and 2003, the club took on a coach who has managed to stay with them since and who, with time, has been able to steer the

[20] www.elmundo.es, 31 October 2001.
[21] www.elmundo.es, 7 February 2001.

team towards the long-awaited sporting triumphs of two La Ligas and a Champions League.

In conclusion, instability in management was associated in both cases, Real Madrid CF and FC Barcelona, with disappointing sporting results, while more stability in management was accompanied by competition success.

4.3.2 Team composition[22]

The high level of competition that currently characterizes the main European football leagues (Italy, England, Germany and Spain) has made it necessary for the clubs to get the best players in the world on board and back this up with huge financial commitments to sustain the strategy.

Real Madrid CF and FC Barcelona are no exceptions to this trend, and from different perspectives have been able to build teams made up of a combination of players of three different types: stars, intermediate players and young reserve players (Figure 4.3). The first group comprises those players who have international prestige,[23] the second is made up of high-level players who come from other national and international clubs, and the third, of those who have trained in the club's youth team and have managed to make it into the first team. In the graph below we can see the team composition of both clubs in accordance with these three categories of players.

Real Madrid CF

We can see from Real Madrid CF's graph that their main objective over the whole period (2000 to 2006) was to maintain a team with the highest possible number of internationally recognized players. These star players were joined by young players from the youth team, who were committed to the club, involved in the Real Madrid project, capable of personifying the club's values and who, moreover,

---

[22] For more information on the personnel composition see Appendix 4.2.

[23] These are players who have been recognised as the best in the world, who have been awarded the Golden Ball or Golden Boot, and who have a huge potential media and commercial impact worldwide. Nevertheless, there is difference between the stars who have gained international acclaim before being taken on by the club (Zidane, Ronaldo, Figo, Beckham, Owen) and those who have achieved such acclaim during their time with a particular club (Ronaldinho and Eto'o).

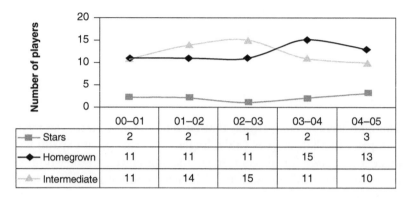

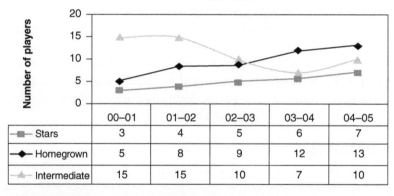

Figure 4.3 Team composition (2000–2003)
Sources: Marca 2001; Marca 2002; Real Madrid 2002; Marca 2003; Marca 2004; Marca 2005; Marca 2006

provide a balance for the high cost associated with contracting the top-level players. The so-called 'Zidane and Pavón' policy (where star players, such as Zidane, are mixed with the 'cantera' or youth players, such as Pavón (Urrutia de Hoyos, 2005)), involved the almost total elimination of intermediate level players from the team. Until then these had been the backbone of the team but now, due to their higher cost, they were seen to contribute little or nothing to the club's main objective.

It should not be forgotten that this strategy not only had a sports dimension which the fans enjoyed, but also a commercial one which, when well managed, could generate significant income based on player merchandising and image rights. In this sense, the team composition and the effect the star players had on the club's income made it viable for them to finance this policy and achieve a balanced P&L.

The actual implementation of this strategy was loyally carried out by Real Madrid FC in the case of the 'Zidanes'. In only three years (2000–2003) they bought Figo, Zidane and Ronaldo, all of whom enjoyed international prestige and excellent media impact. Meanwhile, the number of intermediate players was reduced from fifteen to ten and the number of young reserve players continued increasing over the whole 2000–2006 period, even, from 2003 onwards, exceeding the number of intermediate players.

In the second phase (2003–2005), Florentino Pérez stuck with the same strategy that had brought the team so many sports victories between 2000 and 2003, continuing to buy star players (Beckham and Owen) although it is clear that the new signings were more to do with media impact than the team's sports needs (Figo and Beckham played in the same position, just as Owen and Ronaldo were constantly competing to be the team striker). Similarly, the tendency to reduce the number of intermediate players and increase the number of young reserves continued. It was then that problems arose because not all the stars could play at the same time, and the 'Zidane and Pavón' policy came under attack. Too many stars caused an increase in the average age, a reduction in the intermediate players and a low level usage of the young reserves.

FC Barcelona

FC Barcelona followed a different strategy in their team composition: fewer star players, who although still lacking established superstar status[24] were growing as players, and a group of intermediate players and young reserves that made up the base of the team. In the

---

[24] There is a difference among the star players: those who have attained international recognition before being signed by the club – the type of stars bought by Real Madrid CF – and those who have attained acclaim over the time they have been with the club – such as those bought by FC Barcelona.

2003–2004 season the number of young reserve players exceeded that
of the intermediate players, while the number of stars stayed pretty
much the same throughout the whole 2000–2005 period. This composition favoured the development of the young players and allowed
the club to get the most out of the intermediate players and stars, since
the proportion of each type of player in the team could be replicated
on the pitch.

To conclude, in their latest sporting phase, Real Madrid CF initiated a signing policy focused on star players, supported by young
reserves on the bench, which in practice meant the elimination of
intermediate players from the team and low participation for the
youth reserves.

On the other hand, in their signing policy FC Barcelona looked
for a balanced base of young reserves and intermediate players, who
were highly likely to become established players while in the team
and go on to be internationally recognized, plus a lower number of
stars.

4.3.3 Player participation in the season[25]

Although the composition of the team reflects the signing policy and
the sports strategy of the club, it is not necessarily related to the reality of the first team or to the minutes played by the players over the
thirty-eight matches played during the La Liga season. The analysis
of player participation allows us to see the relationship between the
signing policy or the sports strategy and the reality on the field. The
figures below give an idea of the participation of players of each category in the La Liga seasons between 2000 and 2005.

Real Madrid CF
The Real Madrid graph confirms the suspicion that, the increase in
youth reserves has not led to their increased participation over the
season.[26] Despite the fact that in the second period the number of

---

[25] In order to calculate the player participation we have used the average
minutes played per season according to each category of player (youth
reserves, intermediate players and stars) and then calculated a percentage
based on the total number of minutes in a La Liga season.

[26] Guti and Casillas have been excluded given that their participation in the
season is so far from the average minutes played by the rest of the youth
reserve during the season.

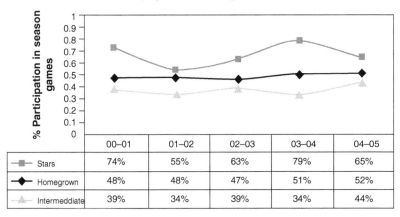

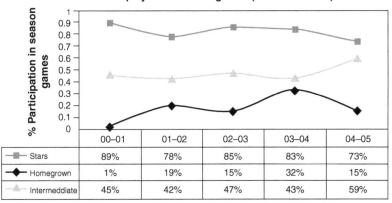

Figure 4.4 Player participation in the season (2000–2005)
Sources: Marca 2001; *Marca* 2002; Real Madrid 2002; *Marca* 2003; *Marca* 2004; *Marca* 2005; *Marca* 2006

youth reserves was increased with respect to 2000–2003, the proportion of minutes played by this group of players was very much lower than that of the intermediate players, and for lower than that of the star players of the team. The data reveals a lack of coherence between the composition of the team in general and the real participation of the players throughout their season in Real Madrid CF.

FC Barcelona

On the other hand, at Barcelona the distribution of playing time among the three categories was more balanced throughout the period 2000–2006. It is interesting to note that the junior players had almost as much playing time as the "quarry" or "workhorse" players. There is more balance in the team among the three categories of players and, thus, a concordance between the sports strategy and the composition of the first team, who actually get to go out on the field.

4.3.4 Sports results

The efficiency of the sports management, team composition and player participation over the season, can be verified by looking at the clubs' sports results (Figure 4.5). At first glance, it seems that both teams won a similar number of matches with a very similar number of goals, and that perhaps the final position in La Liga could have been different.

The first period (2000–2003), was an era of sporting triumphs for Real Madrid CF who won two Ligas and a European Cup, while FC Barcelona remained in the wings as far as results were concerned. In the second period (2003–2006), by contrast, FC Barcelona started to improve to the point where they won La Liga twice and the European Cup once, while Real Madrid CF were overshadowed, failing to achieve any significant success.

The differences in the results between the two periods can be seen more clearly if we look at the relationship between matches won, lost and drawn (Figure 4.6). In the first period (2000–2003) FC Barcelona shows an increase in the matches lost and a reduction in those won, a trend which then changed direction from 2003 onwards, where the club went through a considerable increase in matches won and a decrease in those lost, giving rise to their improved La Liga results. However, the position of Real Madrid CF throughout the whole 2000–2006 period is less clear; we can only conclude that their 2003 La Liga triumph came about through few lost matches and many draws and wins.

Both clubs' international competition results, particularly those of the UEFA Champions League, follow the same patterns as observed in La Liga over the same period (Figure 4.7). In the first

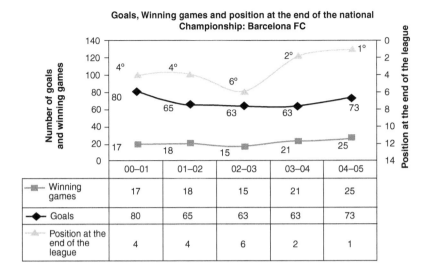

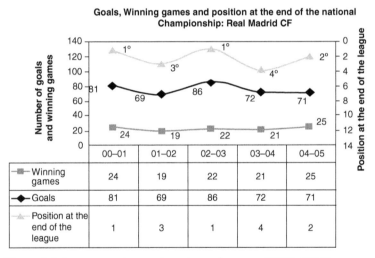

Figure 4.5 League results, goals and matches won (2000–2005)
Sources: Marca 2001; Mca 2002; Real Madrid 2002; Marca 2003; Marca 2004; Marca 2005; Marca 2006.

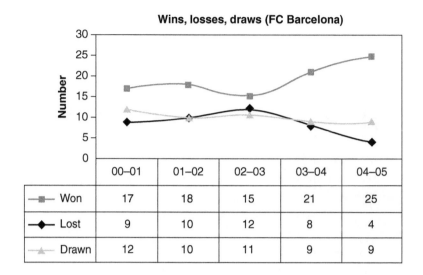

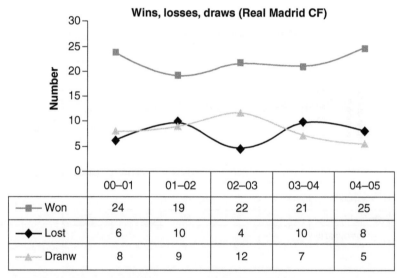

Figure 4.6 Matches won, lost and drawn (2000–2005)
Sources: Marca 2001; Marca 2002; Real Madrid 2002; Marca 2003; Marca 2004; Marca 2005; Marca 2006.

period (2000–2003) Real Madrid CF achieved significant wins but, since 2003, despite managing to qualify for the international competition, they haven't been anywhere near winning. FC Barcelona played a less significant role in La Liga until the 2005–2006 season when they won it. At least both the results curve for La Liga and the UEFA Champions League were moving up towards the end of the period.

4.4 Consequences of both models

The sports strategy which can be seen from the team composition, player participation in the season and management stability data, has produced results in terms of triumphs and disappointments (Figure 4.8). Yet each strategy also brings with it its own consequences depending on the model followed, determining how long it is in place for.

Figure 4.8 shows the risks of Real Madrid CF's model, characterized by a relatively imbalanced team, sustained by a group of star players, of a high average age, who take part in the whole season, while others spend almost the whole season on the bench. These established players are, in general, older than the rest of the players and significantly increase the average age of the team. As we can see in the graph, not only are they ageing, but they also tend to participate less in the season and contribute fewer goals. If we also consider that these players take part in many international matches, reaching intense sporting activity levels – probably much higher than the rest of the team – the risk of injury and exhaustion is significantly increased.

In FC Barcelona we observe that, during the first period, the star players were of high average age and their participation in the season was considerably lower, as was the number of goals but, from 2003 onwards, the star players' average age dropped, their participation in the season increased and so did the number of goals.

Therefore, the model of incorporating lots of established star players in the team carries with it the risk of age and exploitation of players who, within a short timeframe, begin to decline. The balance of the team and prudent substitution of the stars may go some way to avoiding a reduction of star players taking part in the season

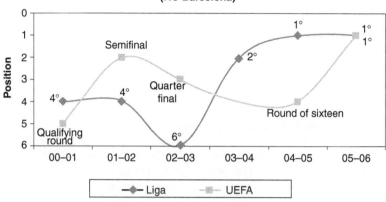

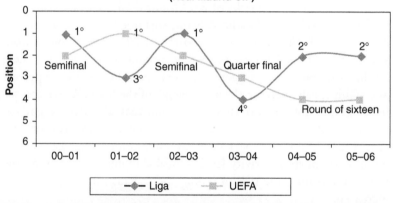

Figure 4.7 Results of La Liga and the UEFA Champions League
Source: www.uefa.com (accessed 19 April 2007).

and, consequently, the reduction in the number of goals that this may signify.

4.5 The commercial and sporting strategic matrix

The analysis of the business and sports data of Real Madrid FC and FC Barcelona has allowed us to see the differences between the two

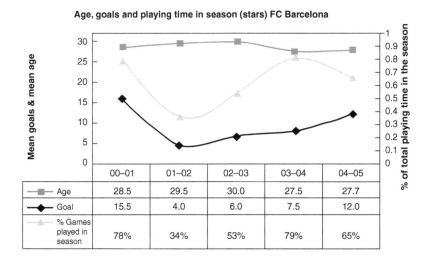

Figure 4.8 Age, goals and star player participation in the seasons (2000–2005)

Sources: *Marca* 2001; *Marca* 2002; Real Madrid 2002; *Marca* 2003; *Marca* 2004; *Marca* 2005; *Marca* 2006

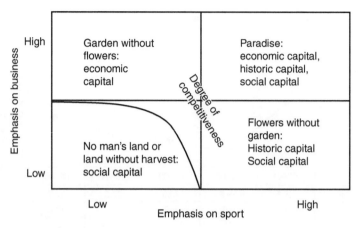

Figure 4.9 Sports emphasis/business emphasis
Source: IESE – CSBM.

clubs in these two areas. These differences can be seen even more
clearly through a matrix (Figure 4.9) relating the two dimensions,
aimed at understanding the emphasis of each of the strategies and the
paths they have mapped out for the clubs.

The sport-business emphasis matrix comprises four quadrants
where the clubs can be positioned. We have used a gardening meta-
phor because of the similarity between the ground and the financial
aspects on one hand, and flowers and the sports aspects on the other.
The financial side is a base upon which a club focused on sporting
success can be founded (to get the flowers). Good financial management allows the club to buy good players, technical support, sports
resources, etc. However, while these elements increase the probability
of achieving sporting success, they do not assure it, just as flowers
may or may not grow.

Where a club has unfavourable financial management and performance as well as bad sports results, they will be positioned in the lower
left quadrant of the matrix, that is in 'unworked land' – they have
potential, but it isn't exploited. If they manage to achieve sporting
success, but still have deficient financial aspects, they will be placed
in the lower right quadrant, in 'flowers without a garden' – the land
produces flowers, but there is a risk that it won't do so if a need to sell
an important player or other resource arises.

The quadrant above is where clubs who have achieved good financial performance belong. The top left quadrant shows all those clubs who, despite their overflowing coffers, have been unable to achieve sporting success, and the top right, 'paradise', which is where financial and sporting success coincides.

By applying the matrix to the two clubs we are dealing with here, it is possible to position them in different quadrants according to the elements emphasized by each of them. FC Barcelona's financial weakness in the first period, together with their lack of sports results, puts the club in the lower left quadrant of the matrix, 'unworked land'. Nevertheless, thanks to the decision to syndicate their debts, FC Barcelona went on to accumulate sporting triumphs which, in turn, allowed them to sort out their financial situation. FC Barcelona then went on to become the club with the second highest turnover in Europe, after Real Madrid, positioning them in the 'flowers without a garden' quadrant.

For their part, Real Madrid CF found themselves in a good financial position between 2000 and 2003 with solid sporting results, placing the team in the top right of the matrix, in 'paradise'. In the last few years of Pérez's presidency, the sporting success of the club sloped off under his business-style leadership and thus they moved to the upper left quadrant of the matrix, the 'garden without flowers'.

Combining the financial and sporting results over the period 2000–2005 we can see the paths both clubs have followed according to their strategies. FC Barcelona's lack of sporting success in the first period and their three important wins in the second, show a movement from 'unworked land' to 'garden without flowers', while Real Madrid CF's sports triumphs in the first period and their lack thereof, takes them from 'paradise' to 'garden without flowers'.

The use of the sport/business matrix confirms that the positions and the trajectories of Real Madrid CF and FC Barcelona are different, confirming what Deloitte Money League, and the results of La Liga and the UEFA Champions League seem to reflect (Figure 4.10). The analysis of specific variables concerned with sporting and business aspects of the clubs has allowed us to compare their strategies, revealing that even apparently-similar clubs follow different strategies and, as such, achieve results in different spheres.

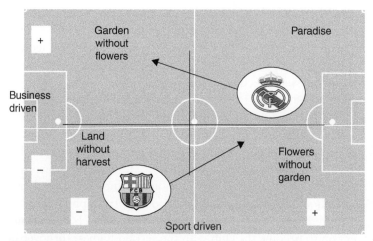

Figure 4.10 Sports emphasis/business emphasis: club trajectory
Source: IESE CSBM

Thus, Real Madrid CF demonstrates healthy financial status through the P&L and balanced accounts, along with a team composition that doesn't reflect the real needs of the team, the average age of its players, or the internal training of the players, giving us a glimpse of a very commercial orientation in player signings. All of this points us to the conclusion that the strategy of Real Madrid is very business-orientated. On the other hand, FC Barcelona demonstrates less favourable financial status – albeit drastically improved. The composition of the team is focused on the training of youth reserves, with intermediate players also playing a key role, and star players who are younger but less numerous; all of which has allowed them to attain increased sporting success over the years. Therefore, their strategy is more focused on sport than on business.

4.6 Conclusion

This chapter has used a conceptual framework to guide us in analysis of the strategies of two leading European football clubs of comparable size in terms of audience, resources and reputation. This analysis has permitted us to relate these strategies to sporting success and financial results over two specific significant stages during 2000–2006. The difficulty of this sector lies in being able to achieve a balance between an emphasis on sport and an emphasis on business, in order to prevent any possible technical or financial failure while also taking precautions against the excesses implied by professionalization.

The hypotheses obtained from this analysis, that we will go on to develop in future studies, are the following:

(1) In the short term, sports results do not need to be supported by a balanced financial position.
(2) In the long term, the financial situation is decisive for the maintenance of the clubs' sporting success.
(3) Where there is continuity and clarity in the organization and division of responsibilities on the sports side, the probability of achieving positive sports results is significantly increased.
(4) The design of the signing policy and success in achieving a balanced team composition, between the different categories of players and their average age, is reflected in the sporting results.

Appendix 4.1 Financial results and balance sheets of Real Madrid CF and FC Barcelona

Table A4.1 *Financial results 2003 (in millions of euros)*

	Real Madrid CF		FC Barcelona	
Income from members and stadium	41	21%	34	28%
Income from friendlies and international competitions	37	19%	8	6%
Income from broadcast rights	46	24%	43	35%
Income from marketing	38	20%	24	20%
Other income	30	16%	15	12%
Total Operating Income	**193**	**100%**	**123**	**100%**
Expenditure on supplies	9	5%	1	0%
Expenditure on personnel (sports and non-sports)	139	72%	103	83%

Table A4.1 (*cont.*)

	Real Madrid CF		FC Barcelona	
Operational expenditure	42	22%	46	38%
Provisions variation	2	1%	2	2%
Ordinary amortization	23	12%	44	36%
Total Operating Expenditure	**214**	**111%**	**196**	**159%**
Operating result	(22)	–11%	(26)	–21%
Financial income	4	2%	6	5%
Financial expenditure	(5)	–2%	(5)	–4%
Financial result	(1)	–1%	1	1%
Ordinary result	(23)	–12%	(71)	–58%
Profit from transfer of players	6	3%	4	3%
Profit from sale of fixed assets	129	67%	8	6%
Extraordinary income	8	4%	2	2%
Total extraordinary income	**142**	**74%**	**14**	**2%**
Early amortization	76	40%	44	12%
Provisions variation for fixed assets	26	13%		0%
Expenditure brought forward from previous years	6	3%	11	9%
Other extraordinary expenditure	2	1%		0%
Total extraordinary expenditure	**110**	**57%**	**112**	**91%**
Extraordinary result	32	17%	(98)	–79%
Pre-tax profits	9	5%	5	0%
Corporation tax	3	2%		4%
After-tax profits	**6**	**3%**	**(164)**	**133%**

Source: Annual reports of Real Madrid CF and FC Barcelona.

Table A4.2 *Balance sheet 2003 (in millions of euros)*

Liabilities	Real Madrid CF	FC Barcelona
Capital	74	(75)
Share capital	59	77
Legal reserve (Royal Decree 7/96)	9	12
Profit over period	6	164
Distributable income	40	65

Table A4.2 (*cont.*)

Liabilities	Real Madrid CF	FC Barcelona
Risk and expenditure provisions	32	135
Long-term creditors	183	33
Long-term debts with credit entities		22
Other creditors	183	11
Sports entity creditors for player transfers	45	4
Tax authority creditors for deferred tax	98	4
Long-term creditors for broadcasting	20	
Long-term creditors for purchase of fixed assets	19	
Short-term creditors	169	137
Short-term debts with credit entities		39
Debts with group or associated entities	1	
Commercial creditors	38	19
Creditors for purchases and rendering of services	34	13
Sports entity creditors for rendering of services	3	6
Non-commercial liabilities	95	78
Sports entity creditors for player transfers	29	24
Creditors for the acquisition of fixed assets	4	27
Public administration for VAT, Income Tax and Social Security	7	12
Tax authority creditors for deferred tax	2	8
Personal creditors	53	7
Prepayments and accrued income – income to be attributed to the next financial year	35	1
State income	27	
Competition income	6	
Total liabilities	**498**	**294**

Source: Annual reports of Real Madrid CF and FC Barcelona.

Table A4.3 *Balance sheet 2003 (in millions of euros)*

Assets	Real Madrid CF	FC Barcelona
Fixed assets	212	239
Intangible sports assets		110
Player acquisition rights	372	241
Amortization	(372)	(131)
Other intangible assets		2
Cost	99	3
Amortization	(99)	(1)
Fixed assets	113	104
Cost	138	139
Amortization	(24)	(34)
Provisions	(1)	
Financial fixed assets	99	22
Distributable expenditure	0	7
Current assets	286	48
Stocks	2	0
Debtors	141	45
Broadcasting rights debtors	8	
Stadium income debtors	15	
Marketing income debtors	21	
Group or associated company, short-term debtors	1	
Sports entity short-term debtors	16	
Short term debtors for sale of fixed assets	64	
Personal debtors	1	
Public administration debtor for short-term tax credit	24	
Public administration debtor for other matters	0	
Provisions	(10)	
Various debtors		

Table A4.3 (*cont.*)

Assets	Real Madrid CF	FC Barcelona
Temporary financial investments	140	3
Liquid assets	3	1
Pre-payments and accrued – expenditure to be attributed to next tax year	0	0
Total assets	**498**	**294**

Source: Annual reports of Real Madrid CF and FC Barcelona.

Table A4.4 *Financial results 2005 (in millions of euros)*

	Real Madrid CF		**FC Barcelona**	
Income from members and stadium	71	26%	45	22%
Income from friendlies and international competitions	23	8%	21	10%
Income from broadcast rights	65	24%	79	38%
Income from marketing	117	42%	48	23%
Other income		0%	14	7%
Total operating income	**275**	**100%**	**207**	**100%**
Expenditure on supplies	(9)	0%	(3)	–1%
Expenditure on personnel (sports and non-sports)	(144)	–52%	(102)	–49%
Operational expenditure	(74)	–31%	(43)	–21%
Provisions variation	(1)	0%	0	0%
Ordinary amortization	(16)	–6%	(40)	–19%
Total operating expenditure	**(245)**	**–89%**	**(188)**	**–91%**
Operating result	30	11%	19	9%
Financial income	3	0%	1	0%
Financial expenditure	(3)	0%	(8)	–4%
Financial result	0	0%	(7)	–3%
Ordinary result	30	11%	12	6%

Table A4.4 (*cont.*)

	Real Madrid CF		FC Barcelona	
Profit from transfer of players	24	9%	9	4%
Profit from sale of fixed assets		0%	28	0%
Extraordinary income	3	1%		14%
Total extraordinary income	**27**	**10%**	**37**	**18%**
Early amortization	(48)	–17%		0%
Provisions variation for fixed assets		0%		0%
Expenditure brought forward from previous years		0%		0%
Other extraordinary expenditure	(1)	9%	(13)	7%
Total extraordinary expenditure	**(49)**	**–18%**	**(13)**	**7%**
Extraordinary result	(22)	–8%	24	11%
Pre-tax profits	8	3%	36	17%
Corporation tax	(2)	–1%	(1)	1%
After-tax profits	**6**	**2%**	**35**	**18%**

Source: Annual reports of Real Madrid CF and FC Barcelona.

Table A4.5 *Balance sheet 2005 (in millions of euros)*

Liabilities	Real Madrid CF	FC Barcelona
Capital	86	(37)
Share capital	71	(86)
Legal reserve (Royal Decree 7/96)	9	12
Profit over period	6	37
Distributable income	27	45
Risk and expenditure provisions	8	78
Long-term creditors	192	121
Long-term debts with credit entities	0	64
Other creditors	192	56
Sports entity creditors for player transfers	36	50
Tax authority creditors for deferred tax	85	2
Long-term creditors for broadcasting	16	

Table A4.5 (*cont.*)

Liabilities	Real Madrid CF	FC Barcelona
Long-term creditors for purchase of fixed assets	55	4
Short-term creditors	245	170
Short-term debts with credit entities		29
Debts with group or associated entities		18
Commercial creditors	41	18
Creditors for purchases and rendering of services	38	
Sports entity creditors for rendering of services	3	
Non-commercial liabilities	140	123
Sports entity creditors for player transfers	37	26
Creditors for the acquisition of fixed assets	27	38
Public administration for VAT, Income Tax and Social Security	7	25
Tax authority creditors for deferred tax	16	
Personal creditors	53	34
Prepayments and accrued income – income to be attributed to the next financial year	64	
State income	32	
Competition income	5	
Total liabilities	**558**	**376**

Source: Annual reports of Real Madrid CF and FC Barcelona.

Table A4.6 *Balance sheet 2005 (in millions of euros)*

Assets	Real Madrid CF	FC Barcelona
Fixed assets	302	243
Intangible sports assets		100
Player acquisition rights	379	
Amortization	(379)	
Other intangible assets		3
Cost	101	
Amortization	(101)	
Fixed assets	209	123

Table A4.6 (*cont.*)

Assets	Real Madrid CF	FC Barcelona
Cost	244	
Amortization	(34)	
Provisions	(1)	
Financial fixed assets	93	17
Distributable expenditure	1	12
Current assets	254	121
Stocks	5	
Debtors	80	103
Broadcasting rights debtors	2	
Stadium income debtors	7	
Marketing income debtors	38	
Group or associated company, short-term debtors		
Sports entity short-term debtors	12	
Short-term debtors for sale of fixed assets		
Personal debtors	2	
Public administration for short-term tax credit	19	
Public administration debtor for other matters	10	
Provisions	(10)	
Various debtors		
Temporary financial investments	157	6
Liquid assets	3	12
Pre-payments and accrued – expenditure to be attributed to next tax year	8	
Total assets	**557**	**376**

Source: Annual reports of Real Madrid CF and FC Barcelona.

Appendix 4.2 Staff composition by team (2000–2005)

Table A4.7 *Staff composition by team (2000–2005)*

Real Madrid CF

Season	Goalkeeper	Defence	Midfield	Forwards
2000–2001	César Sánchez – Casillas	Hierro – Campo – Karanka-Salgado – R. Carlos	Celades – Figo – Geremi – Flavio – Guti – Helguera – Makelele – McManaman – Solari – Sanchís – Rivera	Morientes – Munitis – Raúl – Tote – Savio
2001–2002	Carlos Sánchez – César Sánchez – Casillas	Hierro – Karanka – Campo – Salgado – Miñambres – Bravo – Geremi – Pavón – Rubén – R. Carlos	Celades – Figo – Flavio – Helguera – Makelele – McManaman – Solari – Valdo – Zidane	Guti – Morientes – Munitis – Savio – Raúl
2002–2003	Casillas	Helguera – Hierro – Salgado – Miñambres – Pavón – Raúl B. – R. Carlos – Rubén	Borja – Cambiasso – Celades – Figo – Guti – Makelele – McManaman – Solari – Zidane – Flavio	Morientes – Portillo – Raúl – Tote – Ronaldo

Table A4.7 (*cont.*)

Real Madrid CF

Season	Goalkeeper	Defence	Midfield	Forwards
2003–2004	Casillas – César Sánchez	Helguera – Mejía – Salgado – Miñambres – Pavón – Rubén – R. Bravo – R. Carlos – Samuel	Cambiasso – Beckham – Borja – Núñez – Figo – Guti – Juanfran – Jordi López – Solari – Zidane	Portillo – Morientes – Raúl – Ronaldo
2004–2005	César Sánchez – Casillas	Helguera – Samuel – Mejía – Salgado – Miñambres – Pavón – Arbeloa – Palencia – R. Bravo – R. Carlos	J. García – Jotha – Juanfran – Borja – Celades – Baptista – Beckham – Gravensen – Guti – P. García – Solari – Figo – Zidane	Owen – Morientes – Portillo – Raúl – Ronaldo

FC Barcelona

Season	Goalkeeper	Defence	Midfield	Forwards
2000–2001	Arnau – Dutruel – J.M. Reina	Abelardo – F. de Boer – Puyol – Reiziger – Berjuan	Cocu – Gabri – Gerard – Guardiola – L. Enrique – Petit – De la Peña – Simao – Xavi – Zenden	Dani – Kluivert – Overmars – Rivaldo – Pérez – Santamaría

2001–2002	Bonano – J.M. Reina	Puyol – F. de Boer – Christnaval – Coco – Berjuan – Reiziger – Andersson – Abelardo – Fernando Nav.	Xavi – Cocu – Gabri – Rochemback – L. Enrique – Geovanni – Motta – Gerard – Jofre – Trashorras	Saviola – Kluivert – Rivaldo – Overmars – Pérez – D. García
2002–2003	Bonano – V. Valdés	F. de Boer – Puyol – Reiziger – Zorín – Fernando Nav. – Christnaval – Andersson – Oleguer – O. López	Mendieta – Riquelme – Cocu – Xavi – Gabri – Gerard – Motta – Rochemback – L. Enrique – Iniesta – Geovanni	Kluivert – Saviola – Overmars – D. García – Nano
2003–2004	V. Valdés – Rustu – Jorquera	Van Bronckhorst – Reiziger – Puyol – Márquez – Oleguer – Gabri – O. López – Andersson – Mario – Ros	Cocu – Xavi – L. García – L. Enrique – Quaresma – Motta – Gerard – Davids – Iniesta – Santamaría	Saviola – Ronaldinho – Kluivert – Overmars – S. García
2004–2005	V. Valdés – Jorquera – R. Iván	Puyol – Oleguer – Márquez – Belleti – Van Bronckhorst – Silvinho – Damiá – Edmilson – Fernando Nav. – Rodri	Iniesta – Xavi – Deco – Ronaldinho – Giuly – Gerard – Motta – Messi – Albertini – Gabri	Eto'o – Larsson – Maxi López

References

Deloitte (2005). *Annual Review of Football Finance 2004*. London: Deloitte Touche Tohmatsu.

—— (2007). *Football Money League*. Manchester.

—— (2008). *Annual Review of Football Finance 2007*. London: Deloitte Touche Tohmatsu.

Marca (2000–2006). *Guía de la Liga*. Madrid.

Murillo, E. and Murillo, C. (2005). *El Nuevo Barça: contado por sus protagonistas*. Madrid: Peninsula.

Real Madrid (2002). *Informe Económico 2001/2002*. Washington, DC: Brookings Institution Press.

Urrutia de Hoyos, I. (2005). 'Analysis of the Economic and Athletic Effects of the Innovative Recruiting Methods of Real Madrid: Zidane and Pavones'. Unpublished paper, Madrid.

5 The proto-image of Real Madrid: implications for marketing and management

KIMIO KASE, IGNACIO URRUTIA AND
MAGDALENA OPAZO

5.1 Introduction

The value creation model of Real Madrid is analysed and found to follow the culture-bound and vision-based strategic management style, albeit anchored to careful consideration of the cash-flow generation. It is also discussed that Real Madrid under the presidency of Florentino Pérez tried to move away from the dependency on sport events much in the same vein as Disney moving away to more stable revenue generation in the form of theme parks.

The relevance of sport in the economic field has experienced an extraordinary growth in recent years. Not only has it won a significant place in economic publications, but also in economic departments and programmes at universities (Szymanski, 2003), reflecting an increased popularity among economists and in the economic field.

Sports in general have become increasingly relevant in social life, as can be perceived just by looking at everyday news. There is a vast diversity of sport-related television programmes and even television channels showing only sport topics. Recent data show that, of the television news usually watched by 70 per cent of the Spanish population, approximately 20 per cent of airtime is given to topics related to sport, the same amount of time as politics.[1] This social exposure of sport-related topics also contributes to the rise in fame of those who are involved in the world of sports, giving sport stars the same or even greater prestige than many politicians.

Originally published as: Kase, K., Urrutia, I., Martí, C., Opazo, M. (2007). 'The Proto-Image of Real Madrid: Implications for Marketing and Management', *International Journal of Sports Marketing and Sponsorship*, 8 (Spanish and Latino Special Edition): 212–33. Reproduced with permission.

[1] Consumer Eroski carried out a study on national and local television news in Madrid. The sample consisted of 648 television programmes and 16,752 news programmes.

Two examples of the global relevance of sports are the Olympic movement and world football (soccer) (Amara *et al.*, 2005), and it is interesting how events like these can paralyse a country. The Olympic Games have become a multi-billion dollar business, helping the host countries to change their physiognomy, both physical and economic. A 2004 study by PricewaterhouseCoopers, an audit and professional services firm, estimated that the economic impact of the 2000 Sydney Olympic Games on Australia's economy represented 2.78 per cent of its GDP, compared to 2.41 per cent impact on the US economy by the 1996 Atlanta Games.

The impact of professional football in Spain is approximately 1.7 per cent of the GDP and 2.5 per cent on the GDP in relation to the service sector, generating 8.066 million euros in 2003, according to research from the LFP (Liga de Fútbol Profesional).

So far, relatively little attention has been paid to this phenomenon from the viewpoint of business administration and related social science fields, with the exception of marketing, brand management, etc. Nevertheless, multiple paradigms have been offered such as positivism, pragmatism, critical social science, postmodernism, and a combination of these (Frisby, 2005). The success or failure of a sport team has not been captured in a theoretical framework.

Since Florentino Pérez was elected Real Madrid's chairman, the club has experienced an amazing increase in its revenues, even becoming the richest football club in the world (Table 5.1).

This chapter analyses this economic success and uses various business concepts in order to understand, *ex post facto*, the process experienced and the strategy underlying the Real Madrid model during Florentino Pérez's presidency[2] 2000–2006 (see Appendix 5.1). This chapter attempts to discover the design patterns of their strategy and a coherent explanation for the implementation of it. Following this our interest centres on answering such questions as:

(1) Can it be explained through business administration and marketing?
(2) Is the sponsorship scheme sustainable?
(3) Does it depend more on the figure of leadership? If so, could it be replicated by subsequent presidents, and why wasn't the scheme used in the past?

[2] For the ease of description the present tense is used throughout the chapter as if Pérez's presidency is an ongoing process.

Table 5.1 *DTT ranking of football clubs by income in 2006*

Position 2005 (prior year)	Club	Revenue (millions of euros)
1 (2)	Real Madrid	275.7
2 (1)	Manchester United	246.4
3 (3)	AC Milan	234.0
4 (5)	Juventus	229.4
5 (4)	Chelsea	220.8
6 (7)	FC Barcelona	207.9
7 (9)	Bayern Munich	189.5
8 (10)	Liverpool	181.2
9 (8)	Internazionale	177.2
10 (6)	Arsenal	171.3
11 (12)	AS Roma	131.8
12 (11)	Newcastle United	128.9
13 (14)	Tottenham Hotspur	104.5
14 (17)	Schalke 04	97.4
15 (n/a)	Olympique Lyonnais	92.9
16 (13)	Celtic	92.7
17 (16)	Manchester City	90.1
18 (n/a)	Everton	88.8
19 (n/a)	Valencia	84.6
20 (15)	SS Lazio	83.1

Source: Deloitte (2006).

In pursuit of an adequate theoretical framework with a high level of explanatory power on these questions, we heed Pitts' (2001) words calling attention to the issue that sport management study has often been nothing more than the study of management of college athletics. He suggests that the scope of research be expanded and that the many other areas of the sport industry be added. The general management point of view may be one such groundbreaking focus that responds to Pitts' calling.

The traditional Porter framework (1980, 1985) centres on the business-level strategy and may not provide an integrated view of Real Madrid's working scheme. The resource-based view of the firm (RBV) school of strategic thinking (Barney, 1991, 1995, 2001, 2002; Barney *et al.*, 2001; Mauri and Michaels, 1998; Spanos and Lioukas, 2001; Ulrich and Barney, 1984; Ulrich and Smallwood, 2004) sheds an interesting light on some questions such as the star players' contribution, but may not furnish the general management viewpoint (Goold *et al.*, 1994; Grant, 2004).

The economic approach (Dobson and Goddard, 2001: 11) may help us to understand some concrete aspects such as the link between the distribution of resources among the members of sports leagues, and the degree of competitive balance. Industrial economics may construe the workings of the industry or its branch nicely (Magaz González, 2003). Non-discipline-based authors such as Conn (1997) may give us a nicely rounded picture of the workings of football clubs, but they stop short of giving a managerial view and catering to the interests of entrepreneurial readers.

One approach that may help us to capture an overall general management view of the Real Madrid phenomenon is one based on the business approaches, identified by Kase *et al.* (2005), followed by successful business leaders. In the research these authors studied four entrepreneurs from Japan. Emphasis on timeframe was different – while one of them attached more importance to longer-term profit maximization, the other prioritized shorter timeframe cash flows. The former, namely the proto-image of the firm (PIF) approach, in contrast to the profit-arithmetic (PA) approach, facilitates a high-degree of explanation of the behaviour observed at Real Madrid's strategic configuration. First of all, let's turn our attention to the business approach.

5.2 Proto-image of the firm (PIF) approach

The four outstanding business leaders studied by Kase *et al.* (2005) have two distinctive strategic approaches. On the one hand Sony's president, Ohga, has a clear image of what the essence of Sony is and should be. On the other hand, Shin-Etsu's president, Kanagawa, acts based on his extraordinary business acumen which allows him to discern what levers should be pulled if profit is sought. Both succeed despite the differences in their business approaches.

Kase *et al.* (2005) call Ohga's way of basing his judgment on a specific image of a firm the 'proto-image of the firm' (PIF) approach. In contrast, Kanagawa clearly operates on the basis of processing data and information through a mental model which enables him to discern which are profit levers and which are not. Kase *et al.* (2005) call this the 'profit arithmetic' (PA) approach. The PIF approach tends to view long-term prosperity of the firm, while the PA approach sets more store by shorter term flows of cash (for the main traits of PIF and PA, see Table 5.2).

People and organizations must make sense of every situation they face (Weick, 1979, 1995, 1996, 2001), and this involves simplifying the situation (Bateman and Zeithaml, 1989; Calori *et al.*, 1994). Kase *et al.*'s (2005) thesis is that the simplification takes place in the mind of business leaders. PIF and PA approaches help them in this process. Needless to say, however, there must be a certain level of trust and belief among the organization members (Amis *et al.*, 2004). The PIF approach, above all, may have a head-start in this regard since it is based on shared values.

5.3 Real Madrid and its business approach

Real Madrid bears, under the leadership of Florentino Pérez, all the hallmarks of a PIF firm. First of all, it repeatedly stresses[3] the importance of some emotion-laden values such as honesty, discipline, fighting spirit, leadership, camaraderie, chivalry, nobility ('señorío'), etc., associated with Real Madrid and summarized as 'Madridismo' (Martínez-Jerez and Martínez de Albornoz, 2004). Tradition is highly emphasized when reference is made to the legendary player, Alfredo Di Stéfano, and to the founder of the club as it is now known, Santiago Bernabéu (president 1943–1975) as an inspiration and stimulation for leadership, proper behaviour, discipline and the will to triumph.[4]

Secondly, it is also possible to see a mid- to long-term goal orientation in their aim to eliminate heavy debt and to reorganize the revenue structure by buying back commercial activities such as television broadcasting rights; both were done by Real Madrid as a foundation for future consolidation.[5]

Thirdly, wide new competences and products are fostered in connection with this long-term concern. Merchandising of Real Madrid-branded goods, Real Madrid television channel, etc., are some

[3] Speech of Florentino Pérez on 27 May 2001.
[4] Speech of Florentino Pérez on 19 October 2003.
[5] Speech of Florentino Pérez on 23 September 2001.

Table 5.2 *Comparison of PIF and PA approaches*

	PIF	PA
Essential element	Image of the firm	Actions oriented to profit levers
Shaping or constituent factors	Professional background, environment, firm's business culture and institutionalization	Professional background, environment, knowledge of firm and industry and sense for business
Familiarity with the firm	Necessary	Not so essential
Timeframe	Focus on mid- to long-term	Penchant for short-term
Domain	Wide, new competences and products are fostered	Narrow, existing portfolio
Cash-flow position	Affluence required	At the time of crisis, the only option is to survive
Explicit or implicit instructions from the top	Implicit, second-guessed	Explicit
Applicable when changing firms?	Difficult	Possible
Succession	Relatively easy to find a person with a similar approach, if they share the belief	Imitability or replicability low
Combination with the other approach	PIF – top management PA – lower management	If PA at the top, PIF not possible at lower levels

Source: Kase *et al.* (2005: 48).

examples. In fact, box office revenues have come to represent only a small part of Real Madrid's P&L account.

Fourthly, instructions and guidance coming from the top are often ambiguous, but the shared proto-image of the firm helps the staff intuitively to guess what is expected to be done.

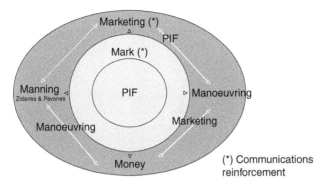

Figure 5.1 The four Ms of Madrid's marketing-centred model
Source: Kase and Jacopin (2007: 217)

Hence, these four characteristics provide evidence for Real Madrid's PIF way of working, based on the importance of values and mid- to long-term orientation in their financial, marketing and manoeuvring performance.

5.4 The four Ms of Madrid's modus operandi

Figure 5.1 represents our theory about the way Real Madrid operates.

Our interviews with Real Madrid-related people and industry experts, and an analysis of published materials in journals and magazines, all point to the probable fact that, at the heart of Real Madrid's strategy, lies the proto-image of the firm (PIF) which its players, managers and '*socios*' or club members share. The PIF cannot be built overnight; it sometimes takes several decades. Time-compression diseconomics (Collis and Montgomery, 1997) exists, which signifies that its path-dependency, namely the dependency on the path of time, creates a barrier to entry. This is something money cannot purchase, because the PIF needs to be bought with conviction.

Based on the PIF, the current Real Madrid management defines its business as being 'an exciting challenge to build a story of value upon simple concepts: brand and content' (Quelch and Nueno, 2004). For its president the action needing to be taken was 'to equip the club with a professionalized structure, which may enable Real Madrid to position itself as a universal brand'.[6]

---

[6] Speech of Florentino Pérez on 23 September 2001.

Therefore the PIF and the brand (based on the former) are the pillars of Real Madrid's strategy. Revolving around these two core strategic elements are:

(1) marketing;
(2) manning;
(3) manoeuvre; and
(4) money.

We will proceed to explain how these elements work. First of all, we will analyse the role of the PIF and the brand in Real Madrid's strategy and afterwards the other four elements.

5.4.1 Real Madrid's proto-image of the firm (PIF)

In a sport club with such a brilliant history and image as Real Madrid, the shared understanding of what the club is or should be does not require much discussion. This shared understanding facilitates decision-making. In its implementation there could be divergence of opinions, but we should not confuse strategic decision-making (what to do) with its implementation (how to do it).

The proto-image of the firm serves as a system for the identification of priorities, more often than not, to know what must not be done rather than what should be done. This will also impede issues of particular interest prevailing over issues of general interest. Many people might aspire to take advantage of Real Madrid's social prestige for their personal prosperity but to the detriment of the club's interest. It is difficult for such things to take place however, since, thanks to the shared PIF, people know what actions cannot fit with Real Madrid, and therefore are able, or even forced, to avoid them. Unless a paradigm shift occurs in the mindset of the club-related people, such actions will be a non-starter or will signify an unusually high cost (mainly psychological). Then, really, what is the PIF of Real Madrid?

The core part of the PIF of Real Madrid may be elucidated as nobility ('señorío'), class or prestige. Thanks to the PIF, the club has become recognizably the 'best' football club in the world. The brand and content, defined as Real Madrid's business by Florentino Pérez and his staff (Quelch and Nueno, 2004), are built upon that. The spirit of continual self-improvement ('espíritu de superación') and the respect for adversaries ('respeto por el adversario') are two principal ingredients of the Madridismo.

Santiago Bernabéu, the president (1943–1978) who brought about the club's glory, can be credited with giving shape to Real Madrid's PIF. During his tenure, the club forged a culture that was later to be transmitted from father to son and, for many of the club's members, it consolidated the club's position in the world in such a way that it came to be considered something apart from the common run of sport clubs. Its history as twenty-nine-times champion of La Liga, seventeen-times champion of the Copa, and nine-times Champion of Europe, among numerous other victories, is beyond comparison.

Real Madrid, for many of its members, represents a way of life, something they cannot view objectively – profound emotion and profound feeling. It's a style, an attitude that one is imbued with when still young. Elegance in winning and losing is appreciated as a key characteristic.[7]

The PIF of Real Madrid is not constrained to static routine; it is more dynamic. The buildings, the stadium, training camps, etc., do not define Real Madrid. The brand and content determines its existence. Likewise, the best football club can project its influence in other parts of the world. Going to Japan, China, etc., is a logical consequence of its PIF. The PIF of Real Madrid is embedded in the four strategic elements to be mentioned below.

5.4.2 Brand

The PIF leads to the brand that sets a guideline for Real Madrid's management. This kind of guideline usually comes from the business leader (Kase *et al.*, 2005). The strategy has more of the designed rather than emerging breed (Mintzberg, 1990, 1991). At the beginning of his presidency at the club, Pérez clearly stated that they structured themselves as a company and thought of themselves as a content provider, which for Martínez Albornoz, its marketing director, signified that their vision was to be the best football club in the world and the club's mission was to nurture and project the Real Madrid brand worldwide (Quelch and Nueno, 2004). Obviously the club's management used the brand-building as its starting point. An emotional commitment was established in the visualized form of the brand. As Campbell *et al.* argue (1990) a sense of mission was created among the club's

---

[7] Speech of Florentino Pérez on the occasion of his visit to the Pope.

personnel. What is the mechanism by which a brand is built? In other words, do dimensions of the brand contribute to its establishment?

Some authors (Gladden and Funk, 2002; Keller, 1993) identified dimensions of brand associations as major contributors to the creation of brand equity, namely the added value contributed by a brand name (Aaker and Joachimsthaler, 1999).

These dimensions are attributes (success, head coach, star players, management, stadium, logo design, product delivery and tradition), benefits (identification, nostalgia, pride, escapism and peer-group acceptance), and attitude (importance, knowledge and affect). Accordingly, we may contend that some of these dimensions contribute to strengthen the brand when they operate well. For example, a well-chosen coach and star players will facilitate the team's success and enhance the pride of 'belonging' felt by the fans, who, at the same time, feel euphoric at the victory of their traditional, favourite club, etc. Any noise that may impair the brand image must be brought under control, and to this end the club has always striven for rapid and effective damage limitation following improper declarations or actions by players.[8]

Figure 5.2 shows how the inclusion of star players accompanied an increase in the stadium revenues of the club (memberships, season tickets, VIP places and ticketing), supporting the idea expressed above.

It seems therefore that this brand-building, once set in motion, may unleash a self-perpetuating process, if well designed and implemented. Martínez Albornoz, marketing director of the club, emphasized that the key to success of this brand-based formula was to develop a series of actions that transform the emotional ('pasional') relations between the brand and the fans into the relations that contribute economic returns (Martínez-Jerez and Martínez de Albornoz, 2004). Thus, managers from Real Madrid quantify the brand success in terms of:

(1) the size of audience;
(2) the frequency with which the audience consents to be influenced by the brand;
(3) socio-economic characteristics of the audience; and
(4) the relations tying the associations of local fans to the brand (Quelch and Nueno, 2004).

The consequences of the work done with the brand brought about some results in the mid-term and they can be seen in Table 5.3 related

[8] Speech of Florentino Pérez on 23 September 2001.

Table 5.3 *Brand recognition*

	2001	2002	2003
1	Nokia	Nokia	IKEA
2	IKEA	IKEA	Virgin
3	Absolut	Mini	Nokia
4	Virgin	BMW	Mini
5	BMW	Absolut	BMW
6	Orange	Volkswagen	Vodafone
7	Red Bull	Vodafone	Real Madrid
8	Guinness	Orange	Absolut
9	al Qaeda	BBC	Diesel
10	Volkswagen	easyGroup	Puma

Source: Interbrand (2003).

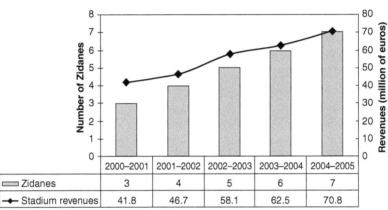

	2000–2001	2001–2002	2002–2003	2003–2004	2004–2005
Zidanes	3	4	5	6	7
Stadium revenues	41.8	46.7	58.1	62.5	70.8

Figure 5.2 Real Madrid's stadium revenues and star players
Source: Authors

to brand recognition, where the data reveal that, in 2003, Real Madrid gained a remarkable place at Interbrand's brand recognition ranking, three years after Florentino Pérez becomes president of the club.

5.4.3 Manning

The brand shows the PIF in an intuitive way. That Real Madrid is the 'best football club in the world' and, accordingly, the best brand in

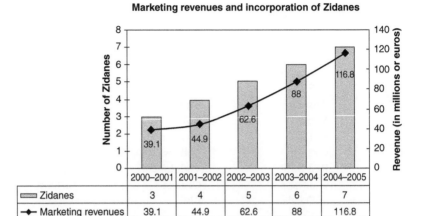

Figure 5.3 Real Madrid's marketing revenues and Zidanes
Source: Prepared by the authors based on *Marca*'s yearbooks

the field, must be translated into reality in concrete terms. The brand is supported by the image. The image in the professional sports field is grounded in players and in how they play. As 'señorío' or noble behaviour is one important attribute proclaimed by Real Madrid, it is expected for players to be responsive to that – if they don't play fairly, then the club's projected image will not be validated by the fans. This explains why the recruitment of adequate players becomes an essential component of the brand. The consequences of this can be seen in the relationship between marketing revenues and the recruitment strategy of star players. Figure 5.3 shows that the incorporation of every 'new Zidane' corresponded to an increase in marketing revenues.

The 'theory' of star players ('Galácticos') was thus born. By 2002, Zidane and Ronaldo had arrived, while the contracts with twenty-three players were finalized either by transfer to other teams or by being rescinded. The purpose of this reorganization was to right-size the dimension to the club's real need. Carlos Sánchez, Miñambres, Pavón, Raúl Bravo, Cambiasso, Tote, Portillo, Casillas, Guti and Raúl constituted the core team.[9] Five of the top ten contenders for the 2003 FIFA player-of-the-year award were Real Madrid players (Martínez-Jerez and Martínez de Albornoz, 2004). Star players are mixed with

---

[9] Speech of Florentino Pérez on 6 October 2002.

the 'cantera' or youth players – what Real Madrid dubbed the 'Zidanes and Pavones' combination – whereby a star player, 'a Zidane', is put with a young player, 'a Pavón' (Urrutia de Hoyos, 2005). For this reason, scouts were sent to countries such as Brazil, Uruguay, Argentina, France and Portugal in search of new talent.[10]

Urrutia de Hoyos (2005) holds that:

(1) the player-recruiting method of Real Madrid has reinforced the international image of the club and its brand;
(2) the recruiting method has permitted the club to achieve sport success; and
(3) the recruiting method has consolidated the economic and sport structure and consolidated the club's long-term viability.

(As to the cups won by Real Madrid in its history, see Table 5.5.) There is some circumstantial evidence, however, that, in the recruitment of players, the basic consideration is the balancing of the cash flow portfolio contributed by each and every player (the balanced cash flow model of recruitment), on which we are currently conducting research. What is also important to note is that the cost of players and personnel has been kept under control so that it oscillates less than 60 per cent of the total revenue in contrast to García del Barrio and Pujol's (2004) thesis that the monopsony[11] profits revert to star players from the clubs.

Figure 5.4 shows the attempt to control personnel costs and the number of employees during the last five years. When personnel costs were rising too high, an attempt can be seen to reduce them during the 2003–2004 season, but the opposite proved true and, in 2005, personnel costs were at an even higher level.

Florentino Pérez explains the emotional side of football: 'People go to a football match to see how Zidane stops a ball, how Ronaldo breaks through, how Raúl strikes with great composure and how Roberto Carlos strongly kicks. They come to the stadium expecting to see spectacular play, even though we sometimes lose matches' (Pérez, 2001). Table 5.4 lists the championships won by Real Madrid.

[10] Speech of Florentino Pérez on 23 September 2001.
[11] In economics, a monopsony (coined by Joan Robinson in 1933) is a market form with only one buyer facing many sellers. It is an instance of imperfect competition; symmetrical to the case of a monopoly, in which there is only one seller facing many buyers.

Table 5.4 *Championships won by Real Madrid*

League champion

1931–32	1932–33	1953–54	1954–55	1956–57
1957–58	1960–61	1961–62	1962–63	1963–64
1964–65	1966–67	1967–68	1968–69	1971–72
1974–75	1975–76	1977–78	1978–79	1979–80
1985–86	1986–87	1987–88	1986–87	1989–90
1994–95	1996–97	2000–01	2002–03	

Champion of la COPA de S.M. el Rey

1904–05	1905–06	1906–07	1907–08	1916–17
1933–34	1935–36	1945–46	1946–47	1961–62
1969–70	1973–74	1974–75	1979–80	1981–82
1988–89	1992–93			

Champion of European Cup

1955–56	1956–57	1957–58	1958–59	1959–60
1965–66	1997–98	1999–2000	2001–02	

Source: www.realmadrid.com (accessed 5 May 2003).

Personnel expenditure and number of employees

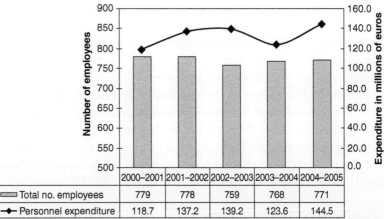

	2000–2001	2001–2002	2002–2003	2003–2004	2004–2005
Total no. employees	779	778	759	768	771
Personnel expenditure	118.7	137.2	139.2	123.6	144.5

Figure 5.4 Real Madrid's personnel expenditure and number of employees
Source: Prepared by the authors based on *Marca*'s yearbooks

Likewise, the ingredients of brand dimension also include other human factors, concretely, the coach and management. For example, Kellett (1999) holds that professional sport seems to provide a close analogy to corporate environments, so coaches may be considered leaders.

From the very onset of his presidency, Florentino Pérez paid maximum attention to equipping the club with qualified professionals.[12] The Marketing Management department was created and José Angel Sánchez was appointed its head, supervising twenty staff.[13] They and other 'responsibility centres' were expected to position Real Madrid as a universal brand.

For these professional managers the management of Real Madrid is a science based on 'best practices' learnt from other clubs, industries and business schools. José Angel Sánchez, scouted from a Japanese multinational firm (cited by Quelch and Nueno, 2004), maintains that 'the task of marketing is similar to any other business activity – a plan is designed, grounded in the definition of the values of a brand, its differentiating traits and in the study of the audience, segmented to determine what products to offer and how much demand to be expected'.

5.4.4 Marketing

On the basis of the PIF, Pérez defines the business of Real Madrid as brand and content. The brand was analysed in Section 5.4.3 as being based on several dimensions. Adequate manning, or human resources, including players, coach, and management team, was required to substantiate the brand dimensions.

Marketing is the next element of Real Madrid's strategy in pursuit of its implementation. In the words of Pérez: 'Real Madrid does not recruit players to sell T-shirts; when the board of directors (La junta) decides to recruit star players, what it is doing is handing over, to the marketing department, a football player who has a set of assets with a high potential market value, even though he is signed up as a player' (Pérez, 2002). The content is a set of products generated by football and its players, comparable with a film. This is developed

[12] Speech of Florentino Pérez on 23 September 2001.
[13] Speech of Florentino Pérez on 23 September 2001.

live and through the media and can give rise to multiple forms of exploitation: box office tickets, television broadcasting rights, events, T-shirts, etc. (Martínez-Jerez and Martínez de Albornoz, 2004).

Real Madrid's management argues that the best players contribute more than they are paid for (Real Madrid Club de Fútbol, 2003); the club's image is bettered, and fans enjoy the club's improved image, not only by watching matches but also buying T-shirts and other merchandising items.

At the beginning of Florentino's period in 2000, stadium revenues and marketing revenues were at the same level as in 2003. It was only in the 2002/2003 season that marketing revenues experienced a relevant increase, enabling Real Madrid to become the richest football club in the world in the year 2006.

The so-called 'halo effect'[14] benefits the P&L account of sponsoring firms such as Adidas, the sportswear manufacturer that had a sponsoring contract with Real Madrid until 2008. Audi, Pepsi, Telefónica, Mahou-San Miguel (beverage producer), Unilever and Sanitas (group of medical insurers) also feature on the list of sponsors.

In selecting sponsoring firms, Real Madrid is insistent about one thing – that they share similar values such as tradition, leadership, standards of high performance, contribution to progress in society, etc.[15]

There are three levels of sponsorship:

(1) main sponsors that enjoy worldwide rights of coverage (e.g. Siemens Mobile);
(2) international sponsors with slightly more limited rights to cover worldwide (e.g. Adidas, Audi, Pepsi); and
(3) national sponsors with rights covering only their domestic national market (e.g. Mahou, Unilever).

Licences for Real Madrid products are highly sought after. Licensing revenue amounted to €51 million in 2004 with eighty licences for 450 products (Martínez-Jerez and Martínez de Albornoz, 2004). The club also opened retail shops, preferring not to franchise them in order to protect the integrity of the brand.[16] In the shops, television

---

[14] The halo effect refers to a cognitive bias whereby the perception of a particular trait is influenced by the perception of related traits or interpretations.

[15] www.realmadrid.com (accessed 5 May 2003).

[16] Speech of Florentino Pérez on 23 September 2001.

monitors replay matches, and players' pictures and team memorabilia are displayed.

Real Madrid standardized licensing, which involved both homogenizing the licensing contracts and selecting first-class licensees. In order to combat piracy, the club developed the 'Hala Madrid' collection to cater to certain market segments without cannibalizing the line developed with Adidas (Martínez-Jerez and Martínez de Albornoz, 2004).

5.4.5 Manoeuvre

Anthony (1988) contends that an organization is a group of people that has one or more leaders without whom they cannot accomplish their goals and that the implementations of strategies require control function. Budgetary process is one of the frequently used control functions. But it does not cover non-financial objectives for the achievement of organizational goals (Goold and Quinn, 1990). Longer-term, non-financial objectives in addition to financial, budgetary targets are needed. In other words, strategic control is required (Goold and Quinn, 1990).

Therefore, in this section which touches upon the implementation aspects of strategy, namely, manoeuvre, we will have a wider look at the implementation process and structure of Real Madrid, which as we have seen is based on the PIF and the brand, which are supported by manning and marketing. Budgetary process, organizational structure, strategic review process, monitoring, personal rewards and sanctions, and ownership structure are reviewed below (Goold and Quinn, 1990).

The annual plan starts to be developed when team directors and executives define the objectives for the coming exercise in early May. The annual budget is produced on the basis of the objectives, and forms part of a three-year plan. The former is approved by the club's members (*socios*), whereas the latter is not, since it is used only for internal control. Martínez-Jerez and Martínez de Albornoz (2004: 9) explain the process as follows:

With the guidance of the strategic objectives and the assumptions provided by the Corporate Manager, each operating unit prepares a preliminary budget ... This document is an action plan that includes a description of all the initiatives the unit intends to undertake ... and the Key Performance

Indicators (KPIs) against which the management performance will be evaluated ... The resources requested in the preliminary budget are assessed by the respective corporate units (Human Resources, Insurance, etc.) ... The resulting plans are then consolidated ... before being sent for approval to Management Committee, the Board and the *socios* ... The board of directors ... votes on the budget during the weekend of the first official home game of the season (late August or early September). Once approved ... the budget is submitted to the Liga de Fútbol Profesional (LFP) and the Consejo Superior de Deportes (CSD). Failure to submit ... budgets ... will exclude the team from official competitions ... In early October the general assembly ... approves both the financial statements for the past fiscal year and the budget for the current season ... Budget ... follow-up is carried out monthly by each area ... according to its Balanced Scorecard ... financial and non-financial KPIs.

Regarding the organizational design, the concept of responsibility centres was introduced in 2002, while centres managing revenues and expenses and centres developing activities to generate future revenues were distinguished.[17] Four main units – Sport Area, Corporate Area, Marketing Area and Presidency Area – were created to address Pérez's strategic priorities (Martínez-Jerez and Martínez de Albornoz, 2004). Increase in revenue generation would be attempted by the presidency unit and the marketing unit. Sport Area would be closely watched by the Corporate Area to bring about the necessary financial discipline, since the former's expenses represented the major portion of the club's expenditures. A variable pay structure was introduced for better employee motivation. As cited before, financial and non-financial targets were linked to departmental and company-wide business plans based on the Balanced Scorecard framework (Martínez-Jerez and Martínez de Albornoz, 2004).

One thing which differentiates Real Madrid from other major premium clubs is its ownership structure. Whereas Manchester United and Juventus are owned by shareholders, and dominated by majority shareholders such as John Magnier and J.P. McManus in the case of Manchester United, and the Agnelli family in the case of Juventus, Real Madrid is owned by its *socios* or members.

The motivational structure must therefore be different. Shareholders ultimately seek the increase of their share price or the club's market capitalization. *Socios* care for the club's economic and financial

[17] Speech of Florentino Pérez on 6 October 2002.

performance, but their basic interest must lie in the emotional satisfaction the club may be able to provide them with. It means that
the club's centre of gravity shifts. Quarterly or daily ups and downs
of share price is not the indicator it has to play with, enabling it to
concentrate on fewer performance indicators such as winning the
matches, mid-term restructuring of team players, etc.

5.4.6 Money

Money, or the financial aspect of the strategy, is analysed here.
First the financial situation that faced the newly elected president is
explained, followed, second, by the course of actions that were taken.
Third, the result of financial management is presented.

Upon taking charge of the presidency of Real Madrid, Pérez realized that the club was in dire straits (see Table 5.5 for financial data).
Ewing (2004) attribute the financial problems of many European
football clubs to:

(1) runaway salaries;
(2) organization of the league system, in which membership is fluid
    and revenues may drop by half if a team slides to the second
    league;
(3) managers, often ex-players, who lack basic business expertise;
    and
(4) difficulties of teams popular only in their home regions, whose
    declining revenues leave them unable to recruit stars, in turn fur-
    ther depressing sponsorship and ticket sales.

An immediate antidote was needed. Pérez speculated that it would
have been an easy solution if he had sold star players as an emergency
stopgap.[18] He refrained from it, because it was obvious to him that
Real Madrid was an 'institution' and as such needed a long-term survival plan. The PIF he formed of Real Madrid went against such a
measure. As head of a large construction company, Pérez set store by
the balance of incoming and outgoing flows of cash, since construction projects required the injection of a huge amount of money for a
long period and any imbalance in the flows of cash might easily mean
the demise of the firm.

---

[18] Speeches of Florentino Pérez on 27 May 2001 and 23 September 2001.

Table 5.5 *Real Madrid's financial data*

	1999*	%	2000*	%	Rate	2001*	%	Rate
Ticketing	2.64	0.11	4.70	0.15	0.78	3.97	0.08	−0.16
TV rights	5.38	0.22	5.85	0.19	0.09	7.50	0.16	0.28
Advertising	3.42	0.14	4.25	0.14	0.24	3.85	0.08	−0.09
Sporting revenues	11.45	0.48	14.80	0.48	0.29	15.31	0.33	0.03
Season tickets' revenues	3.66	0.15	3.79	0.12	0.04	4.32	0.09	0.14
Net import of the business	15.10	0.63	18.60	0.61	0.23	19.63	0.42	0.06
Subsidies	0.10	0.00	0.03	0.00	−0.73	0.02	0.00	−0.30
Revenues from transfer rights	2.78	0.12	0.07	0.00	−0.97	0.17	0.00	1.33
Renting	0.03	0.00	0.17	0.01	4.25	0.23	0.00	0.34
Merchandise selling	1.28	0.05	0.86	0.03	−0.33	1.93	0.04	1.23
Other	0.07	0.00	1.81	0.06	26.74	0.97	0.02	−0.47
Other exploitation revenues	4.26	0.18	2.95	0.10	−0.31	3.31	0.07	0.12
Total ordinary revenues	19.36	0.80	21.55	0.70	0.11	22.95	0.49	0.06
Revenues from selling players			0.00			0.00		
Total Sum	6.74	0.28	0.00	0.00		0.00	0.00	
Cost	2.02		0.00	0.00		0.00	0.00	
Net	4.72	0.20	3.46	0.11	−0.27	4.79	0.10	0.38
Merchandising rights /selling C. Deportiva	0.00	0.00	5.70	0.19		19.30	0.41	
Real Madrid's total net revenue	24.08	1.00	30.71	1.00	0.28	47.04	1.00	0.53
			0.00			0.00		
			0.00			0.00		
Wages	11.89		12.89	0.08		19.75	0.53	
Immobilize players	3.63		4.89					
pay-off						7.92		

* In millions of pesetas

Source: Prepared by the authors based on Real Madrid annual reports.

2002*	%	Rate	2003*	%	Rate	Budg. 2004*	%	Rate
4.16	0.05	0.05	6.19	0.11	0.49	7.59	0.17	0.22
7.83	0.09	0.04	7.73	0.14	−0.01	11.71	0.26	0.51
3.75	0.04	−0.03	6.32	0.12	0.69	3.76	0.08	−0.40
15.74	0.18	0.03	20.24	0.37	0.29	23.06	0.51	0.14
5.14	0.06	0.19	6.76	0.12	0.32	4.91	0.11	−0.27
20.88	0.24	0.06	27.01	0.50	0.29	27.96	0.62	0.04
0.03	0.00	0.72	0.03	0.00		0.00	0.00	−0.00
0.24	0.00	0.42	0.17	0.00	−0.30	2.48	0.05	13.44
0.26	0.00	0.11	0.04	0.00	−0.83	0.00	0.00	−0.00
2.65	0.03	0.38	3.23	0.06	0.22	7.62	0.17	1.36
1.26	0.01	0.30	1.56	0.03	0.24	0.63	0.01	−0.60
4.44	0.05	0.34	5.04	0.09	0.13	10.73	0.24	1.13
25.32	0.29	0.10	32.04	0.59	0.27	38.69	0.85	0.21
0.00			0.00			0.00		
0.00			0.00			0.00		
0.00			0.00			0.00		
0.08	0.00	−0.98	0.96	0.02	11.62	0.00	0.00	−0.00
62.22	0.71	2.22	21.39	0.39	−0.66	6.58	0.15	−0.69
87.62	1.00	0.86	54.39	1.00	−0.38	45.27	1.00	−0.17
0.00			0.00			0.27		
0.00			0.00			0.00		
22.84	0.16		23.16	0.01		22.17	−0.04	
44.22			7.97			2.70		

The mounting debts meant that the club was being bled dry between the interest payment and amortization. Newly-bought star players, the success of merchandising, etc., might signify the income of cash in future but, as the saying goes, there's no long-term without short-term. Something had to be done. As Grundy (2004) holds, 'financial strategy options warrant separate exploration'.

Pérez set out to establish two different timeframes, taking the advice of Deloitte & Touche, their firm of auditors. For day-to-day cash requirements, the club resorted to short-term bank loans.

Mid-term, the budgetary deficit and cash position had to be remedied. To his dismay Pérez and his management team discovered that commercial rights had been sold long-term for a fixed price and that they had already been cashed in.

Accordingly, three sets of action were laid out:

(1) to re-negotiate the rights that had been sold by the previous management;
(2) to set up a base for the future launch of Real Madrid into the world market; and
(3) the coordination of activities to celebrate the centenary of the club.

First, the club repurchased 50 per cent of TV Real Madrid, Teletienda (a television shopping channel), and advertising space within the stadium from the television channel Sogecable. Additionally, 136 box seats were repurchased from their title-holders.

Second, products carrying the Real Madrid brand were created. A contract was signed with the firm BRB to develop the worldwide license programme. The franchise of 200 Real Madrid consumer products was awarded. It was intended that ten Real Madrid-owned shops would be opened in Spain, supplemented by 100 franchisee shops. A website was created and, in July 2001 alone, 20 million pages were served. Half a million viewers visited it, of which 60 per cent were from abroad. A member card was issued to enhance the loyalty of its members. Agreements with Mahou, Sanitas, Pepsi and Altadis, among others, were reached, which would contribute 700 million pesetas (€4.2 million) every year, which would ultimately increase to 1,500 million pesetas. Agreements were also established in Japan,

Korea, China, Saudi Arabia, Egypt and South America to develop the Real Madrid brand in those countries.[19]

The new management team negotiated with the Autonomous Government of the Madrid region and Madrid city council to settle the historical debt. The club sold its training ground, named La Ciudad Deportiva (Sport City), which allowed it to cancel its debt. By 2002 the club had paid off all bank loans and its working capital was positive for the first time in many years.[20]

The P&L account shows several interesting characteristics. First, the sum of box office ticket sales plus incomes from 'abonados', or subscribing members, which we may call the primary incomes, represented 26 per cent in 1999, dropping to 17 per cent in 2001 (the year of Pérez's entry), then to 11 per cent in 2002, and finally going up to 23 per cent in 2003, reflecting the higher weight the extraordinary incomes carried during 2001 and 2002 due to the sale of its training ground. The P&L structure therefore has become more dependent on ordinary, recurring incomes rather than extraordinary ones (see Real Madrid's P&L accounts from 1999 to 2004).

5.5 Discussion

We analysed the strategic scheme of Real Madrid during the presidency of Florentino Pérez and found that its basic component is the PIF that was nurtured during 100 years of its history. Nobility, fair play, tradition, elegance, etc., are the expressions used to describe it. The current president and his management team configure their strategy on the basis of the PIF and define their business as being brand and content. The brand is a reflection of the values and beliefs fostered by the PIF. The strengthening of the brand by force passes through the manning, that is, the recruitment of star players, and the creation of a professional management team availing itself of the most advanced management and marketing concepts and techniques.

The brand image substantiated by the manning leads to the marketing, which is supported, in turn, by the manoeuvre, namely, the

---

[19] Speech of Florentino Pérez on 23 September 2001.
[20] Speech of Florentino Pérez on 6 October 2002.

operations and implementation process of the strategy including control system and organizational design. Money integrates all other strategic components and proffers the financial base for the whole strategy.

We are now in a position to answer the questions raised at the beginning of this chapter. Let's go through them one by one and attempt to respond to them.

(1) Could it be explained through business administration and marketing?
(2) Is the scheme of sponsoring sustainable?
(3) Does it depend more on the figure of leadership? If so, could it be replicated by subsequent presidents, and why wasn't the scheme used in the past?

In the first and second place, could this same scheme be applicable to another sport business or to other businesses in general?

The scheme itself is readily copied to other businesses. As a matter of fact, the PIF approach was first identified in business entities such as Sony. The snag is that sport organizations basically diverge from other business entities in one aspect – their dependency on the ups and downs of human beings. Emotion and enthusiasm are the order of the day. Only the business part may be 'systematized' according to the application of the analysis.

Third, in relation to the scheme's sustainability, was Pérez going to be able to sustain this for some years to come? Or, if not him, will his successor be able to keep this afloat after his departure from the presidency?

Our analyses point out that Pérez's strategic scheme was not entirely implemented. The club's P&L account demonstrates that the implementation of the strategy may have seen its first round concluded by 2005. Whether it is sustainable or not can only be seen in coming years. It is still premature to pass the final judgment on Pérez and his management team. However, some threats to the model become visible in a longitudinal analysis of players performance statistics, as in Figure 5.5.

Figure 5.6 shows that 'the Zidanes' are getting older; their participation in international games is higher every year and, at the same time,

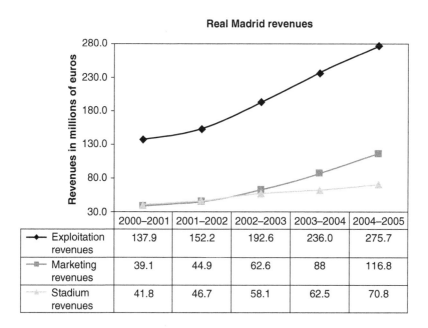

Real Madrid revenues

	2000–2001	2001–2002	2002–2003	2003–2004	2004–2005
◆ Exploitation revenues	137.9	152.2	192.6	236.0	275.7
■ Marketing revenues	39.1	44.9	62.6	88	116.8
▲ Stadium revenues	41.8	46.7	58.1	62.5	70.8

Figure 5.5 Real Madrid's revenues
Source: Prepared by the authors based on *Marca*'s yearbooks

their presence in the national league championship is decreasing. If the centre of Real Madrid's model is marketing, then 'the Zidanes' – the most famous figures – play a vital role for the development of the strategy and in the sustainability of the scheme. As has been said by Florentino, people go to the games to see these figures playing and, if they are not on the field, the consequences could be distressing for the model.

Soon these players will need to be replaced and then an important decision will arise: will Real Madrid find other players with the ability to sustain what these 'Zidanes' have brought about?

On the assumption that this is a successful scheme and Pérez's successor may try to replicate it, how will he or she fare in the attempt? This question may be scrutinized in the light of Pérez's predecessor's behaviour.

Both Pérez and his predecessors, Sanz for example, enjoyed the same 'ingredients' to formulate their strategy – the tradition and values

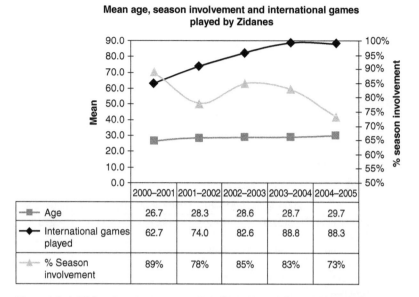

Figure 5.6 Zidane's age, season involvement and international games played

that formed the PIF for Pérez and his management team. If they were not so successful or they mapped out different strategies and courses of action (and this seems to have been the case), then the continuity of the existing scheme may rather depend on the will to continue and most probably on the skills or capability of the successor. As Kase *et al.* (2005) argue, 'the mind of the strategist, therefore is the main unit of analysis in the cognitive perspective of strategic management'.

5.6 Conclusion

This chapter exemplifies the possibility of applying the concepts and technique of business administration to the analysis and understanding of sport activities and their management.

One of the limitations felt during its writing is that the human factors that may affect the ups and downs of a sport team may need a more specific analytical tool. We feel, however, that the elucidation of every nook and cranny of the mystery that is sport may remain beyond reach for many years for the benefit of those who are sport enthusiasts.

The PIF approach we made ample use of in this chapter may have some degree of explanatory power on sport phenomena precisely because it involves such visceral elements as values, beliefs, love and hate.

In concluding we are to add an *ex post facto* analysis of Real Madrid's management after the departure of the former management headed up by Florentino Pérez.

The entry of a new management team, led by a person trained in the law, will change the entire management and, of course, the sport approach. As a matter of fact, some key executives have already begun exiting from the central arena. Our guess hazards that such a change heralds the move from emphasis on business management to emphasis on sport. Likewise we predict the switch from PIF to PA in the management approach at the team.

One good feature of the Florentino regime was the financial consolidation. Accordingly, thanks to the full coffers, the new management will be able to enjoy a lengthy trial-and-error period if the patience of its 'abonados' is overly taxed by too many sport failures.

In brief, one management cycle seems to have ended at this premier Spanish team, but what is certain is that the new cycle will not be lacking the myriad human glories and miseries that make up the beautiful game: football.

Appendix 5.1 Research methodology

Basically, interview survey and a review of relevant literature were the mainstays of our research:

- Interview survey: fifteen in-depth interviews with industry experts including the incumbent executives of football clubs, former Real Madrid players, journalists and academics.
- Literature review: sport newspapers, academic journals, other secondary data.
- Content analysis using Leximancer, an IT application, Version 0.1 for Macintosh.

References

Aaker, D.A. and Joachimsthaler, E. (1999). 'The Lure of Global Branding', *Harvard Business Review* (November–December).

Amara, M., Henry, J., Liang, J. and Uchiumi, K. (2005). 'The Governance of Professional Soccer – Five Case Studies: Algeria, China, England, France, and Japan', *European Journal of Sport Science*, 5(4): 189–206.

Amis, J., Slack, T. and Hinings, C.R. (2004). 'Strategic Change and the Role of Interests, Power, and Organizational Capacity', *Journal of Sport Management*, 18(2): 158–99.

Anthony, R.N. (1988). *The Management Control Function*. Boston: The Harvard Business School Press.

Barney, J.B. (1991). 'Firm Resources and Sustained Competitive Advantage', *Journal of Management*, 17(1): 99–120.

(1995). 'Looking Inside for Competitive Advantage', *Academy of Management Executive*, 9(4): 49–61.

(2001). 'Resource-based Theories of Competitive Advantage: A Ten-year Retrospective on the Resource-based View', *Journal of Management*, 27: 643–50.

(2002). 'Strategic Management: From Informed Conversation to Academic Discipline', *Academy of Management Executive*, 16(2): 53–7.

Barney, J.B., Wright, M. and Ketchen Jr., D.J. (2001). 'The Resource-based View of the Firm: Ten Years after 1991', *Journal of Management*, 27: 625–41.

Bateman, T.S. and Zeithaml, C.P. (1989). 'The Psychological Context of Strategic Decisions: A Model and Convergent Experimental Findings', *Strategic Management Journal*, 10: 59–74.

Calori, R., Johnson, G. and Sarnin, P. (1994). 'CEOs' Cognitive Maps and the Scope of the Organization', *Strategic Management Journal*, 15: 437–57.

Campbell, A., Devine, M. and Young, D. (1990). *A Sense of Mission*. London: The Economist Books.

Collis, D.J. and Montgomery, C.A. (1997). *Corporate Strategy: Resources and the Scope of the Firm*. Chicago: Irwin.

Conn, D. (1997). *The Football Business: the Modern Football Classic*, 5th edn. Edinburgh: Mainstream Publishing.

Deloitte (2006). *Football Money League*. Manchester.

Dobson, S. and Goddard, J. (2001). *The Economics of Football*. Cambridge: Cambridge University Press.

Ewing, J.C. Laura (2004). 'Can Soccer be Saved?', *Business Week*, 19 July, pp. 46–9.

Frisby, W. (2005). 'The Good, the Bad, and the Ugly: Critical Sport Management Research', *Journal of Sport Management*, **19**: 1–12.

García del Barrio, P. and Pujol, F. (2004). 'Pay and Performance in the Spanish Soccer League: Who gets the Expected Monopsony Rents?', Working Paper: 5/04. Facultad de Ciencias Económicas y Empresariales, Universidad de Navarra, Pamplona.

Gladden, J.M. and Funk, D.C. (2002). 'Developing an Understanding of Brand Associations in Team Sport: Empirical Evidence from Consumers of Professional Sport', *Journal of Sport Management*, **16**: 54–81.

Goold, M. and Quinn, J.J. (1990). *Strategic Control: Milestones for Long-Term Performance*. London: The Economist Books.

Goold, M., Campbell, A. and Alexander, M. (1994). *Corporate-Level Strategy: Creating Value in the Multibusiness Company*. New York: John Wiley.

Grant, R.M. (2004). *Contemporary Strategy Analysis: Concepts, Techniques, Applications*, 5th edn. Oxford: Blackwell.

Grundy, T. (2004). 'Strategy and Financial Management in the Football Industry', *Strategic Change*, **13**: 405–22.

Interbrand (2003). *Best Global Brands*. Online, available at: www.interbrand.com (last accessed 2 April 2007).

Kase, K. and Jacopin, T. (2007). *CEOs as Leaders and Strategy Designers: Explaining the Success of Spanish Banks*. Hampshire: Palgrave Macmillan.

Kase, K., Sáez, F. and Riquelme, H. (2005). *Transformational CEOs: Leadership and Management Success in Japan*. Cheltenham: Edward Elgar.

Keller, K.L. (1993). 'Conceptualizing, Measuring, and Managing Customer-based Brand Equity', *Journal of Marketing*, **57**(January): 1–22.

Kellett, P. (1999). 'Organizational Leadership: Lessons from Professional Coaches', *Sport Management Review*, **2**(2): 150–72.

Magaz González, A.M. (2003). *Una Aproximación al Análisis del Sector de Fútbol Profesional desde la Perspectiva de la Economía Industrial*. León: Universidad de León.

Martínez-Jerez, F.A. and Martínez de Albornoz, R. (2004). *Hala Madrid: Managing Real Madrid Club de Fútbol, the Team of the Century*. Boston: Harvard Business School.

Mauri, A.J. and Michaels, M.P. (1998). 'Firm and Industry Effects within Strategic Management: An Empirical Examination', *Strategic Management Journal*, **19**: 211–19.

Mintzberg, H. (1990). 'Strategy Formation: Schools of Thoughts', in J.W. Fredrickson (ed.), *Perspectives on Strategic Management*. New York: Harper and Row, pp. 105–236.

—— (1991). 'Learning 1, Planning 0: Reply to Igor Ansoff', *Strategic Management Journal*, 12: 463–6.

Pérez, F. (2001). *Discurso pronunciado por el Presidente del Real Madrid C.F., D. Florentino Pérez en la Asamblea Extraordinarios de Socios Compromisarios celebrada el día 27 de mayo de 2001.* Madrid: Real Madrid.

—— (2002). *Discurso pronunciado por el Presidente del Real Madrid C.F., D. Florentino Pérez, en la Asamblea General de Socios Compromisarios celebrada el día 6 de octubre de 2002.* Madrid: Real Madrid.

Pitts, B.G. (2001). 'Sport Management at the Millennium: A Defining Moment', *Journal of Sport Management*, 15(1): 1–10.

Porter, M.E. (1980). *Competitive Strategy: Techniques for Analyzing Industries and Competitors*. New York: The Free Press.

—— (1985). *Competitive Advantage: Creating and Sustaining Superior Performance*. New York: The Free Press.

PricewaterhouseCoopers. (2004). 'The Economic Impact of the Olympic Games'. Online, available at: www.pwcglobal.com/gx/eng/ins-sol/spec-int/neweurope/epa/EEOJun04_SectionIII.pdf (accessed 4 April 2004).

Quelch, J. and Nueno, J.L. (2004). *Real Madrid Club de Fútbol*. Boston: Harvard Business School.

Real Madrid Club de Fútbol. (2003). 'Informe Económico'.

Spanos, Y.E. and Lioukas. S. (2001). 'An Examination into the Causal Logic of Rent Generation: Contrasting Porter's Competitive Strategy Framework and the Resource-based Perspective', *Strategic Management Journal*, 22: 907–34.

Szymanski, S. (2003). 'The Economic Design of Sporting Contests', *Journal of Economic Literature*, 41(4): 1137–87.

Ulrich, D. and Barney, J.B. (1984). 'Perspectives in Organizations: Resource, Dependence, Efficiency, and Population', *Academy of Management Review*, 9(3): 471–81.

Ulrich, D. and Smallwood, N. (2004). 'Capitalizing on Capabilities', *Harvard Business Review* (June): 119–204.

Urrutia de Hoyos, I. (2005). 'Analysis of the Economic and Athletic Effects of the Innovative Recruiting Methods of Real Madrid: Zidane and Pavones', unpublished paper, Madrid.

Weick, K.E. (1979). 'Cognitive Process in Organization', in B.M. Staw (ed.), *Research in Organizational Behavior*, Vol. 1. Greenwich, CT: JAI Press, pp. 41–74.

(1995). *Sensemaking in Organizations*. Thousand Oaks, CA: Sage Publications.

(1996). 'Prepare your Organization to Fight Fires', *Harvard Business Review* (May–June): 143–8.

(2001). *Making Sense of the Organization*. Malden: Blackwell.

6 Value creation from the organizational structure of a sports entity

SANDALIO GÓMEZ, CARLOS MARTÍ AND
MAGDALENA OPAZO

6.1 Introduction

The relationship between the structure and performance of sport-related entities is analysed in this chapter. Using the concept of virtuous circle, namely, the unleashing of a chain of positive reactions, Gómez and Martí shed light on how structures can make best of the value creation process. Types of organizations, challenges and objectives are analysed. Stakeholders are evaluated with regard to their expectations. Financial resources and their linkage to the organizational structure are assessed. Based on the analysis and assessment, an ideal organizational design for sport entities, in this case football clubs, is suggested.

As we pointed out at the beginning of the book, professionalization of sports entities is related to value creation in the sports sector. Sports entities are not only part of the virtuous circle, but they also have an important role to play in how much their financial, sporting and social performance affects whether the circle remains virtuous or becomes vicious. This relationship between the structure and performance of an organization leads us to look at the structural design, in order to ensure that the type of structure is such that it will help these entities create the most value in financial, sporting and social terms.

An organization's structure is frequently associated with the division and coordination of the tasks and responsibilities, as well as the relationship between this and the running of the organization. Thus, an appropriate structure would include clear lines of authority, correct distribution of responsibilities, as well as effective differentiation and integration to help the organization achieve its goals (Hodge *et al.*, 2003). However, there is no single format that represents the key to success for structuring all organizations, rather this will depend on the individual goals, environment, technology, size and internal culture of each organization. Having said this, the basic aims of a sporting entity and the special characteristics of the sports sector tend to determine the most suitable structural design for this type of entity and the extent to which their operations are oriented towards value creation. We will start by looking at which area has created most value for football clubs in recent years.

This chapter aims to look in detail at the key structural elements of a sports entity, in terms of helping instigate the virtuous movement of the value creation circle in the sector. In order to do this we must first distinguish between the different types of sports organizations, since each type is influenced by different circumstances. We will then go on to consider the special traits of the Spanish football sector, finishing with a particular look at the case of Spanish professional football, noting the influence of the basic tasks and the conditions of the environment in the structural design of today's sporting entities.

6.2 Types of sports organizations and the challenges they face

Sports organizations are all those corporate entities that take part in the sports sector, that are results orientated and carry out a rigorously structured activity, the limits of which can be established with certain clarity (Slack, 1997). The interesting thing about this definition is that it distinguishes these organizations by the fact that they belong to a particular industry or sector. Given that the rest of the definition is common to the concept of an organization, it can be understood that the special feature of sports organizations is simply that they belong to the sector they do.

However, the magnitude of the concept allows a vast number of organizations belonging to the sports world to be included in the definition of a sports organization; organizations that differ in terms of the relationship with their environment, their mission, their tasks, and the media and resources used to achieve their goals, in such a way that the term 'sports organization' seems to encompass sporting goods manufacturers, sports event planners, sports broadcasters, sports promotion entities, and so on. Yet each of these organizations' structural design is based on very different goals and value creation models within the sports sector, they operate with different resources and deal with different protagonists in their environments.

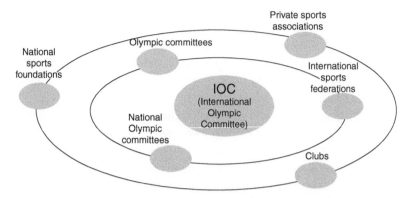

Figure 6.1 The world of sports organizations focused on the promotion and development of sport
Source: Based on www.olympic.org (accessed 7 April 2008).

In this chapter we will focus our attention on organizations whose objective is the promotion and development of sport. Within this category, however, further distinctions can be made between those with different tasks and objectives, despite their orientation towards the same overall aim. We classify these sports organizations into three types:

(1) sports governance organisms;
(2) private organizations for physical activity; and
(3) sporting events producers.

Drawing a distinction between these three types of sports organization is especially interesting in order to understand the complexity of the sports world, the limits within which the organizations operate, and the special features that their different structures may have (Figure 6.1). Despite the fact that the organizations differ in their main object, the activity which they carry out and the level they operate on, sports organizations and the specific entities which they represent in each country have an overall aim of promoting and developing sport within certain limitations. Table 6.1 reflects the main characteristics of each of these organizations.

The table is a response to the classification proposed by Gómez and Opazo (2006), in which three types of sports organization are considered, according to their mission, object, principal activity and members, in order to distinguish those organizations focused on the promotion and development of sport. Despite the fact that in reality

Table 6.1 *Typology of sports organizations focused on the promotion and development of sport*

	Sports governance organizations[a]	Organizations which provide sports activities[b]	Private organizations which organize sporting events[c]
Overall aim Mission	Promote and develop sport. Promote sport on all levels with competence limited by territory and according to the type of sport.	Satisfy a community's interest in undertaking physical activity and socializing through taking part in sports activities.	Articulate the interests of teams or individuals to take part in the competitions organized by the entity.
Main objective	Regulate a sport assuring its promotion and development on both an amateur and professional level, managing the administration, organizing periodic competitions and ensuring the rules of the game are respected.	Provide entertainment to a community through sport, on a recreational or competitive level, to achieve sporting success and social integration.	Organize a system of periodic competitions which assure meetings between teams or individuals who compete professionally in the same type of sport.
Main activity Members	Regulate one or more type of sport. Clubs, individual sportsmen and women, referees, trainers, private associations.	Provide sports activities. Individual members and season-ticket holders.	Generate competition arenas. Clubs and teams that participate in official competitions on a professional level.

Notes: [a] Examples: national associations, federations, national sport organizations, Olympic committees.
[b] Examples: sports clubs, community centres, gymnasiums, fitness centres, universities, schools.
[c] Examples: leagues, associations, circuits, tours.
Source: Authors.

these organizations can carry out any number of functions at the same time (sports governance, physical activity programmes and competitions), this classification is aimed at helping us to understand the structural characteristics of sports organizations. According to some authors (Chandler 1982; Miles and Snow, 1978) these will differ depending on the object and tasks which each organization undertakes, or indeed, the relationship and characteristics of the environment surrounding the organization (Hannan and Freeman 1977; Lawrence and Lorsch 1967).

The distinction between these three types also allows us to see that most discussion on the structure of sports organizations has been focused on sports governance organizations and little is known about the structural characteristics of sports providers or events organizers. In this chapter we will look at the case of professional football clubs in Spain and, as such, we will focus our attention on sports organizations of the 'sports activity provider' variety.

Aside from the differences between these three types of organizations focused on the promotion and development of sports, the environment in which they operate brings with it certain common conditions. In this way, there are two important challenges that affect all sports organizations: the professionalization and commercialization of the sports activity. However, the effect of these has not been the same in all types of sports organizations, in all sports disciplines, or in the diverse sports culture of each country. This is another reason for us to expect each type of sports entity dedicated to the promotion and development of sport to exhibit different structural characteristics. In the text below we will see what these processes refer to and the effects that they have had on sport in general.

Professionalization of sport

The professionalization process refers to the step taken by sportsmen and women from practising their sport as an amateur, to practising it as a professional and/or the rationalization of the way of creating and operating organizations. Over the past few decades, the high level of competition and the speed of change within the sector has created a need for highly trained sports people. This in turn, has caused skilled sports men and women to stop focusing on sport as a hobby and transform it into their vocation and main source of income. The injection of money into sport, in the form of salaries for sports people, has created a clear boundary between professional and amateur sportsmen and women. This is a difference which is also carried further into professional sports with the rise of the sports star.

However, a professionalization process has also taken place at the sports organization level. This professionalization has largely come about due to the need to make these organizations more efficient, and ensure they meet their objectives within a limited budget. Objective-based work makes it all the more necessary to define functions, posts and responsibilities, as well as an increased level of formalization in the activities of sports organizations.

Commercialization of sport

The process of commercialization is more recent than that of professionalization, but it has nonetheless affected the traditional activities that a sporting entity, whose product is sport, carries out. The dissemination of sports events, via different media, has created important income-generation opportunities and supply of resources for organizations linked to the sports product. The sale of television rights, image licences, and the development of a whole host of commercial activities associated with the media exposure of sports teams, players and stars, has greatly increased the number of spectators, the income and professional remuneration. This has happened in such a way that sports organizations have gone way beyond the traditional way of operating and have been pressed into developing new strategies orientated towards marketing and commercial activity (O'Brien and Slack, 2004).

These changes have had such a strong influence on the world of sport that the majority of the discussion on structural characteristics has had to do with them (Gómez and Opazo, 2006). Whether from the perspective of organizational change, organizational efficiency or structural configuration, the academics who have studied these organizations have sought to solve the internal question of whether sports organizations have risen to the challenges they have set themselves.

Similarly, this can be from the perspective of their environment or whether such successes have been a product of the actual evolution of sport. The professionalization and commercialization processes have challenged all organizations focused on the promotion and development of sport – irrespective of the type – and to a large extent explain the emergence of a sector sustained by sport as a main product and composed of a particular type of organization.

The basic work of the organization and the sector characteristics are fundamental to an understanding of the structure of a sports organization. However, the value creation opportunities within the sector are not the same for all sports, nor for all entities within the same sport. With this in mind, we have decided to focus on the structural characteristics, looking in detail at the case of Spanish professional football. In terms of tasks, professional football clubs are sports organizations which are fundamental in their value creation within the sector, whose main aim is such. As far as being characteristic of the sector, Spanish professional football has faced intense professionalization and commercialization processes.

6.3 Professional football in Spain

There is a long tradition of professional football in Spain – most of the professional clubs have already celebrated their centenary or are close to doing so – but the circumstances they now face are quite different to those of their founding years. Both the basic tasks of these entities and the environment they operate in have undergone significant changes. These are mainly associated with the consequences that the professionalization and commercialization processes have had on the Spanish football sector in particular, as we will see later.

Professionalization has had effects at both the player and the organizational level, where a consequence has been a redefinition of the work undertaken by the organization. As early as 1979 special regulations were put in place to cover the labour relations of professional sportsmen and women. From the perspective of the players, this was a mere formalization of their employment relations, but for the clubs within the entities it meant they began to be considered as companies (*Spanish State Gazette*, 15 December 1979). In terms of the structure of clubs, this underlined the need to implement a set of formalities for contracting and paying players, making the management of the entity more complex.

Professionalization of professional footballers in Spain

The process of professionalization of Spanish professional footballers can be seen through the specific laws brought into Spanish labour legislation. Through these we can observe the key features of this work category in detail, and note that dedication to sport is also a form of employment where both parties should be able to enjoy the formal protection of the laws and rights offered to other areas of work.

Spanish Royal Decree 2806/1979 established the special regime for professional footballers for the first time, and includes them within the Social Security system, under a special scheme.

Spanish Royal Decree 1066/1985 recognizes the special feature of a professional sports person, the essence of which is the regular relationship with a sport and voluntary dedication to it, limited to the organization and management of a sports club or entity, in exchange for remuneration. In this piece of legislation the characteristics and specifics of contracting professional sports people are established; working day, compensation, breaks and holidays, seasonal sessions, fouls and sanctions, and collective rights. In other words, the regulatory framework of the Spanish Statute of Workers is recognized, although within the special features of the employment relations of professional sports people.

Spanish Royal Decree 2622/1986 establishes that professional football players go from being subject to the special Social Security scheme, to joining the General Social Security regime, as well as allowing them unemployment protection.

Throughout the 1990s sports organizations were encouraged to become Limited Liability Sports Companies ('Sociedades Anónimas Deportivas'). This was due to the increasing necessity to find a legal persona to suit the needs of professional or spectator sport, which was becoming more and more distant from amateur or practical sport (Cazorla, 1990). In addition to this distancing in the characteristics of the sports activity carried out, the strong sports-results orientation, so much a part of Spanish football (Ascari and Gagnepain, 2006) and the need to sign the best players to get those results, was causing the clubs to accumulate significant debts, which in all likelihood were going to continue increasing. All of this reflected a lack of control over the responsibilities of these entities and their managers. As such, professionalization of the management had to happen, in order to establish a legal persona and a type of sports organization that would fit the needs of the new characteristics of the sport.

Professionalization of professional sports entities in Spain

The Limited Liability Sports Company scheme was intended to make clubs belong to a limited liability company – that is, to make them financially responsible, with a specific legal status – yet it was also intended to be a solution to the clubs' indebted situation. This new legal form imposed certain rules on the clubs in terms of their structure, aimed at reinforcing the sports emphasis of these entities (Cazorla, 1990). As such, shareholders were given preference over the Board of Directors in the decision-making process and certain limits on the composition of the Board were established. These changes, proposed by the national sports public governance organization (Supreme Council of Sports 'Consejo Superior de Deportes') reflect an interest in emphasizing the sports character of these organizations and limiting the clear financial interests behind the huge sums of money involved in the sector.

The appearance of the Limited Liability Sports entities is not only related to the professionalization of the management of sports entities, but is also a response to the development of commercial activity which had started to take shape in the professional sports arena. The sale of television rights for the broadcast of the matches, the concession of licences and image rights, along with merchandising and sponsorship, were activities that began to be incorporated into the main activity of professional football clubs, demonstrating the commercialization of the sector.

Commercialization of professional football in Spain: income from television

The broadcast of sports events through different media has brought significant income-generation opportunities for sports organizations, via the sale of television rights, image licences and other commercial activities, products of media exploitation of the teams, players and sports stars. All this sales and marketing activity linked to the media exploitation has meant that today's sport is quite a different beast to its traditional ancestor, in terms of the way sports organizations are run.

Until the 1997–1998 season, the negotiation of television rights for Spanish professional football was carried out by the Professional Football League. However, once their contract with the Spanish Federation of Independent Radio and Television Broadcasters (FORTA) was over, two television companies started to compete for the television rights to Spanish professional football. This signalled an important change in the P&L of the clubs, in such a way that, in the 1995–1996 season, television rights represented around 20 per cent of the income of a club, while just one season on (1996–1997), they represented 39 per cent of a club's income as Figure 6.2 shows (García Villar and Rodriguez, 2003).

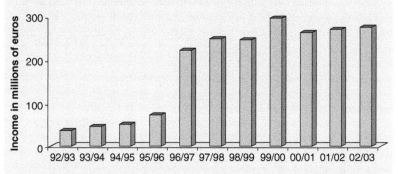

Figure 6.2 Increase in income from television in Spanish Premier Division football (1992–2003)
Source: Ascari and Gagnepain (2006)

The possibility of broadcasting the matches opened up infinite potential for the football clubs and has meant a complete restructuring of the sources of income of these entities, adding the television rights and commercial activities (which the frequent media exposure now allowed) to the traditional source of ticket sales.

Commercialization of professional football in Spain: income structure of the richest clubs

The average budget of the clubs playing in the Spanish Premier Division, 'La Liga', has increased considerably over the last ten years, and so has the gap between the richest clubs and the rest, in such a way that the twenty clubs playing in the premier division can be divided into three ranks: 1) those that have a budget of between ten and thirty million euros; 2) those that have one of more than thirty million but less than 100 million euros; and 3) those that have a budget of more than 100 million euros. There are only three clubs in the latter group: Real Madrid, Barcelona and Valencia, the same three clubs which appeared amongst the world's top twenty richest clubs in 2004–2005.

The effects of commercialization not only have to do with the fact that football clubs achieve extraordinarily high levels of income, but also with the composition of that income. Where football clubs' traditional source of income was the sale of match-day tickets and season tickets, their relationship with the media has opened up new sources of income, television contracts and commercial activities, thanks largely to the media impact of the teams (Figure 6.3).

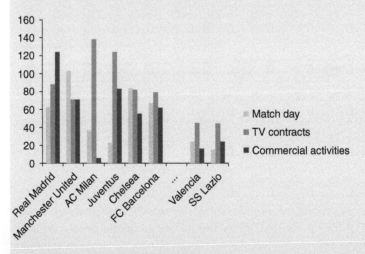

Source: Deloitte (2005). Football Money League.

Figure 6.3 The three clubs among the world's richest clubs in the 2004–2005 season
Source: Deloitte (2005)

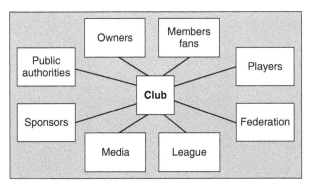

Figure 6.4 Key players in the environment of a sports entity today
Source: Authors

The undertaking of commercial activities associated with football and the constant media exposure of the teams has made the football sector an interesting one for an ever increasing number of key parties on players surrounding and interacting with this club. Nevertheless, each of these players has its own expectations and agenda for value creation in the sector. Thus, the football clubs are facing an increasingly complicated environment, in terms of the number of players surrounding them and the type of relationship they should establish with each of them (Figure 6.4).

The relationship with each of these players will depend on how they expect to become incorporated into the sector. The entity's capacity to meet these expectations will determine their chances of success and the virtuous or vicious movement of the value creation circle. From this perspective, the efficiency of an organization becomes a difficult concept to grasp: an elite professional football club is not an entity exclusively oriented towards sport, although sport continues to be the essence of their activity. The current conditions mean that clubs must take a business perspective on their activities, putting in place sales, marketing and communication objectives in order to cope with these key players and their expectations. For this reason, a traditional glance over the sports results puts sports entities at the crossroads between a sports focus and a business focus, despite the fact that they are in transition (Kase *et al.*, 2006).

In summary, the characteristics of the Spanish professional football sector today (the type of product it offers, the relationship with the key players/parties in the environment of the club, the expectations of

Table 6.2 *Expectations of parties involved in the Spanish professional football sector*

Party	Expectations
Owners	Carry out the sport, promote the image of the city, success for the club, notoriety and prestige.
Players	Sports triumphs, good working conditions, compensation, professional development, media influence.
Fans	Entertainment and excitement.
Public authorities	Visibility and benefits for the community.
Media	Circulation, audience, etc.; relevant, interesting information on matches, trainers and players.
Federation	Adhesion to the rules, promote values and look after the essence of the sport.
The League	Sources of income, enhancement of viewing. Media importance for the sport
Sponsors	Media impact, visibility to the fans and the public in general, increase in sales, image.

Source: Authors

each of these and the solution to the dilemmas they face) will influence the daily objectives and activities carried out by the club, and therefore, the organizational structure of the entity (Table 6.2). We will go on to look at the relationship between the characteristics of the sector, and the structure that football clubs have come to define through the adjustment and creation of value in the sports sector, experienced over the last ten years.

6.4 Organizational structure of the elite professional football clubs in Spain

A significant part of the research on organizations is concerned with the way in which these divide and coordinate the tasks they undertake, oriented towards the achievement of a particular goal. This division of work is a defining aspect of the structure of the organizations, also known as differentiation. However, once the work is divided into various tasks, it is also fundamental to coordinate the parties in order to achieve a common objective, a process known as integration. Differentiation and integration are two processes key to the understanding of the structure of an organization (Hodge *et al.*, 2003).

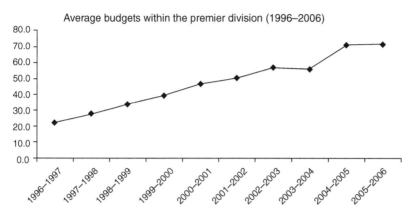

Figure 6.5 Average budgets within the premier division (1996–2006)
Source: Authors

These processes are also related to the level of complexity of the organization, in such a way that the higher the differentiation, the more need there is for coordination and control and, as such, the more complex the organization. Organizations can have different levels of complexity, which allows us to explain the variety of structural compositions they take on. Yet the degree of complexity of an organization is not only related to the differentiation and integration, but also to the influence the organization's environment has on it. Thus, the complexity can be associated with the organization's internal and external factors and not solely with the traditional association between size and complexity (Hall, 1973).

The internal differentiation of an organization is concerned with horizontal or vertical differentiation, or with the spatial dispersion of the organization (Hall, 1973). The first, horizontal differentiation, refers to the way in which tasks undertaken are divided up into routine and uniform tasks (standardization), or by the degree of specific knowledge required to carry them out (specialization). Vertical differentiation is associated with the control and decision-making levels of the organization's hierarchy (centralization/decentralization). Finally, spatial dispersion is related to the spatial distribution of personnel or the organization's activities (Hall, 1973).

Looking at how the budgets of the Spanish clubs forming part of La Liga have evolved (Figure 6.5 and Table 6.3), we can see much greater disparity than that observed among the clubs considered in Deloitte's Football Money League report.

Table 6.3 *Budgets of the La Liga football
clubs 2005–2006 (in millions of euros)*

Football clubs	2005–2006
Alavés	17
Valladolid*	18
Osasuna	20
Málaga	22
Celta de Vigo	23
Mallorca*	24
Racing	27
Sevilla	30
Villarreal	32
Español	33
Betis	35
Zaragoza	35
Real Sociedad	37
Athletic	41
Atlético de Madrid	60
Deportivo La Coruña	77
Valencia	133
Barcelona	242
Real Madrid	346

Source: Spanish Profesional League (Liga Fútbol
Profesional, in Spanish), *Football Clubs* (2007)
('Clubes de Fútbol de la LFP (2007)').

In Spain, the ratio is very inconsistent (1 in 20) while in Deloitte's
Football Money League report, the relationship is 1 in 3. This uncom-
petitive balance is very typical of European structure (see Chapter 2
on the national context). Similar to a monopoly, it reduces the relative
attraction of La Liga since only three teams seem to have the tools to
win the league. The American system appears to solve this issue by
harmonizing budgets, as happens in the NFL for American football.

If we consider the massive contrast in the level of organizational
development of the clubs a segmentation between the different teams
of La Liga arises, of which an evolution is given in Figure 6.6.

- Teams with a budget of more than 100 million euros: Real Madrid,
  FC Barcelona and FC Valencia.

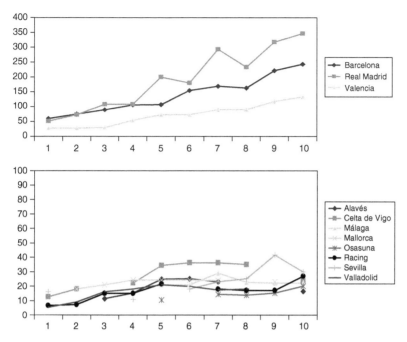

Figure 6.6 Budget evolution in the Spanish clubs from 1995 to 2006
Source: Authors

- Teams with a budget of between forty and eighty million euros: Deportivo La Coruña, Atlético Madrid and Athletic Bilbao.
- Teams with a budget of between seventeen and thirty-seven million euros: the other fourteen La Liga teams.

As the graphs on the budget evolution over the last ten years show, the original increase in available budget was apparent in the three big clubs, which presumes the coexistence of various growth models in football clubs and their management. This suggests that it would be interesting to look at how the richest clubs started on the new path towards an organized management structure, and to what extent the rest of the clubs followed this path.

We will go on to look at the structural characteristics of the top Spanish football clubs.[1] By looking at the information that these clubs provide annually on their structure, we will see the evolution they have

[1] Spain's elite clubs are those in the premier division of the main national level competition, La Liga.

undergone, taking into account the professionalization and commercialization processes discussed earlier. Taking an organizational differentiation perspective we will consider those areas that the elite football clubs incorporate within the management body of the entity.[2]

Professional football clubs are sports organizations that can be classified as 'entities providing sports activity' type. However, the activity they promote is not recreational, but rather at a professional competitive level. As such, the fundamental task of an entity like this is to form a competitive team to take part in official competitions on a professional level. This will then determine the rest of the activities carried out by the organization.

A sports department aimed at forming and developing this team is essential in such entities, since it is directly related to the fundamental task noted above. On the other hand, from a commercial perspective, the competitive team is also the product of the entity, which justifies the importance of a sports department within the management of a professional football club. However, in the majority of the football clubs in La Liga, the sports department seems to have been kept at a distance from the management of the club, in as much as the head of the sports department has not been considered part of the management body, but rather its technical team. Only from the 2002–2003 season onwards has the head of the sports department started to play a role within the board (Figure 6.7). Perhaps this has to do with the fact that the sports department has stopped being seen as merely concerned with product development and has incorporated itself in the strategy of the club.

The other fundamental task of a professional football club is financial management of the entity. The survival of the organization depends on how well this key task is carried out, and the available resources which make this possible. In addition, as noted above, these entities handle large budgets and undertake considerable transactions in the sale and purchase of players, also justifying the importance of the financial department within the management of the club.

---

[2] All the graphs and data used in this section are part of the research project 'Structural Characteristics of Sports Organizations: Differentiation of the Spanish Elite Professional Football Clubs' by the CSBM (unpublished). The project studies the structural characteristics of the Spanish elite professional football clubs which took part in at least 60 per cent of the ten seasons between 1996 and 2006.

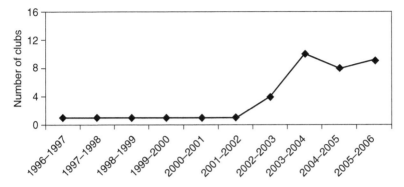

Figure 6.7 Clubs which have a sports department within their management body (1996–2006)
Source: 'Structural Characteristics of Sports Organizations: Differentiation of the Spanish Elite Professional Football Clubs' by the CSBM (unpublished)

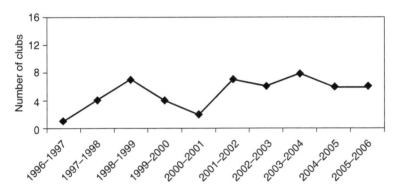

Figure 6.8 Clubs which have a finance department within their management body (1996–2006)
Source: 'Structural Characteristics of Sports Organizations: Differentiation of the Spanish Elite Professional Football Clubs' by the CSBM (unpublished)

However, financial departments rarely have representatives on the board of the club (Figure 6.8). Less than half of the clubs playing in the premier division have a specific department dedicated to the financial and economic management of the entity. This does not mean that the Spanish professional clubs do not financially manage the entity, but rather that this management is run by a director who carries out a range of other functions. The finance department can comprise a treasurer, a financial resources manager and a finance director. Currently, this latter post is the one most used in professional football clubs and, indeed, has begun to play a stronger role in the management body of the football clubs since the 2001–2002 season.

Until now we have alluded to differentiation in terms of fundamental operations that these sports entities carry out, yet differentiation can also refer to internal and external elements of the organization. From the perspective of the organization's operations, differentiation refers to the way in which the organization goes about dealing with the difficulties imposed on it by growth or change within its operations. The division of responsibilities becomes a way of making the work of the employees, directors and sub-departments easier (Blau, 1970). Thus, the changes experienced by Spanish professional football have affected the fundamental task of the clubs, bringing the sports department from the technical to the management body of the club, and generating an increasing need to appoint someone exclusively responsible for the financial management of the entity.

In terms of the influence of external elements on the differentiation of an organization, where organizations try to adjust to their environment, they tend to respond by splitting into different units, each of which is responsible for taking control of a share of the conditions outside of the organization (Lawrence and Lorsch, 1967). We will now look at some of the structural responses that professional football clubs have put in place in order to face the challenges coming from their environment.

When considering this, it is especially important to look at the development in communication with the Spanish professional football clubs (Figure 6.9). The data shown does not necessarily mean that the clubs have, necessarily, developed a specific communication department, but rather that we can see that the majority of clubs have incorporated a Head of Press Relations into their management body, i.e. a person who deals exclusively with the club's media relations. This reflects the idea that media relations require special and constant attention.

However, the fact that the clubs' communication is undertaken by a person holding the position of Head of Press Relations, rather than a department, reflects the urgency and speed with which this person was put in place. That is to say, that rather than a strategic move aimed at developing communication, clubs simply needed someone specific to be responsible for the communication tasks, able to respond constantly to the media. This has meant that other areas of communication in need of development, such as with members, fans and supporters, have been left aside.

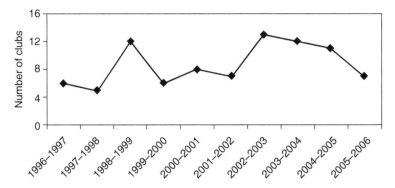

Figure 6.9 Clubs which include a communication post within the management body (1996–2006)
Source: 'Structural Characteristics of Sports Organizations: Differentiation of the Spanish Elite Professional Football Clubs' by the CSBM (unpublished)

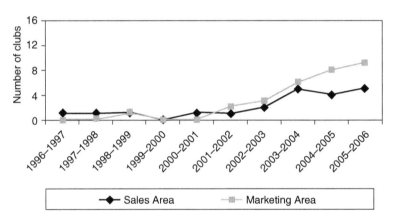

Figure 6.10 Clubs which have sales and marketing departments within their management body (1996–2006)
Source: 'Structural Characteristics of Sports Organizations: Differentiation of the Spanish Elite Professional Football Clubs' by the CSBM (unpublished)

The sales and marketing departments are also indirectly associated with the fundamental task of a professional football club (Figure 6.10). Although, again, not many clubs incorporate these areas within their management body. Nevertheless, the evolution of these areas within the structure of the clubs over the last ten years is interesting. Sales and marketing hardly existed five years ago in the management of professional football clubs, but from the 2002–2003 season onwards this

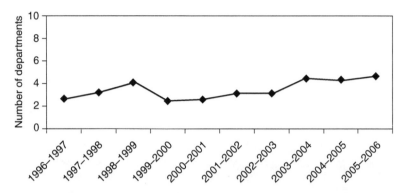

Figure 6.11 Average number of separate departmental areas in place in elite Spanish football clubs between the 1996–1997 and 2005–2006 seasons
Source: 'Structural Characteristics of Sports Organizations: Differentiation of the Spanish Elite Professional Football Clubs' by the CSBM (unpublished)

area started to appear more frequently in the management body of the clubs. It is interesting to note that these two areas in the clubs are almost treated as one, in such a way that it is highly likely that if a club incorporates marketing, it also incorporates sales. Naturally, the sales and marketing departments are inextricably linked with the commercialization of the sport. The carrying out of commercial activity around the sports product has meant that sports entities have had to develop strategies to exploit the new sources of income appearing in the sector.

Over the last ten years, the changes experienced in Spanish football in terms of the income structure (commercialization) and the legal persona of sports entities (professionalization of sports organizations) have led to significant changes in the structure of these organizations. The traditional concept of complexity was concerned with size, that is, the bigger the organization, the more complex. Although seemingly insignificant at first glance, the number of departmental areas incorporated by the football clubs into their management body, when looked at in detail, has meant a significant change in the concept of sports entities focused on professional football.

Since 1996, the number of separate departmental areas in place in most of the elite Spanish football clubs has seen a slight increase from an average of two areas in the 1996–1997 season, to an average of four areas in the 2005–2006 season (Figure 6.11).

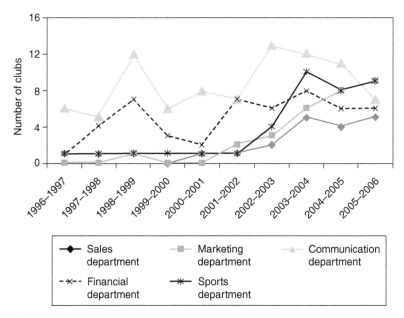

Figure 6.12 Main separate departmental areas in place in elite Spanish football clubs between the 1996–1997 and 2005–2006 seasons
Source: 'Structural Characteristics of Sports Organizations: Differentiation of the Spanish Elite Professional Football Clubs' by the CSBM (unpublished)

We have discussed the essential areas associated with the fundamental task of these entities, such as the sports and financial management departments, and looked at the areas related to a club's adaptation to its environment, such as the communication, sales and marketing departments. Beyond these three most important areas there are a number of other areas associated with external relations, asset management, facilities management, legal and employee matters. The fact that each of these areas exists does not necessarily mean that all clubs include all these departments in their organizational structure; indeed, they probably only have between two and four of those mentioned above.

Despite the fact that the management of an elite Spanish professional football club is generally divided into a minimal number of departments within their management body (as we will see from Figure 6.12), most clubs have traditionally had a communication department and a financial management department. This gives them one inward-looking department and one outward-looking department: one directly related to the fundamental tasks of a football club and the other concerned with the club's relationship with its environment. What is interesting is the increase seen in the other areas; the exclusivity enjoyed by the financial and communication departments in the management of the club is now open to competition from the sports, sales and marketing departments. Today there is more of a balance between the departments, in such a way that clubs nowadays have around four separate areas within their management. Relating this to the increase in the average number of departments within the management body of a professional football club, these are likely to be communication, finance, sports and sales and marketing.

The changes that professional football has experienced over the last ten years have put the structural characteristics of the clubs under pressure. The survival of the organization, previously the direct result of effective financial resource management, has been challenged by the arrival of new sources of income. This in turn has led to the need to incorporate sales and marketing areas into the management of the club. Similarly, the sports department, traditionally considered a technical area, has started to carry more weight in the management of the club. This has meant that the running of this area has gone beyond a purely technical level, towards being responsible for the development of the product offered by the entity; it therefore has to be close to the management.

Finally, we would like to note that, looking at the structure of elite Spanish professional football clubs, it seems that their structural design is based on managerial posts, rather than on the definition of functional departments. As such, their organizational structures seem to be focused more on the definition of specific, fixed tasks and not on the definition of any strategic plans from which those specific tasks later stem. For example, within the management of the club, many clubs have a head of press relations, but no communication department, or tend to appoint a technical secretary, but no sports department.

We will now conclude this chapter by reflecting on the structural characteristics and their relationship with value creation within the football sector. We will focus our attention on the areas on which a football club should base their structural design today, bearing in mind the evolution of the sector and the effects that professionalization and commercialization have had on professional football.

6.5 Conclusion

Taking the characteristics of the Spanish professional football sector today into account, it is clear that clubs have stopped being entities exclusively focused on sports, despite this continuing to be the essence of their activities. Their sources of income, the amount of their budgets, the parties involved in the sector, the characteristics of today's players and entities, force professional football clubs to take more of an overview of their management. Exclusive focus on sports results has been superseded by a set of other priorities, which guide the behaviour of the entity today. On top of sports objectives and the financial survival, the commercial aims of marketing and communications, previously only present in manufacturing or services organizations, are also important. For this reason, a traditional glance over the sports results puts sports entities at a crossroads between a sports focus and a business focus, despite the fact that they are in transition (Kase *et al.*, 2006).

As we have discussed, a plethora of new parties have become involved in the football sector, seeing it as an activity with potential for value creation in its organization. This has meant that a virtuous circle of value creation can be created from the sports product by all who take part in it (Urrutia, 2006). However, value creation is determined by the functioning of the entity and, as such, the structure which defines that functioning. The performance of the organization and the way it deals with the players around it will determine the extent to which it is able to create value within the sector.

The undertaking of a regression analysis between the evolution of the clubs' budgets and the development of a business-driven structure does not yet seem positive, with the exception of the marketing and sports departments. The development of the marketing department is one of the most positive results of the study, since it opens a substantial area for improvement in the management of these clubs and justifies the contribution of traditional management to sport. In contrast, the positive regression analysis which arises between budget and creation of a sports department indicates that all the new income has gone on expenses directly related to the sports structure. This could suggest that there are some doubts about the maximization of the resource allocation.

Sport continues to be the essence of these organizations, yet their survival depends on the resources the organization gets hold of or manages to generate to continue the pursuit of its objective. The professionalization and commercialization processes directly affect this essence and represent significant challenges for the organizations. In any event, we are particularly interested in these entities' structural response to deal with the changes in the sector.

Labour laws formalizing the relationship between the club and the players, making them employees, signified a need to formalize contracts and working conditions. As such, it has become necessary to put someone in place to comply with the new employment law requirements imposed on this type of organization. At the same time, the Sports Law, granting football clubs a new legal persona, was intended to professionalize these entities in terms of decision-making and liability for their actions. This requires clubs to produce reports on their performance supervision mechanisms, particularly in the finance area; an area which has created many conflicts within the professional football sector. From this it follows that professional football clubs should at least consider placing directors responsible for carrying out the administration of the club within their structure, as well as managers in charge of monitoring and controlling the financial aspects of the entity.

The commercialization process gives the club the possibility of accessing new resources, which not only assures the survival of the organization, but also the possibility of generating income. This means that the club can offer its product, in addition to creating collateral products related to the match, the players or the entity itself. However, the carrying out of commercial activity by the clubs shows that, in addition to designing the product on offer, a strategic plan to sell it should also be developed. Today, therefore, a professional football club should consider including product design and sales departments within their structure, in order to take advantage of the new sources of income which the commercialization process has opened up for them.

The media is closely associated with the commercialization process. The possibility of selling television rights for the broadcast of matches was the main source of income opened up for clubs, who had traditionally relied on the sale of match-day and season tickets. At the same time, the media generates a large amount of information concerning the matches, players and football clubs, such that media relations with the clubs have remained independent. Clubs and the media rely on each other equally and thus, for some time now, football clubs have ensured that someone responsible for communication is on board.

Nevertheless, the number of key players/parties present in the club's environment imposes communication needs beyond those of the media. This has meant that, rather than one person dealing with media relations, clubs have seen a need to create a department which manages communication with all the relevant players in the football sector.

Before proposing a classic organizational chart, we suggest that clubs should consider creating a new department focused on corporate social responsibility. This would allow the sports entity to remain faithful to its spirit in an ever-more professionalized environment. In fact, these values are already in place as seven clubs in La Liga have charitable foundations to promote this type of incentive.

In line with what we have discussed up to this point, we would like to propose how the basic structure of a professional football club today should look like. We have taken into account the sector characteristics and the effects that professionalization and commercialization have had on this. Based on this simple structure we will go on to put forward a more detailed organizational structure, where we will suggest the functions needed in each of the main areas proposed in Figure 6.13.

The sports, sales and marketing, communication and administration departments are responsible for the creation, preparation and development of the product offered by football clubs today. Their work determines the product quality, the collateral products which may be on offer, the sales channels and the product's links with any of the parties interested in it. However, in as far as a football club depends on its infrastructure for product development, facilities management should also be included as a related area. As such, in addition to the departments concerned with the production, commercialization, communication and administration of the 'competitive team', the maintenance department must also be considered as equally important. This department is responsible for ensuring that the facilities allow adequate training and development, keeping the product (and the collateral products) offered by the club attractive.

Value creation depends on the extent to which the organization orients its functions towards the creation of an attractive product, which entertains and excites those moving the virtuous circle of value creation: the fans (Urrutia, 2006). Figure 6.14 is a proposal for an organizational structure, which bears all of this in mind, considering

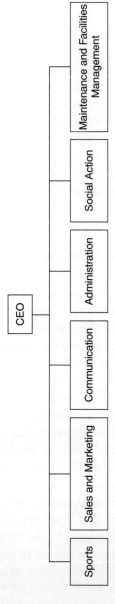

Figure 6.13 Basic departments in the structure of a professional football club
Source: Authors

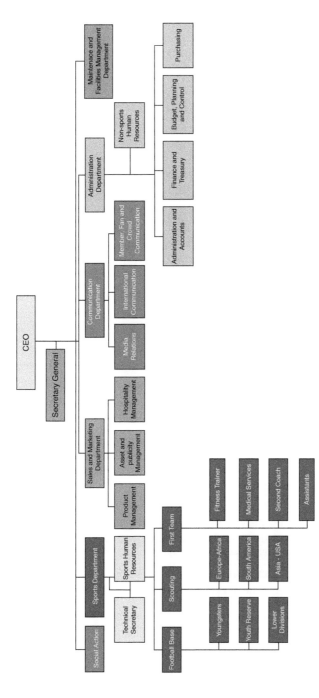

Figure 6.14 Organizational chart proposal. Proposed organizational design for an elite professional football club
Note: the shading refers to the departments proposed in Figure 6.12.

the challenges of the sector, the key players/parties involved and the opportunities of value creation.

Based on the organizational chart proposed, we would like to end by including a brief description of the characteristics of the five main areas we consider crucial in order to carry out a professional football club's objectives.

Sports department

The sports department continues to be the essence of a professional football club, in as much as the object is still linked to the promotion and development of sport, and the main aim of the club is to form a team to represent the club in national and international competitions. The traits of this team and the tasks it carries out will determine the product type and quality offered later. As such, the sports department is not only the source of activities in these organizations, but also decides whether the entity survives, advances or grows.

The sports department includes activities such as selection, training and preparation of the team, physically, technically and tactically, and overcoming the differences to ensure a cohesive, successful team. Moreover, this is the department which should put the medium- and short-term objectives in place; on the one hand, getting around the short-term emphasis traditionally brought about by the desire for weekly results while, on the other, assuring that the values and culture of the club are maintained.

The professionalization of the sport has implied significant changes in this area, not only in terms of the incorporation of players with extremely high compensation levels and a huge media presence, but also because designing a short-, medium- and long-term sports policy requires formalization, specialization and a coordination of the different activities. Only then can the organization achieve the agile, effective operation, so necessary to get key sports results and ensure the survival and growth of the entity.

Sales and marketing

Commercialization of the sport has caused the rise and increased importance of a sales and marketing department, capable of generating new resources to finance the sports activities. In order to come up with the best possible strategy, this department should start with a clear definition of the product and an image of the customers these products are aimed at.

Related to their main objective of forming a competitive team, the product offered by professional football clubs is the sporting event and everything that goes with it, sometimes called the 'total experience' (Van Uden, 2005). As the club expands its commercial activity, new products appear (although they are always associated with the principal one) such as merchandising, the use of the sports facilities for non-sport activities, guided tours of the stadium, the sale of image rights, television rights, and so on. The different products are associated with customers related to professional football clubs.

Thus, the customer may be a direct customer, that is a member, fan or direct consumer of the rest of the products on offer, or an institutional customer, the sponsor companies, advertisers and media.

Members and fans are direct customers: they buy the different products offered by football clubs, starting, of course, with the ticket to see the match or the member's season ticket. Additionally, this department is the engine behind the virtuous circle of value creation in the sector, so much so that clubs should give great importance to their relationship with fans. Within the departments of a club, there should be a department focused especially on the relationship with the direct customer, without forgetting the different 'groups' focused on capturing new members and increasing the member loyalty of the club.

Companies deal with these entities through sponsorship and advertising. This relationship is also very important, given that companies contribute a significant proportion of a club's resources. Thus, the clubs should also set up a department especially oriented towards capturing new corporate clients and increasing the loyalty of those existing ones.

Communication department

The media is a key player in the professional football clubs' environments. Every day, it handles and publishes a huge amount of information and is instrumental in forming public opinion. Therefore, strong media relations allow media exposure which promotes the image of the club and helps capture new members and fans. A professional football club has to be in constant contact with the media and needs to have a department in place to define a strategy and facilitate the maintenance of the relations, in order to take maximum advantage of them. However, the communications department should go beyond media relations and also work on external relations with local authorities and sports associations, where good management can be very beneficial for the organization.

The importance of the media, on one hand, and the need to maintain contact with the members and fans, on the other, creates a need to define a specific department focused on communication. This could also include the launch of the club's own media, whether in printed or broadcast format.

Administration department

Bearing in mind the complexity of the activities undertaken by a professional football club today, it is vital that there is a department monitoring the attainment of the club's different objectives.

The high budgets handled by the clubs require planning, management and control. Since the correct administration of the resources will also determine the organization's potential survival and growth, this department is of key importance to the whole organization.

Of course, the club not only manages financial aspects, but also infrastructure, assets and human resources, and therefore the administration department aims to efficiently manage all the resources of an organization, and monitors the club's attainment of objectives set within the confines of the relevant budget.

Maintenance and facilities management department

Given that the main activity of a football club is the formation of a competitive team, the facilities of the club which allow for the preparation of such a team and the infrastructure necessary to bring together all parties interested in entertaining, exciting spectator football, are invaluable.

Essentially, a football club needs a training ground, facilities for the physical and psychological preparation of players and a stadium where the fans can congregate. Facilities which, as well as being used for sport, are also useful for the carrying out of the club's commercial activity.

Social activity

The recent professionalization of football clubs has distanced them from their initial social function. However, the development of charitable foundations – seven in the Spanish professional football league – shows sports entities' increased consciousness of value creation through one of their key assets – young people. Actions such as (1) that taken by FC Barcelona of creating competitive advantage through their social mass and (2) its sponsorship contracts with UNICEF have helped to produce an important change in the minds of people.

References

Ascari, G. and Gagnepain, P. (2006). 'Spanish Football', *Journal of Sports Economics*, 7(1): 76–89.

Blau, P.M. (1970). 'A Formal Theory of Differentiation in Organizations', *American Sociological Review*, 35(2): 201–18.

Cazorla, L.M. (1990). *Las Sociedades Anónimas Deportivas*. Fuenlabrada, España: Ediciones Ciencias Sociales.

Chandler, A. (1982). *Strategy and Structure: Chapters in the History of the Industrial Enterprise*. Cambridge, MA: MIT Press.

Child, J. and Smith, C. (1987). 'The Context and Process of Organizational Transformation – Cadbury Limited in its Sector', *Journal of Management Studies*, 24(6): 565–93.

Deloitte (2005). *Football Money League*. Manchester.

García Villar, J. and Rodriguez, P. (2003). *TV Revenues in Spanish Football: Old Solution, New Problems*. Barcelona: Congreso Mundial de Gestion Economica del Deporte.

Gómez, S. and Opazo, M. (2006). 'Sport Organizations Structure: Trends and Evolution in the Research Field', 14th EASM Congress (European Association of Sport Management), Nicosia, Cyprus.

Hall, R. (1973). *Organizaciones: estructura y proceso*. Englewood Cliffs: Prentice-Hall.

Hannan, M.T. and Freeman, J. (1977). 'The Population Ecology of Organizations', *The American Journal of Sociology*, **82**(5): 929–64.

Hodge, B.J., Anthony, W.P. and Lawrence, M.G. *et al.* (2003). *Teoría de la Organización: un enfoque estratégico*. Madrid: Pearson Prentice Hall.

Kase, K., Gómez, S., Urrutia, I., Opazo, M. and Martí, C. (2006). 'Real Madrid CF – Barcelona FC: Análisis de las estrategias económica y deportiva del período 2000–2006', CSBM (Centre for Sport Business Management), O. paper, Madrid, IESE Business School, p. 29.

Lawrence, P.R. and Lorsch, J.W. (1967). 'Differentiation and Integration in Complex Organizations', *Administrative Science Quarterly*, **12**(1): 1–47.

Miles, R. and Snow, C.C. (1978). *Organizational Strategy, Structure and Process*. New York: McGraw Hill.

O'Brien, D. and Slack, T. (2004). 'The Emergence of a Professional Logic in English Rugby Union: The Role of Isomorphic and Diffusion Processes', *Journal of Sport Management*, **18**: 13–39.

Slack, T. (1997). *Understanding Sport Organizations: The Application of Organization Theory*. Champaign, IL: Human Kinetics.

Urrutia, I. (2006). *Caso Atlético de Madrid: diario de dos añitos en el infierno*. II Foro de Entidades Deportivas, IESE Business School, Madrid.

Van Uden, J. (2005). 'Transforming a Football Club into a "Total Experience" Entertainment Company: Implications for Management', *Managing Leisure*, **10**(3): 184.

Appendix I
Why NGOs matter for the success of sporting events: the case of the America's Cup

TANGUY JACOPIN AND IGNACIO URRUTIA

Activist NGOs are the shock troops of the Civil Society.

(SustainAbility UN Global Compact, 2003)

Introduction

The role of NGOs (non-governmental organizations) in the success of sport events is analysed in the light of their relevance to other stakeholders in the events. The assumptions on which the analysis is based are twofold: first, the professionalization of sport events requiring the participation of NGOs, and, second, with the consumers being increasingly more reactive to the events, proactive players such as NGOs are needed to capture value forces. On the basis of these assumptions, the hypothesis that the NGO activists' behaviour has become a better indicator of the success or failure of sport events is verified by the examination of the 32nd America's Cup.

Much of the literature about corporate social responsibility (CSR) and sporting events is suffused with cause-related marketing (CRM). Little has been done, however, to foster CSR in terms of stakeholder analysis. The aim of this appendix is to consider the benefits of considering non-governmental organizations (NGOs) as key drivers in the success of not only the sporting event but also the success of the other stakeholders in the 'orbit' of that event – these stakeholders may include citizens, the city, the sponsors, and even other related sport events. In short, our aim is to show that the benefits stemming from a connection to the NGOs' behaviours are also conferred upon the sporting event and all its stakeholders.

The insights provided by NGOs' collaboration with companies have been widely described in literature (Austin, 2000; Drumwright, 1994 and 1996; Waddock and Smith, 2000). However, there were no studies concerning the NGOs' impact on sporting events.

Instituto Noos financed part of the study. Having been written before the final of the 32nd America's Cup, this appendix does not provide a post- but pre-event framework due to the difficulties that arose between 2005 and 2006.

209

This appendix is based on two main assumptions:

(1) As sporting events are becoming more and more professional, they can be likened to companies. Therefore, collaboration with NGOs has to be encouraged.
(2) Consumers can no longer be considered as the most relevant key actor for companies and sporting events because they are reactive to change, whereas the necessity to create or capture value forces sporting events to look for proactive partners. Besides, the emergence of 'civil society governance' is based on social, environmental and ethical criteria. In both cases, NGOs are more relevant partners than consumers.

From these two assumptions, we can deduce that the new key figures of the upcoming governance are those NGO members that will be called 'NGO activists' in the rest of this appendix. Indeed, contrary to consumers that remain reactive to the company supply, NGO activists are proactive in their queries to companies or governments. For instance, the case of Shell and Greenpeace in the North Sea in 1995 is paradigmatic of this situation where the behaviour of the NGO activists sets in relief emerging trends. In that case, the attack of the oil platforms revealed a growing interest for environmental issues, first by these activists and, later on, by consumers, society and companies.

Such a change means that the activists do not exclusively represent a threat of attack against a sporting event but can also constitute an intangible asset if a business niche is associated with an emerging need. Therefore, the planning of sporting events should consider the incorporation of NGOs in order to increase their chances of success.

The 32nd America's Cup in Valencia (Spain) will be used to consider the advantages of incorporating NGOs into the management of a sporting event. We will look at its success due to the major financial knock-on effect of the sporting event, and at its lack of cooperation until now with the NGOs. This is in contrast to the management of two other major sporting events, namely the Olympic Games and the Football World Cup, which did consider and act upon issues of CSR and sustainability. The possibility of highlighting some benefits to the major promoters and stakeholders of the regatta will open new perspectives on the collaboration among NGOs and sporting events.

Hypotheses

To minimize the uncertainties often linked with consumer responses, the assumption taken in this appendix is that the NGO activists' behaviour has become a better indicator (than consumer response) of the success or failure of sporting events, and can help to forecast the future evolution of those events.

The lack of insights provided by consumer responses in favour of sporting event development, coupled with the rising influence of stakeholders – among them, the NGO activists – make it necessary to develop a theory based on the study of activist behaviour (see Jacopin *et al.*, 2008).

Such a theory is necessary for the following reasons. First, their hypothetical actions against the sporting events have to be contemplated to find remedies. Second, the sporting events need to create methodologies to find reliable partners among NGOs. Third, thanks to their predictive perspective, NGO activists are the strategic link that enables the formation of a profitable customer base.

In the first part, the focus will be on the lack of insights provided by consumer responses to guide sporting events ever closer to their customers. This is the reason why the establishment of an alternative model based on the civil society and the different stakeholders is mandatory to unite (at best) sporting events with consumers and citizens. The third part will focus on the specific case of the America's Cup presenting the mapping of the selected NGOs first and then analysing the consequences of the prescriptions provided by NGOs.

Methodology

As it is an exploratory survey, a low number of cases will provide sufficient insights to spur future projects. Our selection of NGOs has been according to their field of expertise, and in four different areas (environment, sport, development and Valencia NGOs). The decision to prioritize these areas can be justified by their direct relationships with this specific sporting event as well as their main relevancy among NGOs.

In-depth interviews with qualitative questionnaires were undertaken, while taking into consideration the fact that, in many NGOs, a very small number of people are involved in decision-making. Greenpeace, WWF/Adena, Intermon – Oxfam, Red Deporte y Cooperación, Deportes sin Fronteras, Dona Lliure, Societat Valenciana de Ornitologia and CIDEAL took part in this exploratory survey, with 42 per cent positive answers.[1]

Theoretical framework

Consumer responses constitute an essential area of study for marketers. Nevertheless, the insights provided by consumers are not as valuable as they

---

[1] Local associations in Valencia (from El Carmen, El Cabanyal and El Campanar) were also going to take part in this survey, but so far it has been impossible to get any feedback from them. Two more NGOs promised to answer the survey, although have not as yet.

should be in the context of generic and sporting literature. An additional problem arises from the governance shift towards 'civil society governance' that forces marketers to contemplate the replacement of the consumer by the NGO activist as being the most important figure in a sporting event.

'Although a handful of studies have investigated the effects of various associations on consumer responses, their results are equivocal (e.g. Bolger, 1959; Clevenger, Hazier and Clark, 1965, Cohen, 1967, Hill, 1962 ...). The inconsistent results leave marketing managers with the intuitive implication that a good image is probably better than a bad image' (Brown and Dacin, 1997). The impact of consumer response has remained unclear – for instance, some researchers such as Belch and Belch (1987), Wansink (1989) and Keller and Aaker (1992) found a positive correlation between positive corporate image and consumer response; Goldberg and Hartwick (1990) found a correlation between consumer response and advertiser reputation, and Keller and Aaker (1992) found a correlation between consumer response and corporate credibility. On the other hand, Shrimp and Bearden (1982) did not find any strong correlation between the reputation of the company and the consumer response. On their side, Brown and Dacin (1997) considered as well that the perceived differences in consumer responses were justified by the fact that 'not all corporate associations are alike'.

More specifically, the study of the correlation between consumer responses and sporting events provides the same uncertainties. Correlation with things such as sponsor recognition, image transfer from event to brand and favourable attitudes towards a sponsor were developed by Gwinner and Eaton (1999), Johar and Pham (1999), Pham and Johar (2001), Speed and Thompson (2000) and Roy and Graeff (2003), yet the latter study found that brand is only moderately related to brand/event fit.

Moreover, there is a problem that has not yet been dealt with – specifically, when the target audience of an event is a very small sample of the general public, then the wider general public can feel alienated by the perceived importance of that event in which they have no interest. In that case, to avoid potential conflicts arising with other stakeholders, the core target audience should no longer be the priority of the sporting event organizers. A multi-stakeholder dialogue approach should be developed to optimize the success of the sport event.

Thus, the trend towards a new governance – what we call civil society governance, in reference to the stakeholders – supposes the rise of a governance based on financial, environmental, ethical and social criteria, and one that is more complex than the previous, mainly finance-driven corporate governance. In that new arena, the NGOs are facing a new role and their exponential growth has brought them recognition from companies

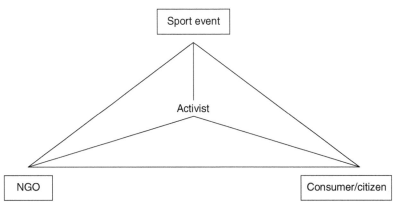

Figure AI.1 The new framework under civil society governance
Source: Adapted from 'Sport Event', Jacopin *et al.* (2008)

and nations. This context can provide sources of competitive advantage for the first companies that collaborate with NGOs. The same can be said for sporting events – the earlier they get involved with the NGOs, the sooner they will be able to reach new target groups, ahead of their competitors.

Despite this, many companies and sporting events have been reluctant until now to contemplate the benefits of incorporating NGOs into their stakeholders, mainly due to their different opinion about the activists' increasing tendency to advocacy[2] and eventual boycotts.

The awareness concerning the stakeholder issue has continuously increased in sport literature (Mahony *et al.*, 2005; Mason and Slack, 2001; Mason *et al.*, 2006; Trail and Chelladurai, 2000; Wenner, 2004). Nevertheless, the benefits and obstacles that NGOs can bring to sporting events have not yet been studied.

Concerning obstacles, if the organization of the boycott has corresponded far more to political and company issues, the 'professionalization' of sporting events changes the way sporting events can be perceived. Therefore, sporting events can become victims of boycott as well if they do not take sufficient care of their different stakeholders and, among them, the NGOs. Events such as the boycott of Areva for the 31st America's Cup by Greenpeace activists in 2001 are likely to occur much more frequently.

[2] The current NGO range of activities includes the 'outreach, direct lobbying, education and research they undertake to raise awareness and contribution to public dialogue on issues at stake on any given relief'. Their transition from service delivery to this new mission was developed to justify their funding with respect to their own stakeholders and to be able to cope with the increasing levels of competition among NGOs.

The segmentation and consideration of NGOs are therefore key issues for sporting events if they want to avoid boycotts or, at least, not to be seen as remote from the preoccupations of their customers or, more broadly, the general public. As a boycott's effectiveness is high in the short-term and then decreases over time (Friedman, 2002), and as the main change in boycott organizations has been the fact that NGOs and activists are now typically the catalysts of the frustration or claim of consumers and citizens, the interest to study the activist, rather than the consumer, is completely justified.

The shift towards civil society governance has favoured a better acceptance of NGOs. Thus, the dialogue with NGOs can be contemplated more easily because of the potential for competitive advantage resulting from collaboration with NGOs. Therefore, sporting events require a new approach when considering their stakeholders. This study deals specifically on how the sporting event organizers can improve their knowledge of the NGOs involved in their field.

The America's Cup

The America's Cup is the oldest regular sporting event in the world, and undoubtedly the most prestigious trophy to be won in sailing. The first event took place in 1851 around the Isle of Wight, in England. *The America*, a racing vessel from New York, won the competition and gave its name to the competition previously called 'The 100 Guinea Cup'. The America's Cup is governed by a document called the 'Deed of Gift', which is the primary tool concerning the rules of valid challenge for the America's Cup[3] and on the conduct of the races. Any sailing club from anywhere in the world can challenge the winner of the competition.

The New York Yacht Club managed to keep the trophy for 132 years and twenty-five challenges, a unique phenomenon of superiority in sporting history. Nevertheless, in 1983, an Australian vessel achieved the seemingly-impossible and, due to the ancestral rules bound with this trophy, the 100 Guinea Cup moved to the southern hemisphere for four years before returning to the United States after another US victory. The superiority of the US sailors did not last long, though, as the Cup headed back to the southern hemisphere again four years later and remained for eight years in New Zealand until Alinghi, the Swiss team, won the Deed of Gift.

This meant that Alinghi and Switzerland had to organize the following America's Cup but, as every schoolboy knows, Switzerland has no sea

---

[3] http://en.wikipedia.org/wiki/America's Cup (accessed 1 April 2004).

coast. Therefore, a competition among sixty cities was organized to establish the location of the 32nd America's Cup, with Valencia eventually winning the privilege to host this most prestigious sailing event.

Winning the right to host the America's Cup is not the same as winning the competition itself, and may be considered a far greater challenge.
Indeed, the economic impact of hosting an event lasting from October
2004 until July 2007 is enormous, particularly the impact on the construction and tourism industries. To this end, KPMG (2004) undertook a study
which estimated that the growth impact on Valencia would be around 1.7
per cent, versus 1.1 per cent for the previous America's Cup. Moreover,
it would generate €3,150 million in production, taking into account the
direct and indirect effects, and would create some 27,760 jobs during the
whole duration of the competition, with some 70 per cent of the profits
remaining in Valencia.

Nevertheless, KPMG (2004) pointed out 'the considerable (lack of)
awareness of the actual indicators and development projects generated
by the America's Cup, which leads to a low preparation level in the business community of Valencia'. Informing target audiences of the benefits of
sponsorship could have helped develop the mental associations bound with
the sponsor or the event.

Moreover, there is that other problem that has not yet been dealt with –
that of the target audience being very small compared with the general
public, and thereby the general public possibly feeling alienated by the perceived importance attached to the event. Being a high-profile media event
(and being seen as somewhat elitist), the America's Cup can be considered a
likely case where the effective target groups have been reached successfully
but where the general public has been kept apart from the sporting event
(or at least feels distanced), despite the public's enthusiasm or willingness
to be involved (Factiva, 2005).

That 'lack of awareness' highlighted by KPMG has progressively
decreased in the population of Valencia (Instituto Noos, 2006), and, as
a result, the collaboration between the America's Cup management and
the public authorities of Valencia (united behind the 'Consorcio Valencia')
have succeeded in designing new processes to create value for their main
targets, namely the media, sponsors and sailing teams. The America's Cup
management had ample opportunity for creating value by increasing the
number of tournaments before the final, thereby increasing the exposure of
their own sponsors, and that of the generic sponsors of the event, through
the resulting increased impact on the media.

With that background, this appendix acknowledges the general public's
lack of interest, or lack of opportunity for involvement, by considering the

NGO activists as the most likely to increase the chances of the Valencian people's involvement in the America's Cup. Therefore, the aim of this framework is:

(1) to lower the tension between the America's Cup management and the local organizers (City of Valencia and Generalitat de Valencia) on one hand *and* local inhabitants on the other; and
(2) to show how NGOs can interfere in this conflict and create value for the sporting event.

NGO mapping

In order to use a multi-stakeholder approach, this study undertook a mapping of NGOs bound to the America's Cup. Greenpeace, WWF/Adena, Intermón – Oxfam, Red Deporte y Cooperación, Deportes sin Fronteras, Dona Lliure, Societat Valenciana de Ornitologia and CIDEAL were the eight NGOs interviewed and dispatched according to their status, whether environmental, developmental, sporting or Valencian NGOs. The results of this qualitative survey are presented first, NGO by NGO. Later, we present a new global framework intended to improve communication with the America's Cup as well as to foster change (Figure AI.2).

The beneficial impact of the America's Cup on the Valencian community has until now been considered by all NGOs to be minimal, whether for the general public, for the environment, for the real-estate sector, or even for the sporting event itself. Nevertheless, all the NGOs are willing to get involved with the America's Cup to help things change, and they all consider that they share the same values as found in sailing, such as team spirit, solidarity and sharing. Nevertheless, it has to be noted that only two NGOs, Intermón and Red Deporte y Cooperación, have effectively tried to get in touch with the sporting event organization or sailing teams. Red Deporte y Cooperación announced their intention to lead a project from October 2005 with the South African team.

Thus, the organization and the sailing teams have the opportunity to influence the NGOs and to try to foster a new dynamic that will help to satisfy all the stakeholders and feed back the perception and the psychological associations of the America's Cup. Such a move would be as relevant as the International Olympic Committee's (IOC) decision to involve NGOs in setting standards for the Olympic Games.

Conclusions

Instead of trying to foster consumer response insights from another perspective, this appendix decided to take into consideration the shift towards civil

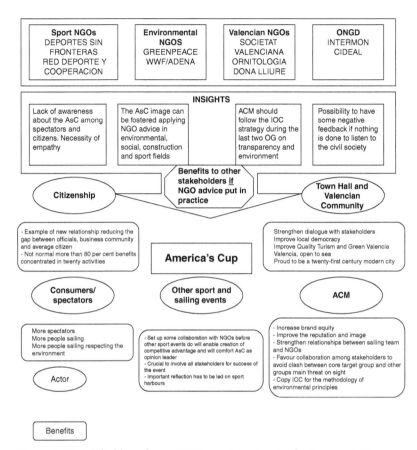

Figure AI.2 Global benefits to NGO participation in the America's Cup
Source: Authors

society governance, where the NGO activist constitutes the main emerging stakeholder for the companies. This work was based on the assumption that sporting events should be likened to companies. Therefore, sporting events 'have to let NGOs be and act as NGOs' (Simmons, 1998) because that is the only way to reach the 'critical cooperation' (Covey and Brown, 2001), defined as 'the possibility to manage not just cooperation or conflict but cooperation and conflict in the same relationship'.

Future contributions should increase the size of the sample and evaluate to what extent the tools of consumer behaviour theory can apply to activist behaviour theory. Specific tools for the theory of activist behaviour will have to be developed in the future to ensure that the CSR practices are improved.

The main goal of this appendix was to provide a new framework that favours the closing of the gap existing between NGOs and sporting events such as the America's Cup. The current situation of mutual ignorance could easily be changed, thanks to the common values shared by sporting events and NGOs. Moreover the current climate of willingness to find ways of improving consumer perceptions about the America's Cup should open new perspectives to this top class event.

References

Austin, J. (2000). *The Collaboration Challenge. How Non-profits and Businesses Succeed through Strategic Alliances*. New York: Jossey-Bass.

Belch, G.E. and Belch, M.A. (1987). 'The Application of an Expectancy Value Operationalization of Function Theory to Examine Attitudes of Boycotters and Nonboycotters of a Consumer Product', *Advances in Consumer Research*, **14**: 232–6.

Brown, T.J. and Dacin, P.A. (1997). 'The Company and the Product: Corporate Associations and Consumer Product Responses', *The Journal of Marketing*, **61**(1): 68–84.

Covey, J. and Brown, L.D. (2001). 'Critical Cooperation: An Alternative Form of Civil Society–Bsuiness Engagement', *IDR Reports*, **17**(1): 1–18.

Drumwright, M. (1994). 'Socially Responsible Organizational Buying: Environmental Concern as a Noneconomic Buying Criterion', *The Journal of Marketing*, **58**(3): 1–19.

(1996). 'Company Advertising with a Social Dimension; the Role of Non-economic Criteria', *Journal of Marketing*, **60**: 71–87.

Factiva (2005). 'Strong Company Leaders Boost Value. Proactive, Persuasive Execs can have Enormous Impact on Brand, Market Valuation', Nikkei Weekly.

Goldberg, M.E. and Hartwick, J. (1990). 'The Effects of Advertiser Reputation and Extremity of Advertising Claim on Advertising Effectiveness', *Journal of Consumer Research*, **17**(2): 172–9.

Gwinner, K.P. and Eaton, J. (1999). 'Building Brand Image through Event Sponsorship: The Role of Image Transfer', *Journal of Advertising*, **28**(4): 47–57.

Instituto Noos (2006). *Valencia Summit: New Trends in Management of Major Sport Events*. Barcelona: Instituto Noos.

Jacopin, T., Poisson, S. and Fontrodona, J. (2008). 'Iberdrola: A Utility's Approach to Sustainability and Stakeholder Management', *Journal of Business Ethics and Education*, **8**: 30–5.

Johar, G.V. and Pham, M.T. (1999). 'Relatedness, Prominence, and Constructive Sponsor Identification', *Journal of Marketing Research*, **36**(3): 299–312.

Keller, K. and Aaker, D. (1992). 'The Effects of Sequential Introduction of Brand Extensions', *Journal of Marketing Research*, **29**: 35–50.

KPMG (2004). *America's Cup 2007: Economic Impact and Expectations of the Business Community in Valencia.* Madrid: KPMG.

Mahony, D., Hums, M. and Riemer, H. (2005). 'Bases for Determining Need: Perspectives of Intercollegiate Athletic Directors and Athletic Board Chairs', *Journal of Sport Management*, **19**(2).

Mason, D.S. and Slack, T. (2001). 'Evaluating Monitoring Mechanisms as a Solution to Opportunism by Professional Hockey Agents', *Journal of Sport Management*, **15**(2): 107–34.

Mason, D., Thibault, L. and Misener, L. (2006). 'An Agency Theory Perspective on Corruption: The Case of the International Olympic Committee', *Journal of Sport Management*, **20**(1).

Pham, M.T. and Johar, G.V. (2001). 'Market Prominence Biases in Sponsor Identification: Processes and Consequentiality', *Psychology and Marketing*, **18**(2): 123–43.

Roy, D. and Graeff, T. (2003). 'Influences on Consumer Responses to Winter Olympics Sponsorship', *International Journal of Sport Marketing*, December–January.

Shrimp, T. and Bearden, W. (1982). 'Warranty and Other Extrinsic Cue Effects on Consumers' Risk Perceptions', *Journal of Consumer Research*, **9**: 38–46.

Simmons, P.J. (1998). 'Learning to Live with NGOs', *Foreign Policy*.

Speed, R. and Thompson, P. (2000). 'Determinants of Sports Sponsorship Response', *Journal of the Academy of Marketing Science*, **28**(2): 226–38.

SustainAbility UN Global Compact (2003). 21st Century NGO: Playing the Game or Selling Out. New York.

Trail, G. and Chelladurai, P. (2000). 'Perceptions of Goals and Processes of Intercollegiate Athletics: A Case Study', *Journal of Sport Management*, **14**(2): 154–78.

Waddock, S. and Smith, N. (2000). 'Corporate Social Responsibility Audits: Doing Well by Doing Good', *Sloan Management Review*, **41**(2): 75–83.

Wansink, B. (1989). 'The Impact of Source Reputation on Inferences about Advertised Attributes', in T.K. Srull (ed.), *Advances in Consumer Research*, Provo: Association for Consumer Research.

Wenner, L. (2004). 'Introduction: Recovering (from) Janet Jackson's Breast: Ethics and the Nexus of Media, Sports and Management', *Journal of Sport Management*, **18**(4).

Appendix II
Strategic evaluation of sponsorship and patronage

KIMIO KASE, IGNACIO URRUTIA AND CARLOS MARTÍ

Introduction

Decisions on sponsorship are, more often than not, taken on the basis of hunch and other judgmental criteria. This appendix proposes a matrix for the systematic assessment of sponsorship options using three variables (the image potential, the proto-image of the firm, and the corporate social responsibility). Its merits are multiple:

(1) the comparison of different options at the same time;
(2) the provision of a homogeneous and across-the-board criterion; and
(3) the visualization of the comparative options in a bidimensional plane, while taking advantage of three indicators.

Nowadays, good corporate citizenship has become an indispensable condition for a company to obtain a socially acceptable image. This concept has made it increasingly normal for companies to take pride in being pillars of the community where they are based. Sponsorship and patronage of cultural and sporting events are, therefore, frequently granted by companies with a view to projecting their image to the society and, at the same time, helping the communities to develop.

However, top management or key decision-makers for this type of business activity are sometimes forced to base their decisions on intuition, in the absence of adequate conceptual tools, while others limit themselves to more or less objective indicators (e.g. media impact in terms of frequency of mentions or the number of spectators who have seen a particular event), despite the fact that the cause and effect relationship between the indicators and the sought after result have not been established (at least academically).

Faced with this lack of evaluation methodology, some sponsors think the 'feel-good factor' of a project should have the last say, which of course is no bad thing, but perhaps reduces the homogeneity a little.

Part of this idea was published in *MK Marketing + Ventas*, No. 203, June 2005, p. 14.

Spurred on by the need to find a conceptual tool, some authors have carried out a review of the literature available on this subject.[1] Cornwell and Maignan's classic study (1998) classifies research into five streams:

(1) the nature of the sponsorship;
(2) the business aspects of the sponsorship;
(3) the measurement of its effects;
(4) the strategic use of the sponsorship; and
(5) the legal and ethical considerations of the sponsorship.

Walliser (2003) emphasizes the importance of developing an evaluation method which is not limited to the degree of consumer awareness. Torres (n.d.) puts forward the need for a strategic aspect to sponsorship and patronage.

At the same time, we are increasingly convinced that it is one thing to wish to occupy a position in the competitive environment[2] and quite another to actually achieve it. This second stream of thought highlights the role played by the internal resources of the firm. This means that it is important for us to see the influence that sponsorship and patronage can have on the internal human resource belief system.[3] Campbell *et al.* (1990)[4] maintain that where the values or belief system are attractive and are taken on by the personnel, it gives staff a sense of mission.

As such, the evaluation of sponsorship/patronage must combine these requirements. That is to say, it must be an evaluation:

(1) that contemplates aspects beyond simply the measurement of image awareness in the consumer mind;
(2) that evaluates the strengthening of the internal values; and
(3) that allows a strategic assessment of the external factors.

While sponsorship is placed within the framework of the consumer marketplace, patronage concerns society, for example the support of art exhibitions.

With this frame of reference we propose a matrix for the evaluation of different sponsorship and patronage projects. First, we will explain the variables comprising the matrix and, second, we will analyse some specific projects by way of applying it. Finally we will argue the significance of

---

[1] Cornwell and Maignan, 1998; Torres, n.d.; Walliser, 2003.
[2] Porter, 1980, 1985 and 1996.
[3] Barney, 2002; Ulrich and Smallwood, 2004.
[4] Campbell *et al.*, 1990.

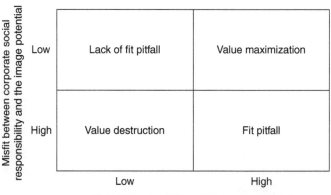

Figure AII.1 Evaluation matrix

this matrix, as well as its limitations. It is also worth highlighting that this evaluation matrix is still in the development phase.

Evaluation matrix

The matrix (see Figure AII.1 and Table AII.1) comprises three variables we need to know:

(1) the belief system, which we will call PIF (the proto-image of the firm);[5]
(2) potential of the image;
(3) CSR (corporate social responsibility).

Proto-image of the firm (PIF)

This refers fundamentally to values or belief systems shared with the company, which consist of:

• Belief (e.g. status as the leading football team).
• Mission (e.g. contribute to labour normalization in Spain through their services; help people to design their own career paths).
• Demarcation in terms of what they would not do as a company (e.g. not intervene in high risk tasks such as operations in high places).
• Mindset (e.g. 'let others say for you, what you would like to say for yourself').

[5] Kase *et al.*, 2005.

Table AII.1 *Strategic map*

	Definition	Analysis
Social responsibility	Definition of social responsibility	Cultivates society Quantify relations
Image potential	Definition of business Union with other businesses Common image Buy-in readiness	Improvement of my differential advantage
PIF	Values Intuitive criteria Direction Formulae Social mission Tacit knowledge	Fortifies a value
Event	Financing of a classical music group Attributes Advantages of the beneficiary Advantages for society	

Note: Proposed by Kimio Kase/Ignacio Urrutia. March 2005.

- Vision (e.g. 'an image is a set of values in the mind of the consumer').
- Slogan (e.g. Leche Pascual's 'fuente natural de salud' ('Natural source of health').

Image potential

- Outward projection (e.g. information provider on new and unknown services – Adecco).
- Image management (e.g. conventional campaign for image improvement: 'temporary work is also decent' – Adecco).
- Image creation (e.g. basketball team El Estudiantes needed better management and Adecco sponsorship arguably brought with it an injection of 'good sense').
- Message (e.g. teamwork as the sum of individual work).
- Sale of branded goods (e.g. Repsol YPF social duties through racing-driver training).
- Information and data (e.g. technical specifications).

- Exteriorization of the PIF (e.g. Adecco people – professionalism, results orientation, enthusiasm, youth, dynamism, a single joint project).

Corporate social responsibility

- Supply of quality goods and services at a reasonable price.[6]
- Protection of the environment.
- Equal rights and no sex discrimination.
- Orientation of public opinion as a leader of the industrial sector.
- Supplement of social needs where the state organisms fail.
- Social justice.
- Good citizenship.
- Regional development of the community.
- Health promotion, sports activities – (Mens sana in corpore sano).
- Endorsement of exemplary social practice.

On one hand, the matrix allows for a fit or compromise between the PIF and the image potential, while on the other, it allows for a lack of fit or compromise between the CSR and the image potential. We use the concept of lack of fit because there is a certain matrix difference (for example, it is not the same to say 'I don't dislike reading' as it is to say 'I like reading').

Application of the matrix

We will look at each quadrant of the matrix, one by one. First, that of value maximization, second those of 'fit and lack of fit pitfalls'. In terms of 'destruction of value', this probably doesn't need further explanation.

Value maximization

Projects positioned in this quadrant are the optimum ones. NH Hoteles sponsor tennis tournaments – Seat Godo Open (Barcelona), ARAG World Team Cup (Düsseldorf), Spanish Women's Open (Madrid), Tennis Masters Series (Rome), as well as the Davis Cup.

The PIF of the hotel chain can be summarized in the phrase 'eye for detail'. Certain touches, such as freshly squeezed orange juice on the breakfast table and providing the right pillows for every client, reflect these service values. The personnel believe in the importance of quality service.

---

[6] Kotter, 1997; Valero *et al.*, 2005.

Tennis fits the PIF with its projection of an image of elegance, health, fashion and classic style. Further, the profile of the sport's spectators coincides with the typical clientele – 69 per cent of tennis spectators are thirty-five years old or above, with a large proportion being university educated (57 per cent).

The lack of fit between the image potential and corporate social responsibility aspects (health, cleanliness, promotion of sports activities) is minimal.

Moreover, the financial impact is far from negligible. NH Hoteles' calculations on the profitability of the sponsorship estimate that, thanks to the high media impact of the Davis Cup final, the advertising effect was worth about 1.4 million euros. In 2004 the number of NH Hoteles rooms booked that were linked to their sponsorship of this event was 2,139.

Fit and lack of fit pitfalls

These quadrants are difficult. First, in that of the 'lack of fit pitfall', although the fit is low, so is the lack of fit; as such, decision-makers often allow projects to be repeated year after year, especially if influential predecessors or people with particular sway within the organization made the original decision.

Second, the projects in the 'fit pitfall' quadrant are particular in that their fit is very high, so top managers or decision-makers often allow themselves to be 'conned' by this positive side and not wish to see the negative side: that the lack of fit is also very high. In the absence of a qualitative (or subjective) evaluation method, it follows that decision-makers allow themselves to be convinced, perhaps by a 'good feeling' about the project.

Repsol YPF's programme for the promotion of Latin American music could be a case of a 'lack of fit pitfall'. Obviously, there are not many cross-over points between Latin American music and the PIF of the company, apart from the Argentinean origins of YPF and their presence in the Latin American market. There is, therefore, scant opportunity for increasing the potential of the image. However, the cost of running the campaign is relatively low and the fact that it also does no harm to the image or to the popular perception of the company's social behaviour seems to have made the company choose this promotion.

In terms of the 'fit pitfall', we can also cite the case of Telefónica's sponsorship of the Paris Dakar Rally, as naming sponsor. The telecoms operator's involvement in an event of this magnitude and repercussion might seem a good fit with their PIF in terms of the international expansion of their brand in recent years. Nevertheless, the image of motor vehicles racing through a desert area, where the ecological balance may be in danger, does not appear to fit very well with people's expectations that an entity of Telefónica's size should be seen as a 'friend' of the environment or at least promote activities aimed at becoming one. Or, indeed, because of the negative connotations generated by this rally on a political level for using developing countries' territory for sports activities, or for the terrible accidents that have taken place during the race in the last few years.

Discussion and conclusion

The advantages of the evaluation methodology provided by the matrix explained above are:

(1) that it is a subjective (judgmental) tool;
(2) that it allows us to get an overview of the whole group of sponsorship and patronage projects that a company may have; and
(3) that it provides homogeneous criteria with which to evaluate them.

First, since they depend on subjective variables such as the PIF and CSR, the decision-makers often feel obliged to make a subjective assessment (perhaps, in many cases personal), i.e. to take sides. Nevertheless, in order to defend their position, they must analyse such implicit and tacitly assumed concepts as shared values and the belief system, and share them with their colleagues.

The second and third advantages lie in being able to use homogeneous criteria which cover projects of different types and get an overview of the sponsorship ensemble; the decision to include or exclude them from the budget can at least be subjected to discussion. Moreover, the inertia which inevitably exists in the sponsorship/patronage project portfolio is highlighted and the possibility of debate on this is opened.

The limitations and areas for improvement of this methodology are various. First, it is a prescriptive methodology whose use and foundation must be consolidated through research into further examples. Further arguments are needed on the possible 'distortability' of the model.[7]

Second, the selection of variables may be different, depending on whether we are dealing with sponsorship or patronage – the former being

---

[7] Chalmers, 1999; Popper, n.d.

understood to be positioned within the frame of reference of the consumer market, while the latter, patronage, refers to society.

In terms of sponsorship, it is likely that quantifiable measures (such as return on investment) are more appropriate for our proposal than CSR.

Third, a question arises with regards to whether it is preferable to use the concept of brand rather than image. A more detailed comparative scrutiny is necessary to assess these ideas.

References

Barney, J.B. (2002). 'Strategic Management: From Informed Conversation to Academic Discipline', *Academy of Management Executive*, **16**(2): 53–7.

Campbell, A., Devine, M. and Young, D. (1990). *A Sense of Mission*. London: The Economist Books.

Chalmers, A.F. (1999). *What is This Thing Called Science*, 3rd edn. Indianapolis: Hackett.

Cornwell, T.B. and Maignan, I. (1998). 'An International Review of Sponsorship Research', *Journal of Advertising*, **27**(1): 1–21.

Kase, K., Saez, F. and Riquelme, H. (2005). *Transformational CEOs: Leadership and Management Success in Japan*. Cheltenham: Edward Elgar.

Kotter, J.P. (1997). *Matsushita Leadership: Lessons from the Twentieth Century's most Remarkable Entrepreneur*. New York: The Free Press.

Popper, K. (n.d.). 'Science: Conjectures and Refutations'. Online, available at: http://cla.calpoly.edu/~fotoole/321.321/popper.html (accessed 5 May 2007).

Porter, M.E. (1980). *Competitive Strategy: Techniques for Analyzing Industries and Competitors*. New York: The Free Press.

(1985). *Competitive Advantage: Creating and Sustaining Superior Performance*. New York: The Free Press.

(1996). 'What is Strategy?', *Harvard Business Review* (November–December): 61–78.

Torres, D. (n.d.). 'Estrategia competitiva y patrocinio: el estado del conocimiento después de una década de investigación científica' ('Competetive Strategy and Sponsorship: The Level of Knowledge after a Decade of Scientific Research'). Unpublished research proposal: Barcelona.

Ulrich, D. and Smallwood, N. (2004). 'Capitalizing on Capabilities', *Harvard Business Review* (June): 119–204.

Valero, Vicente, A. and Lucas Tomas, J.L. (2005). *Politica de Empresa: El Gobierno de la Empresa de Negocios (Company Policy: Governance of a Business Entity*), 6th edn. Pamplona: Ediciones Universidad de Navarra.

Walliser, B. (2003). 'An International Review of Sponsorship Research: Extension and Update', *International Journal of Advertising*, **22**(1): 5–40.

Appendix III
Structural characteristics of sport organizations: main trends in the academic discussion

SANDALIO GÓMEZ, MAGDALENA OPAZO AND
CARLOS MARTÍ

Introduction

This appendix complements the analysis on the relations between the performance and organizational structure and focuses on the characteristics of structures. Its main purpose is the review of the existing literature on the topic.

There exists an abundant literature on organizational structure from 1950 onwards. There is Mintzberg's work on typologies of organization based on different structural designs (Mintzberg, 1979), Burns and Stalker's types of organizational structure according to different environmental conditions (Burns and Stalker, 1961), Child's structuring of activities inside the organization (Child, 1972) and Miles and Snow's conception of structure based on the strategy of the organization (Miles and Snow, 1978), among many others. The interest in studying organizational structure resides in the relationship between organizational design and other organizational phenomena, like performance, distribution of power, or control systems. While there is plenty of literature on organizational structure studying different types of organizations, little is written on the specific field of sport organizations in books and journals.

Some authors have used sports as a context for illustrating organizational phenomenon like organizational loyalty, performance, compensation system, escalating commitment, executive succession, sustainable competitive advantage and human resources, among others. Although research on the particular nature of sport organizations and their structural characteristics is still scarce, the article 'Sport and Organizational Studies: Exploring Synergies' (Wolfe *et al.*, 2005) presents a literature review in which they cover a broad spectrum of research studying organizational phenomena in the context of sports.

This paper was presented at the 14th EASM Congress organized by the European Association of Sport Management in Nicosia, Cyprus at Intercollege on September 2006.

A growing body of knowledge built on experience-based research is expanding and validating a research field particularly dedicated to sport phenomena. The increasing academic interest in the world of sports can be assumed in the proliferation of publications and journals looking into sports from a diversity of disciplines (e.g. history, medicine, psychology, economics, sociology and management), all of which are expanding the knowledge as well as the future opportunities for research and publications on sport-related topics. Today, sports present an interesting research field for academics, especially because of the increasing relevance sports have gained in social life, the various changes experienced by the sport sector, and the still relatively easy data collection opportunities in this field.

Most of the research on sport organization structure has been developed by Trevor Slack and other Canadian academics. In his book on sport organizations, Slack gives the following definition of sport organizations describing their particular nature: 'A sport organization is a social entity involved in the sport industry; it is goal-directed, with a consciously structured activity system and a relatively identifiable boundary' (Slack, 1997: 5). Though their peculiarities can be associated to the context in which they operate, it is still a broad definition, allowing many different types of organizations involved in the world of sports to be considered sport organizations: public, private and voluntary organizations, for-profit and non-profit organizations, organizations producing sporting goods, delivering sport activities, creating competitive sport opportunities, broadcasting sport events, as well as many other organizations connected in one way or another to the sport industry. Therefore, the first question arising when studying sport organizations refers to which type of sport organization we are talking about and what different types can be characterized under this broad concept of sport organizations.

The structural characteristics of an organization are more often than not examined in the context of wider organizational studies. The relationship between the structure of the organization to its performance, effectiveness, control system, adaptability, and to the motivation of its members (Hinings *et al.*, 1980) explains the common use of other organizational topics when discussing organizational structure. Since this relation characterizes traditional organizational studies, it may be likely to characterize research on sport organizations as well. Hence there is a need to clarify the theoretical background in which the discussion on sport organizations takes place.

The economic transformations, the evolution of telecommunications (Stern, 1979) and the peculiarities of the political system (Amara *et al.*, 2005) have had an impact both over sports and, certainly, over sport organizations. Changes in the global context within which sports operate affect the internal functioning of the system, their dependence on external resources, the appearance of new communication channels and the support given by the public system. These are all factors that determine the particular characteristics of the context in which sport organizations are operating. The question arising therefore refers to which are the most important contextual elements influencing sport organization structure, or, in other words, which contextual elements are being considered the most important within the existing research exploring sport organizations.

IESE Business School's CSBM[1] is developing a wider research project regarding the structural characteristics of sport organizations in Spain. In order to correctly address this project we first need to know what other authors have written about sport organization structure, what kind of sport organizations they have studied, within what theoretical background they have contextualized the discussion on sport organization structure and which variables they have considered relevant when discussing sport organization structure. The answering of these questions may lead us to identify the state of scholarly knowledge on sport organization structure, as well as uncover interesting niches for our research and other future work on this field.

Literature reviewed

In a literature review the collection of data refers to the selection of the articles that are going to be analysed. This literature review considered those articles discussing both structure and sport organizations at the same time. Slack (1997: 6) defines the structure of a sport organization as 'the manner in which the tasks of a sport organization are broken down and allocated to employees or volunteers, the reporting relationships among these role holders, and the coordinating and controlling mechanisms used within the sport organization'. Using this definition the structure of an organization refers both to the structural design of the organization (differentiation) and to the relationship among actors (coordination and control), which can be associated to the formal structure and the informal structure of an organization.

If sport organizations are to be considered as all those organizations operating in the sport industry, we can include a wide variety of organizations with different goals and means. For the purposes of this literature review, we are particularly interested in those sport organizations dedicated to the promotion and development of sports. This means that we only considered articles discussing sport organizations oriented towards these final goals,

---

[1] Center for Sport Business Management (CSBM) – IESE Business School, University of Navarra.

and hence most commonly associated to organizations like federations, national associations, sport departments, leagues and clubs.

The number of articles to be analysed in a literature review depends on the topic under study and on the resources of the reviewer. Given that the literature related to research of sport organizations is still scarce, it was important to use multiple sources of information. This review is based on primary and secondary sources (Cooper, 1989), looking not only into journals directly discussing sport management topics, but also journals from other disciplines exploring the issue of sport organization structure, as the former journals were established too recently to cover all relevant discussion on the topic.

Our primary sources of information consist of journals directly associated with sport management to which we had electronic access, such as the *Journal of Sport Management* and *Sport Management Review*. Moreover, we searched through electronic databases of academic articles looking for all articles discussing sport organizations and structure at the same time. After this first review we used a secondary source of information, checking the reference lists of those articles already selected from the primary sources of information. The use of these two sources of information allowed us to have a sample of articles from a variety of journals and disciplines (e.g. management, organizational studies, leisure, sociology and economics).[2]

The use of the secondary sources of information increases the risk of over-representing the work of some authors compared to others, because the bibliography used by one author is associated with his primary network of journals (Cooper, 1989). In order to reduce this limitation we continued the search process until it turned circular, which means we stopped the data collection process when the reviewing process brought us back to previously revised articles.

The articles selected cover the period from 1975 to 2006. This is mainly because, until the mid-1970s, sport management textbooks were centred on administrative principles in physical education and athletics, and essentially ignored management analysis and organization theory (Doherty, 1998; Paton, 1987). Therefore, since in our study of structural characteristics of sport organizations, we are more interested in sport organization structure and its relation to management analysis and organizational theory, than in administrative principles, we have only considered as relevant to our sample articles from the mid-1970s onwards.

---

[2] We searched and selected only articles in English, because it is the language commonly used in academic journals and a language that the authors are all comfortable working in.

The final sample included fifty-five articles published during the last thirty-five years, which we considered to represent an important collection of the relevant articles discussing sport organization structure. Once we had all the articles, a matrix was created in order to analyse and compare the information they contained. The matrix consisted of some dimensions and variables that we considered interesting and that would allow us to determine the main trends in the discussion of the structural characteristics of sport organizations. Among the variables considered were the theoretical perspectives used, methodology employed, and type of analysis, country, sports studied, type of publications, main results of the research, and type of sport organizations considered.

Based on these dimensions we organized our results in three main areas that may be useful for understanding the state of scholarly knowledge on the topic of sport organization structure, and that may also be interesting for future research on the field. The three areas were:

(1) type of sport organizations studied;
(2) the theoretical perspectives from organizational theory most commonly used to discuss sport organization structure; and
(3) the most relevant contextual elements considered when discussing sport organization structure.

Academic discussion on sport organization structure

Types of sport organizations

The discussion associated with the structural characteristics of sport organizations has considered various kinds of organizations among those existing in the world of sports. However, most of them can be classified as dedicated to the promotion and development of sports, e.g. federations, national associations, leagues, clubs or local departments of sport. All these sport organizations are associated to sport activity, and though differing in their goals and means, they all respond to the superior mission of promoting and developing sports in society. The differences we identify between them suggest a possible classification for them into three types: sport governing bodies, sport event organizations and sport-providing entities. The first one refers to those sport organizations administering and regulating sports, focusing on its development at all levels, and guaranteeing the rules both of the game and of the competition; the second one refers to those sport organizations responsible for the production of a competition system aimed at satisfying and articulating the needs of professional sports; and the third type includes those organizations producing and delivering recreational or competitive sport programmes at a local or community level. Table AIII.1 summarizes the main characteristics of these three types of sport organizations involved in the promotion and development of sports.

The articles reviewed include discussions about these three types of sport organizations, although the frequency with which each type has been studied differs significantly. Most of the research discussing sport organization structure refers to sport governing bodies (80 per cent). This type of sport organization is part of the international structure of sport governance, which means that their goals and structure are similar across countries, hence allowing the possibility of generalizing research findings. In contrast, little research exists on sport-providing entities (19 per cent) (sport organizations delivering sport programmes), and almost none on sport event organizations (1 per cent) (sport organizations producing competition events).

Sport governing bodies are sport organizations whose primary goal is to promote and develop sports at all levels in a given territory and sport discipline. This entails control and supervision of a sport, guaranteeing periodical competition at a national and international level, amateur and professional, and from grassroots to senior categories. It moreover encompasses the administration of the sport and definition of the rules of the game, as well as protection of the values of sports promoted by the Olympic Movement. Research related to this type of sport organization tends to discuss the challenges faced by the need to professionalize both entities and their outcomes.

Another type of sport organization is the one whose main activity is associated with the production of sport spectacles (e.g. leagues, circuits, tours). The operations and activities of these organizations are subordinated to the venue and rules of sport governing bodies, as well as of professional teams. The main activity of these sport organizations is to design a competition system articulating the interests of all the actors in order to create an attractive sport event. Sport events present a major opportunity for developing commercial activity, giving these sport organizations the potential to exploit the relationship between the sports sector and the entertainment sector through commercial activities such as ticketing, broadcasting rights, licensing, merchandising, publicity and sponsorship. In the articles reviewed related to this type of sport organization, the discussion of the structural characteristics of sport organizations may refer to the structure of the competition (Cairns, 1987) as well as to the structure of the community of actors involved in the competition (Slack and Cousens, 2005).

The third type of sport organization in the classification is the one we call sport-providing entity, whose main activity is to design and deliver

Table AIII.1 *Classification of sport organizations related to the promotion and development of sports*

	Sport governing bodies	Sport-providing entities	Sport-spectacle organizations
Mission	Promote sports at all levels in a given territory and sport discipline.	To satisfy a community's motivation to practice physical activity and socializing through sport activities.	Represent, promote and safeguard the interests of all actors participating in the competitions they produce.
Goal	Govern the sport, ensuring its promotion and development at all levels, monitor the administration of sport, guarantee the organization of regular competitions as well as the respect for the rules of fair play.	Design and offer sport activities, both at a recreational and competitive level, and at individual and team programmes, oriented towards official competitions in order to achieve sporting success and social integration.	Design a regular competition system ensuring the contest among rival teams or individuals in a given sport discipline and under the same ethic codes.
Main activity	Govern one or more sport discipline.	Deliver sport programmes.	Generate competition opportunities.
Examples	National Associations, Federations, National Organizations, Olympic associations/ committees.	Clubs, community centres, fitness centres, university sport programmes.	Leagues, associations, circuits, tours.

Source: Authors.

sport programmes for a given community such as clubs, local sport programmes, fitness centres and university sport programmes. These are private, non-profit associations, dedicated to the provision of recreational sport activities at a local level. The research related to the organizational structure of this type of sport organization has focused on two dimensions of structure, namely the administrative system (De Knop *et al.*, 2004; Fahlén, 2005 and 2006; Hoye, 2004; Hoye and Cuskelly, 2003; Ørnulf, 2002, 2004; Papadimitriou, 2002; Westby and Sack, 1976) and the membership system (Hall, 1983).

The discussion on sport organization structure has centred on these three types of sport organizations, which differ not only in their goals, level of operation and main activity, but also in names and type of entities representing them in each country. Real-life entities and institutions may not have such clear limits as the ones we have outlined in our classification table. Nevertheless these three ideal types allow us to compare the research under study, looking into the different scenarios within which the discussion on sport organization structure has taken place for these three different ways to promote and develop sports.

Sport governing bodies can be at a national or an international level, but the fact that both of these levels are part of the international structure of promotion and development of sports means that all sport governing bodies are connected to the International Olympic Committee's norms and regulations. The bond between sport governing bodies at a national level and the international structure of promotion and development of sports gives the opportunity to generalize or replicate results. Whereas sport governing bodies from different countries may display a large number of similarities, sport-providing entities and sport-event producers depend on the basic unit of promotion and development of sports defined at a national level, and hence differ more radically from country to country (see Figure A3.1).

Although there are common patterns between sport governing bodies at a national level, the particular sport system defined in each country establishes some differences for those sport organizations providing sport programmes and sport spectacles. This means that, while in one country the sport system promotes and develops sports through the educational system, there are others using local sport services or private associations for the same purposes; and while the most popular sport in a country has probably achieved a complex structure for its promotion and development through a variety of institutions, other sports in the same country are promoted and developed just through the activities of the sport governing body. Hence sport-providing entities and sport event organizations depend on each country's basic unit of promotion and development of sport and on the social relevance of the different sports in a country.

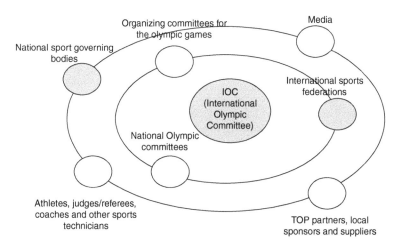

Figure AIII.1 Relationship between sport governing bodies at national and international level
Source: www.olympic.org (accessed 5 May 2007).

The three types of sport organizations may exist within the sport system of any country; however the differences in the basic unit promoting sport activity and the extent to which some sports are more popular in one country than another help explain the differences between countries in relation to the type of sport organizations defining the sport system at a national level. As previously mentioned, similarities are nevertheless found at the level of sport governing bodies. The generalizing opportunities of similarities may explain the over-representation of research of this type of sport organization, but it may also suggest the need to understand and elucidate the results and effectiveness among different sport systems throughout the world.

Organizational theory and sport organizations

The discussion on sport organization structure has usually taken place within the context of wider organizational studies, which means that while there is some research specifically concerned with the structural configuration of sport organizations, most research discussing sport organization structure is situated within the wider theoretical context of organizational change processes and the discussion of organizational effectiveness.

The theoretical background in which to base organizational studies of sport organizations has been of interest to several authors. There are a number of papers specifically concerned with finding theoretical perspectives inside the organizational theory that might be useful in understanding

Table AIII.2 *Distribution of authors in relation to type of sport organization studied*

Sport governing bodies	Sport-providing entities	Sport event organizations
Stern (1979), Frisby (1985), Slack (1985), Frisby (1986), Slack and Hinings (1987), Kikulis et al. (1989), Slack and Kikulis (1989), Chelladurai and Haggerty (1991), Thibault et al. (1991), Kikulis et al. (1992), Slack and Hinings (1992), Slack and Hinings (1994), Theodoraki and Henry (1994), Kikulis et al. (1995, 1995a and 1995b), Amis and Slack (1996), Papadimitriou (1998), Stevens and Slack (1998), Kikulis (2000), Cunningham and Rivera (2001), Frisby et al. (2004), Garrett (2004), Hoye (2004), Amis et al. (2004a), Smith (2004), Thibault and Babiak (2005), Shilbury and Moore (2006), Danylchuk and Chelladurai P. (1999), O'Brien and Slack (1999), Skinner et al. (1999), Thibault et al. (1999), Papadimitriou and Taylor (2000), Shilbury (2000), Amis et al. (2002), O'Brien and Slack (2003), Amis et al. (2004b), O'Brien and Slack (2004), Smith and Shibury (2004), Washington (2004), Nichols et al. (2005), Slack and Mason (2005)	Westby and Sack (1976), Hall (1983), Ørnulf (2002), Papadimitriou (2002), Hoye and Cuskelly (2003), De Knop et al. (2004), Ørnulf (2004), Fahlén (2005), Fahlén (2006)	Cairns (1987), Slack and Cousens (2005)

Source: Data elaborated from the literature review.

organizational phenomena in the context of sports. Among these there are articles considering bureaucratization processes (Frisby, 1985), rationalization processes (Slack and Hinings, 1987), sociological perspectives (Slack and Kikulis, 1989), institutional perspectives (Kikulis, 2000), voluntary sector determinants (Nichols *et al.*, 2005), agency theory (Mason and Slack, 2001) and contextualist approach for change (Thibault and Babiak, 2005).

The main theoretical background within which the discussion on sport organization structure has taken place refers to organizational change theories (45 per cent of the articles in the sample fall into this category). The process of organizational change refers to a shift in the dominant logic that has traditionally determined a certain way of operating within an organizational field (Powell, 1991). In the literature reviewed, this organizational change process was experienced as a rationalization process (Westby and Sack, 1976), a bureaucratization process (Slack, 1985) or a professionalization process (Amis *et al.*, 2002, 2004a, 2004b; Fahlén, 2005; Kikulis, 2000; Kikulis *et al.*, 1992, 1995a, 1995b; Kikulis and Slack, 1995; Nichols *et al.*, 2005; O'Brien and Slack, 1999, 2003, 2004; Shilbury, 2000; Skinner *et al.*, 1999; Slack and Cousens, 2005; Slack and Hinings, 1987, 1992, 1994; Smith, 2004; Stern, 1979; Stevens and Slack, 1998; Washington, 2004). These three 'sub-processes' of organizational change relate to an overall formalization process; a shift from an amateur logic towards a more formalized and professional one. The discussion on sport organization structure in this context refers to the new forms of integration and differentiation inside the organization or inside a network of organizations, which is of particular interest when considering the evolution experienced by sports.

The other theoretical background within which the discussion on sport organization structure has developed refers to organizational effectiveness, which accounts for the overall performance of the organization. In this context, structural characteristics of sport organizations are mentioned as part of:

(1) the variables and models explaining the effectiveness of sport organizations (Chelladurai and Haggerty, 1991; De Knop *et al.*, 2004; Frisby, 1986; Hall, 1983; Shilbury and Moore, 2006);
(2) evaluating the impact or effect of structural configuration on the performance of sport organizations (Cairns, 1987; Cunningham and Rivera, 2001; Garrett, 2004; Papadimitriou, 1998, 2002; Papadimitriou and Taylor, 2000); or
(3) associated with the effectiveness of the articulations between structures or roles in the context of sport organizations (Frisby *et al.*, 2004; Hoye, 2004; Hoye and Cuskelly, 2003; Thibault *et al.*, 1999).

Table AIII.3 *Main contributions of the research related to organizational change in sport organizations*

Author	Publication	Title	Contribution to sport organizations structure research
Westby and Sack (1976)	*The Journal of Higher Education*	The Commercialization and Functional Rationalization of College Football: Its Origins.	Commercialization and rationalization introduced business values to college football.
Stern (1979)	*Administrative Science Quarterly*	The Development of an Interorganizational Control Network: The Case of Intercollegiate Athletics.	Historical transformation of the network generated new structure based on a constant tension between controlling interdependence and autonomy seeking.
Slack and Hinings (1987)	*Canadian Journal of Sport Sciences*	Planning and Organizational Change: A Conceptual Framework for the Analysis of Amateur Sport Organizations.	The introduction of a planning system resulted in a rationalization of amateur sport organizations.
Kikulis *et al.* (1992)	*Int. Review for the Sociology of Sport*	Institutionally Specific Design Archetypes: A Framework for Understanding Change in National Sport Organizations.	Specificities in the design archetype after a change process in the sport sector can be explained through strategic choice.
Slack and Hinings (1992)	*Journal of Sport Management*	Understanding Change in National Sport Organizations: An Integration of Theoretical Perspectives.	Change processes depend on the direction of change and the sources of commitment, and the consequences is a new definition for the division of labour, as well as a new control.

Author (Year)	Journal	Title	Finding
Slack and Hinings (1994)	*Organization Studies*	Institutional Pressures and Isomorphic Change: An Empirical Test.	Though change in a population of organizations tends to move them to similar structures, values and belief can still make a difference between them.
Kikulis *et al.* (1995a)	*Journal of Sport Management*	Does Decision Making Make a Difference? Patterns of Change within Canadian National Sport Organizations.	Decision-making is important for understanding differences between organizational designs, as well as differences between high impact systems.
Kikulis *et al.* (1995)	*Journal of Management Studies*	Sector-specific Patterns of Organizational Design Change.	Design archetypes and patterns of change can be found when analyzing a process of change in an organizational field.
Kikulis *et al.* (1995b)	*Journal of Sport Management*	Toward an Understanding of the Role of Agency and Choice in the Changing Structure of Canada's National Sport Organizations.	Variation in organizational responses to institutional pressures reflects the active role of human agents in the design of organizations.
Stevens and Slack (1998)	*International Review for the Sociology of Sport*	Integrating Social Action and Structural Constraints: Towards a more Holistic Explanation of Organizational Change.	Institutional context do influence change, but types of change are related to the strategic choice of agents.
Skinner *et al.* (1999)	*Sport Management Review*	Amateurism to Professionalism: Modelling Organizational Change in Sporting Organizations.	Change processes have a dual nature: impacts on top positions are not the same as in staff and assistance positions.
O'Brien and Slack (1999)	*Sport Management Review*	Deinstitutionalising the Amateur Ethic: An Empirical Examination of Change in a Rugby Union Football Club.	Institutional pressures and resource dependency are elements determining organizational change.

Table AIII.3 (cont.)

Author	Publication	Title	Contribution to sport organizations structure research
Shilbury (2000)	*Sport Management Rev.*	Considering Future Sport Delivery Systems.	The evolution of the sport industry can be analysed through clusters, in order to see the relation between the industry structure and value creation.
Kikulis (2000)	*Journal of Sport Management*	Continuity and Change in Governance and Decision Making in National Sport Organizations: Institutional Explanations.	Change processes have defined new governance and decision-making structures, and the inclusion of professionals has increased the level of specialization and formalization of the structure.
Amis et al. (2002)	*Journal of Applied Behavioral Science*	Values and Organizational Change.	Values determine both the structure and the operations of an organization, and they are also essential for a transition process.
Ørnulf (2002)	*Voluntas: International Journal of Voluntary and Nonprofit Organizations*	Volunteers and Professionals in Norwegian Sport Organizations.	There is a massive process of professionalization in voluntary sport organizations, which is changing the traditional dependence of these organizations on volunteer work.
O'Brien and Slack (2003)	*Journal of Sport Management*	An Analysis of Change in an Organizational Field: the Professionalization of English Rugby Union.	Change processes in an organizational field tend to move organizations to same structures, though values and beliefs explain the differences still existing.

Author	Journal	Title	Finding
Smith (2004)	*Emergence: Complexity and Organization*	Complexity Theory and Change Management in Sport Organizations.	Change can be intentional or emergent, but the governance structure of the organizations remains to be the most important area on structural change.
Amis *et al.* (2004b)	*Journal of Sport Management*	Strategic Change and the Role of Interests, Power, and Organizational Capacity.	Sub-unit interests, power distribution and leadership activities will have a profound influence on the outcome of large-scale change process.
O'Brien and Slack (2004)	*Journal of Sport Management*	The Emergence of a Professional Logic in English Rugby Union: The Role of Isomorphic and Diffusion Processes.	Change process may be influenced by institutional logics, isomorphism or diffusion, but the different organizational designs can be explained through the decision-making structures.
Amis *et al.* (2004a)	*Academy of Management Journal*	The Pace, Sequence and Linearity of Radical Change.	Even though change may progress at a slower pace at the beginning, when it influences high impact elements, changes become substantive and enduring.
Thibault and Babiak (2005)	*European Sport Management Quarterly*	Organizational Changes in Canada's Sport System: Toward an Athlete-centred Approach.	The impact of change depends on external factors, internal characteristics of the organization and on key individuals.
Slack and Cousens (2005)	*Journal of Sport Management*	Field-level Change: The Case of North American Major League Professional Sport.	Change did occur in the four dimensions considered – communities of actors, exchange processes, governance structure and institutional logics of action – and the consequence of it was a structuration process exhibited in the field.

Table AIII.3 (*cont.*)

Author	Publication	Title	Contribution to sport organizations structure research
Nichols *et al.* (2005)	*Voluntas: International Journal of Voluntary and Non-profit Organizations*	Pressures on the UK Voluntary Sport Sector.	A change in the competing elements of sport market has challenged voluntary sport organizations, as well as the volunteer staff working there.
Fahlén (2006)	*Sport and Society*	Organizational Structures of Swedish Elite Ice Hockey Clubs.	Although clubs are facing similar environmental conditions and are concerned with similar tasks, they exhibit some variation in structural features.

Source: Data elaborated from the literature review.

Table AIII.4 Main contributions of the research related to organizational effectiveness in sport organizations

Author	Publication	Title	Contribution to sport organizations structure research
Hall (1983)	*Management Science*	A Corporate System Model of a Sports Club: Using Simulation as an Aid to Policy Making in a Crisis.	Corporate system model focuses on the learning process of the organization giving the possibility of considering different variables to effectively manage a crisis.
Frisby (1986)	*Canadian Journal of Applied Sport Science*	Measuring the Organizational Effectiveness of National Sport Governing Bodies.	Organizational effectiveness in sport settings is related both to achievement of goals and to the acquisition of scarce resources.
Cairns (1987)	*Applied Economics*	Evaluating Changes in League Structure: The Reorganization of the Scottish Football League.	Changing the league structure can change the nature of the product, affecting the demand of the sport.
Chelladurai and Haggerty (1991)	*Canadian Journal of Sport Sciences*	Measures of Organizational Effectiveness of Canadian National Sport Organizations.	Organizational effectiveness is perceived differently between volunteer staff and professionals. Perception of effectiveness differs between the personnel working in the organization.
Papadimitriou (1998)	*Managing Leisure*	The Impact of Institutionalized Resources, Rules and Practices on the Performance of Non-profit Sport Organizations.	Institutional environment influences, externally, the definition both of the structure and behaviour of the organization. However values, interests and power do it internally, and both have an impact on the performance of the organization.

Table AIII.4 (cont.)

Author	Publication	Title	Contribution to sport organizations structure research
Thibault et al. (1999)	*Managing Leisure*	Interorganizational Linkages in the Delivery of Local Leisure Services in Canada: Responding to Economic, Political and Social Pressures.	Environmental pressures and organizational network determine the organization, and both are needed for achieving goals and acquire scarce resources.
Papadimitriou and Taylor (2000)	*Sport Management Review*	Organizational Effectiveness of Hellenic National Sports Organizations: A Multiple Constituency Approach.	National sport organizations need to identify the most important constituencies and to determine their relationship with the outputs of their organizations in order to achieve effectiveness.
Cunningham and Rivera (2001)	*The International Journal of Organizational Analysis*	Structural Designs within American Intercollegiate Athletic Departments.	Structural design is related to organizational effectiveness and an enabling structure may be better for athletic achievement.
Papadimitriou (2002)	*Managing Leisure*	Amateur Structures and their Effect on Performance: The Case of Greek Voluntary Sports Clubs.	Local sport clubs have arranged their operations around a simple, rather informal structural design.
Hoye and Cuskelly (2003)	*Sport Management Review*	Board–Executive Relationships within Voluntary Sport Organizations.	Effective or ineffective performance of boards in voluntary sport organizations depends on the existence of trust, which is perceived to be responsibility of the board chair.

Hoye (2004)	*Nonprofit Management and Leadership*	Leader–member Exchanges and Board Performance of Voluntary Sport Organizations.	Higher levels of board performance were associated to a perception of higher-quality leader–member exchange between executives, chairs and members.
De Knop *et al.* (2004)	*Sport Management Review*	Quality Management in Sports Clubs.	The use of Total Quality Management model for evaluating traditional sport clubs shows that strategic planning, marketing management and the structure of clubs are the main weakness of these sport organizations.
Frisby *et al.* (2004)	*Leisure Studies*	The Organizational Dynamics of Under-managed Partnerships in Leisure Service Departments.	Some managerial structures are contributing to under-managed partnerships, like the lack of planning and policy guidelines, unclear roles and reporting channels, and insufficient human resources.
Garrett (2004)	*Managing Leisure*	The Response of the Voluntary Sports Clubs to Sport England's Lottery Funding: Cases of Compliance, Change and Resistance.	The response of national sport organizations to institutional pressures is perceived to be more effective from volunteer administrators than from professionals.
Shilbury and Moore (2006)	*Nonprofit and Voluntary Sector Quarterly*	A Study of Organizational Effectiveness for National Olympic Sporting Organizations.	In the relationship between structural orientation and effectiveness, the impact of the rational-goal quadrant (productivity, planning) seems to be the key to effectiveness.

Source: Data elaborated from the literature review.

The third theoretical approach used in the discussion on sport organization structure refers to the patterns of structural design (specialization, standardization and centralization) in the particular case of sport organizations. Within this perspective there are articles proposing structural configuration typologies for sport organizations (Kikulis *et al.*, 1989), articles looking into the differences and similarities between traditional and new sports in relation to patterns of organizational configuration (Theodoraki and Henry, 1994), as well as articles analysing differences and similarities between the design of organizations based on voluntary work versus those that have incorporated professional work (Ørnulf, 2002; Thibault *et al.*, 1991).

Summing up, there are three main theoretical approaches within which the discussion on sport organization structure has taken place: organizational change, organizational effectiveness and structural configuration of organizations. The structural characteristics of sport organizations have existed as a research topic of its own through the latter approach, but most research discussing sport organization structure refers to wider organizational theory studies. The relevance of the two former theoretical approaches can be associated with the significant challenges that have influenced the traditional operation of sport organizations, as well as their traditional way of measuring and conceiving effectiveness.

Context features in the discussion on sport organization structure

More than half of the articles in the sample (64 per cent) considered the influence of the environment when studying sport organizations. Since the moment that organizations started to be conceived as open systems (Hannan and Freeman, 1977), the influence of the environment on their processes and operations has usually been taken into consideration in organizational studies. In the articles reviewed, the environment most commonly refers to the political, economic and social situation within which sport organizations are operating, as well as to those resources existing outside the organization which determine its survival.

In relation to the political, economic and social context of sport organizations, the literature commonly remarks on the increasing relevance of sport in social life and the opportunities brought about by the development of communication and information technologies. Following Stern (1979), the increasing relevance of sports in social life can be explained due to the revival of the Olympic Games in 1986, which in turn strengthened the interest in promoting and developing sports at national level; and due to the development of communication and information technologies, which

Table AIII.5 *Main contributions of the research related to structural configuration of sport organizations*

Author	Publication	Title	Contribution to sport organizations structure research
Frisby (1985)	*Society and Leisure*	A Conceptual Framework for Measuring the Organizational Structure and Context of Voluntary Leisure Service.	The structure of voluntary sport organizations can also be studied through organizational theory, looking into specialization, standardization and centralization.
Kikulis *et al.* (1989)	*Journal of Sport Management*	A Structural Taxonomy of Amateur Sport Organizations.	Eight structural design types can be found on amateur sport organizations based on their different levels of specialization, standardization and centralization.
Slack and Kikulis (1989)	*International Review for the Sociology of Sport*	The Sociological Study of Sport Organizations: Some Observations on the Situation in Canada.	Amateur sport organizations have gone through a bureaucratization process, which until now has been conceived as a uniform process. Nevertheless, there might be some differences based on interdependency and resources.
Chelladurai and Haggerty (1991)	*Canadian Journal of Sport Sciences*	Differentiation in National Sport Organizations in Canada.	National sport organizations were found to be very similar in terms of task differentiation patterns. However, differences were found in the perceived amount of influence between administrative positions.

Table AIII.5 (*cont.*)

Author	Publication	Title	Contribution to sport organizations structure research
Thibault *et al.* (1991)	*International Review for the Sociology of Sport*	Professionalism, Structures and Systems: The Impact of Professional Staff on Voluntary Sport Organizations.	In non-voluntary sport organizations the hiring of professional staff increased the levels of specialization and formalization, changing the structural arrangements.
Theodoraki and Henry (1994)	*International Review for the Sociology of Sport*	Organizational Structures and Contexts in British National Governing Bodies of Sport.	There is no clear difference between structural configuration of organizations related to traditional sports and those related to new sports. Structural analysis should consider a historical, contextual and internal perspective.
Amis and Slack (1996)	*Journal of Sport Management*	The Size–Structure Relationship in Voluntary Sport Organization.	An increase in the size of an organization is not necessarily associated to more decentralization. In voluntary sport organizations volunteers were reluctant to increases in size, in order to retain control over the organization.
Danylchuk and Chelladurai (1999)	*Journal of Sport Management*	The Nature of Managerial Work in Canadian Intercollegiate Athletics.	Size is an important determinant of the number of managerial responsibilities to be distributed in a sport organization.

Cunningham and Ashley (2001)	*Sport Management Review*	Isomorphism in NCAA Athletic Departments: The Use of Competing Theories and Advancement of Theory.	The structure and processes of an organization are more influenced by strategic choice than by environment (population ecology).
Washington (2004)	*Organization Studies*	Field Approaches to Institutional Change: The Evolution of the National Collegiate Athletic Association 1906–1995.	Conflicts and interests can help determining a structuration process in an organizational field.
Smith and Shilbury (2004)	*Sport Management Review*	Mapping Cultural Dimensions in Australian Sporting Organizations.	There are some dimensions related to organizational culture that are important for all types of organizations. However, there are other dimensions which are particularly important for sport organizations like rituals, symbols, size and history and tradition.
Ørnulf (2004)	*International Review for the Sociology of Sport*	The World According to Voluntary Sport Organizations: Voluntarism, Economy and Facilities.	Nowadays, voluntary sport organizations are increasingly pressured when it comes to recruitment, because of the massive process of professionalization taking place in this kind of organization.
Slack and Mason (2005)	*Sport in Society*	Agency Theory and the Study of Sport Organizations.	Principal–agent relationship can also be used for explaining sport phenomena, especially when there are resources to be allocated. Agency theory doesn't work well under conditions of scarcity.

Table AIII.5 *(cont.)*

Author	Publication	Title	Contribution to sport organizations structure research
Fahlén (2006)	*The Sport Journal*	Organizational Structures in Sport Clubs – Exploring the Relationships between Individual Perceptions and Organizational Positions.	Perceptions of organizational structure are associated with the position occupied in the organization, and tension can be found between different organizational positions.

Source: Data elaborated from the literature review.

has expanded sport event transmission possibilities – first through radio and then by television. Both the increasing relevance of sports in social life and the relation of interdependence between sports and the media refer to contextual features challenging sport organizations today.

The changes in the environment of sport organizations can be characterized through the increasing number of actors participating in the sport sector, as well as by the new type of relationships among them. The nature of these relationships has changed from one based on dependency on outside resources for survival, to one based on interdependence and competition among them. The scarcity of resources forces sport organizations to compete in terms of revenue opportunities as well as on the preferences and time of spectators (Nichols *et al.*, 2005). The interdependency that has also come to characterize the relationships between the actors in the sport sector is, however, essential for achieving sporting success, fair competition and survival of the organization.

The professionalization process has been another relevant contextual feature within the research and literature reviewed on sport organization structure. The movement from amateur status to an increasingly professional one has also affected actors and structures involved in the world of sports – from athletes to sport governing bodies. Sport organizations have experienced this change as an organizational change process, commonly associated with the formalization of activities and procedures inside sport organizations, and the integration of paid staff into organizations traditionally based on voluntary work. Either one way or the other, the professionalization process has had an important effect on sport organization structure, and it was considered in 51 per cent of the articles reviewed, including discussion on sport organization structure.

Despite its late appearance in the literature and relatively modest coverage so far, commercialization presents another important process experienced by sports and characterizing the context within which the study of sport organization structure has taken place. The revenue creation opportunities and the exploitation of commercial activities are challenging sport organization's traditional operations and processes, pushing them towards the development of new strategies particularly related to marketing (O'Brien and Slack, 2004). The commercialization of sports has gained considerable place in the research discussing sport organization structure (24 per cent), especially during the last decade, which reflects its importance for future research studying organizational phenomena within the sport sector.

These three contextual features are influencing the internal dynamic of sport organizations, as well as determining the particular nature of organizational studies in the field of sports. The relevance of the constantly changing environment, plus the transformations caused by the processes of professionalization and commercialization, contribute to characterizing sport phenomena on the basis of sport environments' changing nature. Hence, research on sport organizations might encounter all or some of the contextual features discussed, as well as having to consider their influence over the internal operations and processes of sport organizations.

Conclusion

The aim of our literature review was to highlight the state of scholarly knowledge and the main trends of discussions on sport organization structure, looking deep into the key topics underlying the discussion of the structural characteristics of sport organizations. Following this aim, we wanted to identify the types of sport organizations that have been studied, the theoretical background within which those studies have set their analyses, and the main contextual features that have been considered in the discussion of organizational phenomena in the field of sports. More than prepare an exhaustive review of the literature existing on sport organization structure, we wanted to explore and clarify the main trends in studies on sport organization structure today.

The results reveal that most of the discussion concerning sport organization structure has been developed on sport governing bodies, and less so on what we have called sport event organizations and sport-providing entities. The possibility of finding structural homogeneity between countries in relation to sport governing bodies, and hence the opportunity to generalize results, may explain the relevance that these organizations have gained in the literature discussing sport organization structure. Sport-providing entities and sport-event producers on the other hand tend to differ across countries, because the basic unit from which sport is promoted varies from country to country and so do the most popular sports.

Considering the many types of sport organizations that can be identified within the concept of sport organizations, it is very important to specify the type of sport organizations to be studied. When different types of sport organizations have different goals and work with different activities, the discussion on sport organization structure should first be limited in terms of types of sport organizations. The three-category classification of sport organizations proposed here for those sport organizations dedicated to promotion and development is based on the three main elements integrated in the concept of sports itself: physical activity, formal rules and competition – play, game and contest.[3]

---

[3] Definition from the Encyclopædia Britannica Online: www.search.eb.com/eb/article-9108486 (last accessed 16 October 2006).

Dimensions associated with the concept of sport

Structure of the promotion and development of sports

Formal rules

Sport governing bodies

Competition

Physical activity

Sport event organizations

Sport delivery entities

Figure AIII.2 Relationship between the concept of sport and the types of sport organizations promoting and developing these activities
Source: Authors

As Figure AIII.2 illustrates, each of the components of the concept of sports can be associated with one of the three sport organizations promoting and developing sports. Sport-providing entities are providing physical activity, sport event organizations are providing the competition system, and sport governing bodies are defining the rules and procedures to guide a sport discipline and other sport organizations. Despite their differences, the three types of sport organizations respond to the superior goal of promoting and developing sports.

The relevance of the environment and the processes of professionalization and commercialization in the research on sport organization structures reveal the relevance of the contextual circumstances for the evolution of sports and sport organization. Furthermore, the amount of research studying sport organizations from an organizational change perspective suggests the relevance and impact of those contextual features over the internal processes and operations of sport organizations.

The professionalization process refers more to an internal process experienced by sport organizations, where the quality demanded by sport competition imposes a need to formalize their activities, procedures and positions in order to achieve the expected results. Whereas the commercialization process refers more to the relationship with the environment, which has turned from one traditionally based on the dependence of the organization on its environment for survival, to one based on the exploitation of the revenue opportunities existing in the environment today. Both professionalization and commercialization refer to the evolution experienced in the sport sector, which might explain their relevance in the studies of organizational change and performance in the articles reviewed.

The challenges imposed by the new characteristics of sports today have become an incentive for sport organizations to professionalize their activities and define new relationships within their environment. The literature reviewed shows how sport organizations have been searching for efficiency and effectiveness through the improvement of their managerial practices and functioning (Slack, 1998). The new ties between organization and environment are characterized by the interdependence and competition between actors for the acquisition of the necessary resources to survive, and for exploiting the revenue opportunities existing in today's sport sector. Both changes express the new situation in which sport organizations are operating today, which any future research on this field must consider in its analysis. However, as change and performance have been interesting topics in which to frame the discussion on sport organization structure, future research might consider taking a new starting point, in which these two challenges are more a variable to leverage the analysis than the dependent variable to be examined.

References

Amara, M., Henry, I., Liang, J. and Uchiumi, K. (2005). 'The Governance of Professional Soccer: Five Case Studies: Algeria, China, England, France and Japan', *European Journal of Sport Science*, 5(4): 189–206.

Amis, J. and Slack, T. (1996). 'The Size–Structure Relationship in Voluntary Sport Organization', *Journal of Sport Management*, 10(1): 78–86.

Amis, J., Slack, T. and Hinings, C.R. (2002). 'Values and Organizational Change', *Journal of Applied Behavioral Science*, 38(4): 436–65.

(2004a). 'The Pace, Sequence and Linearity of Radical Change', *Academy of Management Journal*, 47(1): 15–39.

(2004b). 'Strategic Change and the Role of Interests, Power, and Organizational Capacity', *Journal of Sport Management*, 18: 158–98.

Burns, T. and Stalker, G.M. (1961). *The Management of Innovation*. London: Tavistock.

Cairns, J.A. (1987). 'Evaluating Changes in League Structure: The Reorganization of the Scottish Football League', *Applied Economics*, 19(2): 259–75.

Chelladurai, P. and Haggerty, T.R. (1991). 'Measures of Organizational Effectiveness of Canadian National Sport Organizations', *Canadian Journal of Sport Sciences*, 16: 126–59.

Child, J. (1972). 'Organization Structure and Strategies of Control: A Replication of the Aston Study', *Administrative Science Quarterly*, 18: 328–48.

Cooper, H.M. (1989). *Integrating Research: A Guide for Literature Reviews*. Newbury Park, CA: Sage.

Cunningham, G.B. and Rivera, C.A. (2001). 'Structural Designs within American Intercollegiate Athletic Departments', *The International Journal of Organizational Analysis*, 9(4): 369–90.

Danylchuk, K.E. and Chelladurai, P. (1999). 'The Nature of Managerial Work in Canadian Intercollegiate Athletics', *Journal of Sport Management*, 13(2): 148–66.

De Knop, P., van Hoecke, J. and de Bosscher, V. (2004). 'Quality Management in Sports Clubs', *Sport Management Review*, 7: 57–77.

Doherty, A. (1998). 'Managing our Human Resources: A Review of Organizational Behaviour in Sport', *Sport Management Review*, 1: 1–24.

Fahlén, J. (2005). 'Organizational Structures in Sport Clubs – Exploring the Relationships between Individual Perceptions and Organizational Positions', *The Sport Journal*, 8(3): 1–25.

—— (2006). 'Organizational Structures of Swedish Elite Ice Hockey Clubs', *Sport and Society*, 3: 57–81.

Frisby, W. (1985). 'A Conceptual Framework for Measuring the Organizational Structure and Context of Voluntary Leisure Service', *Society and Leisure*, 8: 605–13.

—— (1986). 'Measuring the Organizational Effectiveness of National Sport Governing Bodies', *Canadian Journal of Applied Sport Science*, 11(2): 94–103.

Frisby, W., Thibault, L. and Kikulis, L. (2004). 'The Organizational Dynamics of Under-managed Partnerships in Leisure Service Departments', *Leisure Studies*, 23(2): 109–26.

Garrett, R. (2004). 'The Response of the Voluntary Sports Clubs to Sport England's Lottery Funding: Cases of Compliance, Change and Resistance', *Managing Leisure*, 9: 13–29.

Hall, R.I.M. William (1983). 'A Corporate System Model of a Sports Club: Using Simulation as an Aid to Policy Making in a Crisis', *Management Science*, 29(1): 52–64.

Hannan, M.T. and Freeman, J. (1977). 'The Population Ecology of Organizations', *The American Journal of Sociology*, 82(5): 929–64.

Hinings, C.R., Ranson, S. and Greenwood, R. (1980). 'The Structuring of Organizational Structure', *Administrative Science Quarterly*, 25: 1–17.

Hoye, R. (2004). 'Leader-member Exchanges and Board Performance of Voluntary Sport Organizations', *Nonprofit Management and Leadership*, **15**(1): 55–70.

Hoye, R. and Cuskelly, G. (2003). 'Board-executive Relationships within Voluntary Sport Organizations', *Sport Management Review*, **6**: 53–74.

Kikulis, L.M. (2000). 'Continuity and Change in Governance and Decision Making in National Sport Organizations: Institutional Explanations', *Journal of Sport Management*, **14**: 293–320.

Kikulis, L.M. and Slack, T. (1995). 'Sector-specific Patterns of Organizational Design Change', *Journal of Management Studies*, **32**(1): 67–100.

Kikulis, L.M., Slack, T. and Hinings, C.R. (1992). 'Institutionally Specific Design Archetypes: A Framework for Understanding Change in National Sport Organizations', *International Review for the Sociology of Sport*, **27**: 343–70.

(1995). 'Sector-specific Patterns of Organizational Design Change', *Journal of Management Studies*, **32**(1): 67–100.

(1995a). 'Does Decision Making Make a Difference? Patterns of Change within Canadian National Sport Organizations', *Journal of Sport Management*, **9**: 279–99.

Kikulis, L., Slack, T. and Hinings, C.R. (1995b). 'Toward an Understanding of the Role of Agency and Choice in the Changing Structure of Canada's National Sport Organizations', *Journal of Sport Management*, **9**(2): 135–52.

Kikulis, L., Slack, T., Hinings, C.R. and Zimmermann, A. (1989). 'A Structural Taxonomy of Amateur Sport Organizations', *Journal of Sport Management*, **3**(2): 129–50.

Mason, D.S. and Slack, T. (2001). 'Industry Factors and the Changing Dynamics of the Player-agent Relationship in Professional Ice Hockey', *Sport Management Review*, **4**: 165–91.

Miles, R. and Snow, C.C. (1978). *Organizational Strategy, Structure and Process*. New York: McGraw Hill.

Mintzberg, H. (1979). *The Structuration of Organizations*. Englewood Cliffs: Prentice Hall.

Nichols, G., Taylor, P., James, M., Holmes, K., King, L. and Garrett, R. (2005). 'Pressures on the UK Voluntary Sport Sector', *Voluntas: International Journal of Voluntary and Nonprofit Organizations*, **16**(1): 33–50.

O'Brien, D. and Slack, T. (1999). 'Deinstitutionalising the Amateur Ethic: An Empirical Examination of Change in a Rugby Union Football Club', *Sport Management Review*, **2**(1): 24–42.

O' Brien, D. and Slack, T. (2003). 'An Analysis of Change in an Organizational Field: The Professionalization of English Rugby Union', *Journal of Sport Management*, **17**: 417–48.

O'Brien, D. and Slack, T. (2004). 'The Emergence of a Professional Logic in English Rugby Union: The Role of Isomorphic and Diffusion Processes', *Journal of Sport Management*, **18**: 13–39.

Ørnulf, S. (2002). 'Volunteers and Professionals in Norwegian Sport Organizations', *Voluntas: International Journal of Voluntary and Nonprofit Organizations*, **13**(3): 253–70.

—— (2004). 'The World According to Voluntary Sport Organizations: Voluntarism, Economy and Facilities', *International Review for the Sociology of Sport*, **39**(2): 223–32.

Papadimitriou, D. (1998). 'The Impact of Institutionalized Resources, Rules and Practices on the Performance of Non-profit Sport Organizations', *Managing Leisure*, **3**(4): 169–80.

—— (2002). 'Amateur Structures and their Effect on Performance: The Case of Greek Voluntary Sports Clubs', *Managing Leisure*, **7**(4): 205–19.

Papadimitriou, D. and Taylor, P. (2000). 'Organizational Effectiveness of Hellenic National Sports Organizations: A Multiple Constituency Approach', *Sport Management Review*, **3**: 23–46.

Paton, G.A. (1987). 'Sport Management Research – What Progress Has Been Made?', *Journal of Sport Management*, **1**: 25–31.

Powell, W.W. (1991). *The New Institutionalism in Organizational Analysis*. Chicago: University of Chicago Press.

Shilbury, D. (2000). 'Considering Future Sport Delivery Systems', *Sport Management Review*, **3**: 199–221.

Shilbury, D. and Moore, K. (2006). 'A Study of Organizational Effectiveness for National Olympic Sporting Organizations', *Nonprofit and Voluntary Sector Quarterly*, **35**(1): 5–38.

Skinner, J., Stewart, B. and Edwards, A. (1999). 'Amateurism to Professionalism: Modelling Organizational Change in Sporting Organizations', *Sport Management Review*, **2**(2): 173–92.

Slack, T. (1985). 'The Bureaucratization of a Voluntary Sport Organization', *International Review for the Sociology of Sport*, **20**: 145–63.

—— (1997). *Understanding Sport Organizations: The Application of Organization Theory*. Champaign, IL: Human Kinetics.

—— (1998). 'Studying the Commercialization of Sport: The Need for Critical Analysis'. Online, available at: http://physed.otago.ac.nz/sosol/v1i1/v1i1a6.htm (accessed 5 May 2007).

—— (2003). 'Sport in the Global Society: Shaping the Domain of Sport Studies', *The International Journal of the History of Sport*, **20**(4): 118.

Slack, T. and Cousens, L. (2005). 'Field-level Change: The Case of North American Major League Professional Sport', *Journal of Sport Management*, **19**: 13–42.

Slack, T. and Hinings, C.R. (1987). 'Planning and Organizational Change: A Conceptual Framework for the Analysis of Amateur Sport Organizations', *Canadian Journal of Sport Sciences*, **12**: 185–93.

—— (1992). 'Understanding Change in National Sport Organizations: An Integration of Theoretical Perspectives', *Journal of Sport Management*, **6**(2): 114–32.

—— (1994). 'Institutional Pressures and Isomorphic Change: An Empirical Test', *Organization Studies*, **15**(6): 803–27.

Slack, T. and Kikulis, L. (1989). 'The Sociological Study of Sport Organizations: Some Observations on the Situation in Canada', *International Review for the Sociology of Sport*, **24**(3): 179–200.

Slack, T. and Mason, D. (2005). 'Agency Theory and the Study of Sport Organizations', *Sport in Society*, **8**(1): 48–64.

Smith, A. (2004). 'Complexity Theory and Change Management in Sport Organizations', *Emergence: Complexity and Organization*, **6**: 70–79.

Smith, A. and Shilbury, D. (2004). 'Mapping Cultural Dimensions in Australian Sporting Organizations', *Sport Management Review*, **7**: 133–65.

Stern, R. (1979). 'The Development of an Interorganizational Control Network: The Case of Intercollegiate Athletics', *Administrative Science Quarterly*, **24**(2): 242–66.

Stevens, J.A. and Slack, T. (1998). 'Integrating Social Action and Structural Constraints: Towards a more Holistic Explanation of Organizational Change', *International Review for the Sociology of Sport*, **33**: 143–54.

Theodoraki, E. and Henry, I.P. (1994). 'Organizational Structures and Contexts in British National Governing Bodies of Sport', *International Review for the Sociology of Sport*, **29**: 243–68.

Thibault, L. and Babiak, K. (2005). 'Organizational Changes in Canada's Sport System: Toward an Athlete-centerd Approach', *European Sport Management Quarterly*, **5**(2): 105–32.

Thibault, L., Frisby, W. and Kikulis, L.M. (1999). 'Interorganizational Linkages in the Delivery of Local Leisure Services in Canada: Responding to Economic, Political and Social Pressures', *Managing Leisure*, **4**(3): 125–41.

Thibault, L., Slack, T. and Hinings, C.R. (1991). 'Professionalism, Structures and Systems: The Impact of Professional Staff on Voluntary

Sport Organizations', *International Review for the Sociology of Sport*, **26**(2): 83–99.

Washington, M. (2004). 'Field Approaches to Institutional Change: The Evolution of the National Collegiate Athletic Association 1906–1995', *Organization Studies*, **25**(3): 393–414.

Westby, D.L. and Sack, A. (1976). 'The Commercialization and Functional Rationalization of College Football: Its Origins', *The Journal of Higher Education*, **47**(6): 625–47.

Wolfe, R., Weick, K.E., Usher, J.M., Terborg, J.R., Poppo, L., Murrell, A.J., *et al.* (2005). 'Sport and Organizational Studies: Exploring Synergy', *Journal of Management Inquiry*, **14**(2): 182–210.

Index

For EU product safety concerns, contact us at Calle de José Abascal, 56–1°, 28003 Madrid, Spain or eugpsr@cambridge.org.